These were the years when the nation was told to remember Pearl Harbor, but wanted to forget all cares for a few hours in the magic of the movies.

These were the years when the great stars glittered brilliantly, but were outshone by a pair of ex-burlesque comedians.

These were the years when Abbott and Costello made smash hit after smash hit as they saved an entire studio from ruin—and used their incredible success to make their every wild and whacky dream come true.

These were the years and this was the superbly improvised and uninhibited style of comedy that will never come again—and will never be forgotten by anyone who has ever seen Bud Abbott and Lou Costello turn the screen into their personal wonderworld of laughter.

THE ABBOTT AND COSTELLO BOOK

by Jim Mulholland

POPULAR LIBRARY FILM SERIES
Leonard Maltin, General Editor

POPULAR LIBRARY • NEW YORK

Published by Popular Library, CBS Publications, CBS Consumer Publishing, a Division of CBS Inc.

December, 1977

ISBN: 0-445-04138-2

Photograph credits and acknowledgments: Columbia Pictures, Larry Edmunds Cinema Bookshop, Hollywood Book Collectors, The Memory Shop, Metro-Goldwyn-Mayer, Movie Star News, NBC, The New York Public Library at Lincoln Center, Astor, Lenox and Tilden Foundations, RKO Radio Pictures, United Artists, United Press International, Universal, Warner Brothers, Wide World Photos, Inc., and Steve Allen, Sid Fields, Alvin H. Marrill, Joan Shawlee, and Jean Yarbrough.

We welcome your thoughts and comments on the Popular Library Film Series. Address all correspondence to Leonard Maltin, 200 West 79 Street, 5-L, New York, New York 10024.

PRINTED IN THE UNITED STATES OF AMERICA

Contents

ABOUT THE AUTHOR

Jim Mulholland is a successful young comedy writer whose television credits include "The Tonight Show," "The Dick Cavett Show," "The Jack Paar Show," "The Dean Martin Show," "All in the Family" and "The Mary Tyler Moore Show." He is currently working on a play and a screenplay. This is his first book.

ABOUT THE EDITOR

Leonard Maltin has been editing and publishing *Film Fan Monthly* magazine since 1966. In that time he has also written five books on film, including *TV Movies* and *The Disney Films,* edited the Curtis and Popular Library film series, and contributed articles to numerous magazines and journals. He also teaches at the New School for Social Research in New York.

INTRODUCTION

They complemented each other beautifully.

Bud was tall, lean and debonair. He had a perpetually glowering expression and a raspy, staccato delivery. His costume usually consisted of a smartly tailored double-breasted suit and a wide-brimmed fedora. He was the epitome of the city slicker on the lookout for an easy mark. He never had to look very far. He was the greatest straight man in show business.

Lou was short, plump and child-like. His body was a mass of quivering jello contained in a tight-fitting jacket and baggy pants. He wore either a derby that balanced precariously atop his head or a crumpled hat with an upturned brim. He was the little fellow adrift in a world he couldn't comprehend. Yet he always maintained his dignity as he vainly struggled to defend himself against another of his partner's verbal and physical assaults. Then his squeaky, high-pitched voice would explode into a booming shout of protest. He was a comic genius.

Off camera, they were almost the reversals of their screen personalities. Bud was quiet and introverted. Lou was the driving force in the team; outgoing, energetic and industrious.

Together they comprised the most successful comedy team in motion picture history. In the 1940s they were a national craze.

Then why today are Abbott and Costello so neglected by critics and the public? They're generally dismissed as "pretty good comics," and nothing more. Their films are banished to early morning television, and you won't find an Abbott and Costello festival playing at your neighborhood theater. Even the recent wave of nostalgia for the 1940s failed to include Bud and Lou, which is odd since their three service comedies probably capture that era better than most Hollywood films.

Perhaps the reason for this neglect is that today's audiences aren't familiar with their best work. Many of their early comedies—BUCK PRIVATES, HOLD THAT GHOST, RIO RITA, IN SOCIETY, LOST IN A HAREM—have moments of brilliance. But you'll have to awake at 8 A.M. or stay up to 3 A.M. in order to see them on TV. Television has been kinder to the Marx Brothers, Laurel and Hardy and W. C. Fields, often showing their movies intact, and in prime time.

I think that Lou Costello is the most underrated comedian of all time. Director Jean Yarbrough, who worked with the team often, made this comment about Lou: "He was a great visual comedian, like Stan Laurel. But Lou could also do stand-up comedy, jokes—something Stan could never do."

Lou also had a rare gift for improvisation that deserves mention. When you think of improvisation, the name of only one other comedian comes to mind—Jonathan Winters. Most comedians today are at the mercy of cue cards and teleprompters. Lou rarely bothered to read a script. The dialogue director outlined the scene for him and he was turned loose in front of the cameras. He ad-libbed most of his dialogue. In the middle of a scene he would suddenly pick up an obscure prop and launch into an impromptu bit of business that had absolutely nothing to do with the scene, but was uproariously funny.

Lou had another attribute that is sorely missing in most comedians—pathos. You really *cared* about that little fat man who was constantly put-upon. He created some wonderful sympathetic moments in films like KEEP 'EM FLYING, LITTLE GIANT, THE TIME OF THEIR LIVES and BUCK PRIVATES COME HOME.

Throughout their careers Abbott and Costello were lambasted by the critics for performing old burlesque material in films and television. But these critics failed to point out that no one did these routines as well as Bud and Lou. An old routine like "Who's on First" became an American classic due to their rendition of it. Critics also fail to realize that if it wasn't for Abbott and Costello, these great sketches would have been lost forever. Their films have preserved this wealth of material for generations too young to have seen burlesque.

So it's high time that Bud and Lou get the credit they deserve. They never had any pretensions about art. They were much too busy being funny and enjoying life to the fullest.

This book is not meant to be a definitive biography of the team. It is instead a collection of material on the subject of Abbott and Costello, a good deal of which has never appeared in print before. I hope it will answer many of the questions that their fans have been asking over the years. Most importantly, it attempts to recall just how funny they were through detailed discussions of their work on stage, radio, film and television.

Researching this book was a labor of love. I tried to talk to as many of their friends and co-workers as I could. They all confirmed what I always knew the real Bud and Lou must have been like. Words like "kind," "gracious," "unselfish" turned up in all of the interviews.

My deepest appreciation to the following for being so generous to me with their time and effort: Steve Allen, Patty Andrews, Robert Arthur, Joe Besser, True Boardman, Milt Bronson, Hillary Brooke, Ann Corio, Pat Costello, Harry Crane, Sid Fields, Alex Gottlieb, Buddy Hackett, Hank Henry, Arthur Lubin, Joan Shawlee, Jean Yarbrough, Henny Youngman, and Leonard Maltin who made the whole thing possible.

Further thanks are in order to: Mary Pat Kelly, Barbara Meltzer, Nick Arnold, Mike Barrie and his camera and the Lincoln Center Library of Performing Arts and the UCLA Theatre Arts Library.

First and foremost, I want to thank Bud Abbott and Lou Costello, who made me laugh and introduced me to comedy, for which I'll always be grateful.

An early photograph of the team in their burlesque days.

LIFE BEGINS AT MINSKY'S

William "Bud" Abbott was born October 2, 1895, in Asbury Park, New Jersey. To say that the Abbott family led colorful lives would be an understatement. Bud's mother, Rae Abbott, was a bareback rider with the Barnum and Bailey circus and his father, Harry Abbott, Sr., was an advance man for the troupe. While Bud was still an infant, the Abbotts left the circus and moved to Coney Island, where his father helped to organize the Columbia Wheel, the first burlesque circuit. Bud was never very fond of school and he left P.S. 100 after the fourth grade to work as a candy butcher and "shill" for concessions at the Coney Island amusement park. One of his chief duties was to lure customers into the House of Mirrors. Inside the mirrored maze, the customers invariably got lost, whereupon young Bud approached them and offered to show them the way out for the price of ten cents. Already he was establishing his stage and screen character–the glib, fast-talking con man.

At the age of sixteen, Bud got his first taste of the world of burlesque, a world he would inhabit for twenty-two years. His father got him a job as assistant treasurer for the Casino burlesque theater in Brooklyn. In his capacity as assistant treasurer, the young man paid off such stars as Fanny Brice, W. C. Fields and Bert Lahr. Bud often slipped away from the box office to stand backstage and watch these great performers. He had an eye for one day becoming a comedian himself and absorbed everything he could about timing and delivery.

His performing career was rudely interrupted when he entered a bar on Brooklyn's Red Hook waterfront one night. Bud was having a drink with some strangers and suddenly he blacked out. He awoke and found himself shanghaied on a steamer headed for Norway. He spent the next three months on board the ship, stoking coal and cooking for the other crewmen. Six months later he was back in Brooklyn resuming his duties in the box office.

He thought he knew enough about the business by this time to produce his own shows. Borrowing fifteen hundred dollars from an uncle, Bud and his older brother Harry organized "tab" shows around the country. The Abbott Brothers posed no threat to the Shuberts. Their business venture was something less than a success, and Bud took an offer to produce shows at the National Theatre in Detroit. It was here that Bud gained an almost encyclope-

Bud Abbott at age sixty.

dic knowledge of all the classic burlesque scenes. He put this knowledge to good use when he later teamed with Lou Costello. For three years Bud produced a different show every week at the National and he worked with nearly every comic in burlesque. It was also at the National that Bud left the production end of the business to become a straight man on stage.

In 1918, Bud married a pretty burlesque ingenue whose stage name was Betty Smith. Her real name was Jenny Mae Pratt.

The transition from producer to performer was an easy one for Bud. In order to be a good straight man, you must be a good actor. And Bud was. He really made you believe that the first baseman's name was "Who," or that the refusal to buy one jar of mustard would throw the entire nation's economy out of kilter. Bud could make the most audacious statement seem sound and logical.

Soon all of the comics wanted to team with Bud. They discovered that they got more and bigger laughs working with him. This was because he treated comics in a rough-and-tumble manner on stage—pushing and slapping them around whenever they gave a foolish answer to one of his questions. The audience's sympathy was then focused on the comic, and they laughed longer and louder at the silly little man who was outwitted at every turn by his smooth-talking partner.

By the 1930s he was the number one straight man and Harold

Minsky signed him to appear at the Republic Theatre at Times Square, for an unprecedented two hundred and fifty dollars a week. At this time the average salary for a comic was less than a hundred a week. It seems hard to believe today but in those days the straight man was the star of burlesque, not the comic. The straight man traditionally received top billing over the comic and often they split the salary 60-40, with the straight man getting the lion's share.

In 1936, Bud was working with a comic named Harry Evanson at the Eltinge Theatre on West Forty-second Street. A young comedian named Lou Costello was also appearing at the Eltinge that week. Bud and Lou saw each other perform, liked what they saw and decided to team up. Many biographies of the team claim that Bud was a cashier in a theater box office and he teamed up with Lou when the latter's straight man failed to show up one night. This just isn't true. It is difficult to research Abbott and Costello because they loved to confuse biographers by making "improvements" on their life stories. For instance, it has often appeared in print that Bud was a racing car driver in his youth. But the fact is that Bud never drove an automobile in his life.

The young comic Bud saw that fateful day at the Eltinge had led

Bud Abbott was Jewish, but was married in a Christian ceremony in 1918. In the late 1940s, Betty joined the Jewish faith, and she and Bud were remarried by Rabbi Samuel Harris in March 1950. Wide World photo.

an equally exciting, although divergent life.

Louis Francis Cristillo came into the world March 3, 1906, in Paterson, New Jersey. (Lou managed to slip in a plug for his hometown in virtually all of his films and TV shows.) Lou's mother, Helen, was an Irish-American, and his father, Sebastian, was an Italian immigrant. When Mr. Cristillo settled in Paterson he acquired a job as a weaver in a silk mill. He was then employed by the Prudential life insurance company until he retired. Lou had an older brother, Patrick, and a sister, Marie. The Cristillos were devout Catholics and Lou attended mass at St. Anthony's church in Paterson.

The child's chief interests were basketball, baseball and the movies. He once claimed that he saw Chaplin's SHOULDER ARMS twenty-five times. School was definitely not one of his interests. According to Lou it was in P.S. 15 that he adopted his later radio catchphrase, "I'm a ba-a-ad boy!" The first glint of his comedic talents came when he won a prize at a Halloween party for his impression of Charlie Chaplin. Lou attended high school but spent more time on the basketball court than he did in the classroom. Although he was short (5′4″), he was tremendously agile. For three years he was a state champion foul shooter and he once played against basketball great Nat Holman in an exhibition game with the Celtics. Lou also became a skilled amateur boxer at this time, fighting under the name Lou King. He had an impressive record. He fought twelve times, with eleven wins and one draw. One night Lou's father was given a ticket to the fights by a fellow employee at the insurance company. Mr. Cristillo attended the bout and was shocked to discover that his young son Lou was one of the contenders. Lou had never told his father about his boxing career, which his father quickly ended that night.

In 1927, Lou decided to fulfill his dream of one day being a movie star. He borrowed some money from his father and he and a friend, Gene Coogan, headed for Hollywood. The boys hitchhiked and hopped freight cars until they arrived on the Coast penniless. For months they were unable to find work and were forced to sleep in parked cars and dingy pool halls. They dined on oranges and figs picked from trees belonging to Hollywood residents. Every day they awoke at dawn and made the rounds of the movie studios looking for extra work. They landed jobs as carpenters at Metro-Goldwyn-Mayer and occasionally worked as extras. Because of his athletic prowess, Lou was hired as a stunt man. Considerably slimmer in those days, he doubled for Dolores Del Rio in an opus titled THE TRAIL OF '98. Both Coogan and Costello soon realized that moviemaking wasn't as glamorous as they

Lou Costello.

envisioned it to be. Lou had sustained a number of injuries being tossed around the M-G-M backlot as a stunt man and extra. After eighteen months of this, they agreed to head back home. (Fourteen years later Lou Costello returned to M-G-M at the request of Louis B. Mayer himself.) The two boys hitchhiked cross-country, stopping along the way to take odd jobs to buy food. For two weeks they harvested wheat in Colorado. They eventually made their way to Lawrence, Kansas, where Gene Coogan had relatives who provided the boys with a place to sleep and hot meals. Coogan stayed with his relatives and Lou moved on to St. Joseph, Missouri, where he began his career in comedy.

Lou heard that a local vaudeville theater, the Lyceum, was looking for a Dutch comic. Never lacking confidence, Lou applied for the job and was hired. He had never been on a stage before in his life, but he was naturally funny and had no trouble getting laughs. He stayed at the theater for a year, earning sixteen dollars a week. By now he was working under the name Lou Costello. His brother, Pat, who played the saxophone and had his own band, had changed his name to Costello some time before. Lou then returned to his home town, Paterson, anxious to enter the big time in New York. He took any performing jobs he could get for the experience. He put together an act of songs and jokes and he worked in small bars in and around Paterson. In 1930, a show titled TAKE A

CHANCE came to Paterson. The producer of the show, Nat Fields, brother of Lew Fields of Weber and Fields, saw Lou perform one night and gave him his first job in burlesque. That summer Lou was hired as a comic at the Orpheum Theatre in New York.

The first scene Lou Costello did was an old standby, "Go Ahead and Sing." In this scene, Lou is standing on a street corner happily singing a song when a policeman comes along and warns him to stop all the noise. He informs Lou that people in the neighborhood are trying to sleep. As soon as the cop leaves, the straight man urges Costello to "Go ahead and sing!" "You heard what the cop said–there's a lot of people sleeping," says Costello. "So what?" shouts the straight man. "Did you put them to sleep? Is it your fault they're in bed? Go ahead and sing!" Lou resumes his song at the straight man's request and the cop comes running back and begins to pound Lou on the head with his billy club. "I'm not going to warn you again!" hollers the furious policeman. He exits and the straight man convinces Lou to stand up to the cop, who's "just a public servant." Costello sings another chorus, which is violently interrupted by the cop. "Aren't you a public servant?" Lou asks. "Then get me a glass of water!" The officer shouts, "I'm the

Lou with his mother, Helen, on the set of KEEP 'EM FLYING.

boss around here and you're nothin'!" "You got a nice job," concludes Costello. "Boss over nothin'!" Lou then takes a terrible beating from the cop, while the straight man innocently looks on.

Because of his wide-open baby face, Costello played juveniles in scenes like "The Schoolroom," which provided him with his early training in the art of burlesque comedy.

He soon worked his way up to being a "top banana." One scene that Costello loved was "Crazy House." This famous sketch has Lou spending the night in a "rest home" that is overrun by lunatics. In her book *This Was Burlesque,* Ann Corio recalls that Lou was doing "Crazy House" at the Shubert Theatre in Philadelphia when he was paid an unexpected visit by another great burlesque clown.

> One after another the characters come through—but Lou Costello, as the comic, was a bit surprised one night when Rags Ragland came running through the door, then by his bed, then off the stage. Rags wasn't supposed to be in the scene. Lou was even more surprised when a girl raced through the door behind Rags, waving a real pistol and shouting, "Stop, or I'll shoot! You . . .!"
>
> Rags didn't stop, and the girl chased him right up the aisle. The audience roared. A great blackout. The only thing was—it was real. Rags had broken another heart and once again was fleeing for his life.

Lou fell in love with a beautiful brunette chorus girl named Anne Battler while they were appearing together in a show in New York and they were married in 1934. Their first child, Patricia, was born in 1937. The Costellos had three lovely daughters. Carole Lou was born in 1939 and Christine in 1948. Lou's only son, Louis Francis, Jr., was born in 1942.

After Lou was teamed with Bud, everything seemed to click at once for them. It was fortunate that they met when they did because on May 3, 1937, burlesque officially came to an end in New York City. It had gotten too risqué and Mayor La Guardia was pressured to shut down all the burlesque houses. This also meant the end of a great training ground for comedians. A few other comedians who came out of burlesque: Phil Silvers, Bobby Clark, Rags Ragland, Leon Errol, Ben Blue, Red Buttons, Danny Thomas and Red Skelton.

Abbott and Costello spent the first year of their partnership, and the last year of burlesque, with a touring show, "Life Begins at Minsky's." This was probably the most important year of their

joint careers, because during the course of this show they developed a rapport and a sense of timing that placed them above all of the other comedy teams in burlesque. Audiences found themselves roaring with laughter at familiar routines like "Who's on First" and the "Lemon Bit," although they knew the jokes almost as well as the comics. It wasn't *what* Bud and Lou said, it was *how* they said it.

Before teaming with Bud, Lou had met a talented straight man named John Grant. Grant wasn't the right straight man for Costello but the two men became good friends. Grant was also well-

The Costello family celebrates Christmas of 1952.

versed in all the routines and when Abbott and Costello became big stars, they took Grant on as their chief writer. Grant adapted the old routines to their style and removed all the blue jokes. (There were only a handful of clean burlesque scenes, such as "Who's on First.") Abbott and Costello prided themselves in never doing risqué material in burlesque. They didn't have to resort to that in order to get laughs. Unlike many big-name comedians, who hire and fire writers on an almost daily basis, they kept John Grant with them for more than twenty years.

While doing a show in Philadelphia, the team met a bright young agent, Edward Sherman. Sherman immediately saw their potential and offered to be their manager. He was anxious to get them nonburlesque bookings. At this time they were under contract to Emmett Callahan, who managed a large chain of burlesque theaters. Callahan was generous enough to release Abbott and Costello from their contract so they could move on to more lucrative careers in vaudeville. They signed with Sherman and he arranged a ten-week engagement for the team at Atlantic City's Steel Pier, where they were very big hits. One of the reasons why they were so popular on stage was because they never did the same show twice. By 1937, they had accumulated so much comedy material that they could perform for weeks without repeating themselves. They also ad-libbed a great deal. So the same customers kept coming back for more.

Following their appearance at the Steel Pier, the act skyrocketed. They played their first nightclub, Billy Rose's Casa Mañana in New York. In 1938, they were playing Washington, D.C., and a booker for the Loew's vaudeville circuit saw them. This led to a record-breaking run at Loew's State Theatre in New York.

Kate Smith had a very popular radio program in the thirties and forties. A young comedian, Henny Youngman, was featured on "The Kate Smith Show" every week in 1938. Youngman recalls how Abbott and Costello made their radio debut: "I got an offer from Paramount Pictures to go to Hollywood and make a test, but

Lou taking his father, Sebastian Cristillo, on a tour of Universal studios, and introducing him to actress Gladys George.

Lou with wife, Anne, and their third daughter, Christine.

Celebrating his fortieth birthday with daughters Carole Lou and Patricia on the set of THE TIME OF THEIR LIVES. Joining them is Lou's co-star, Marjorie Reynolds.

Lou taking his daughter, Christine, for a ride around the studio during filming of ABBOTT AND COSTELLO MEET THE KILLER, BORIS KARLOFF.

Abbott and Costello's chief writer, John Grant, seen here instructing Bud how to slap Lou properly on the set of HIT THE ICE. With Marc Lawrence and Joe Sawyer.

Abbott and Costello appearing on radio's "The Kate Smith Show."

Ted Collins, the producer of the show, said, 'You can't go unless you get a replacement.' So I went to Loew's State Theatre and I saw Abbott and Costello and they were doing a thing called 'Who's on First.' I closed my eyes and I visualized that this could be very funny on radio. I stayed for a couple of shows and then I called Ted Collins. He came down, saw Abbott and Costello and put them on the show."

The team performed "Who's on First" on "The Kate Smith Show," giving them their first national exposure. They became regulars on the program and this led to their first and only appearance on Broadway in *The Streets of Paris.* All of this had happened in the space of two years.

Publicity still of Bud and Lou taken at Lou's home in the summer of '42.

THE HOLLYWOOD YEARS

The team's success in *The Streets of Paris* led to a one-picture deal with Universal. They moved to Hollywood in 1940 to make their first film, ONE NIGHT IN THE TROPICS, which did little to advance their careers. Universal grudgingly consented to put them in a second film, BUCK PRIVATES, and that started it all. They were paired in thirty-six features, most of which did big business at the box office. If it wasn't for Abbott and Costello, today Universal City would probably be one of the thousands of used car lots that dot the Southern California landscape. Reportedly, their films grossed one hundred and forty million dollars for the studio. Bud and Lou were well aware of their importance to Universal and felt free to make exorbitant salary demands. For several years they were the highest-paid performers in show business. Their other demands upon the studio included two luxurious house trailers designed specifically for the comedians. Between scenes the boys resided in their trailers playing cards with friends. Bud kept a clause in his contract which precluded him from working past four-thirty in the afternoon. Four-thirty was "scotch time" and he headed for a favorite wateringhole, such as the bar in the Knickerbocker Hotel in Hollywood.

Once they hit it big on the Coast, they were like two small boys turned loose in a candy store with a twenty-dollar bill. They were continually trying to outdo each other to see who could buy the biggest and the best. Bud bought a huge, rambling home in Encino. Lou bought a larger one in nearby Sherman Oaks. One of Lou's favorite pastimes was adding rooms to this house. When he bought the house it had eight rooms. He kept adding to it until it eventually had twenty-four. After years on the road in burlesque, this was the first time they really had homes of their own so they stocked them with every conceivable luxury, regardless of cost.

When Bud built a swimming pool, Lou built a pool one foot longer and one foot wider. Lou enjoyed bragging that it was the finest in Hollywood. Bud built a costly pool house. Inside this structure he had a bar that stretched along the length of the swimming pool.

Both men were fascinated with electrical gadgets. Lou installed an amplifying system which allowed him to listen in on anything in the house. At Bud's home, the front gate and garage doors operated by short wave. A visitor drove up to the gate, pushed a button

Lou visits W.C. Fields and director Eddie Sutherland on the set of "Follow the Boys" (1943)

The Costello family celebrates daughter Patricia's eighth birthday at the Costello home.

Clockwise from top left: (1) There were always birthday parties on the set of an Abbott and Costello movie. This time it's Fran Warren's birthday being celebrated during production of ABBOTT AND COSTELLO MEET CAPTAIN KIDD. (2) The boys at Lou's first home in Hollywood. (3) Lou visiting Dinah Shore on the set of THREE CHEERS FOR THE BOYS (1943). (4) Discussing a fine point in the script of KEEP 'EM FLYING. (5) Immortalized in cement at Grauman's Chinese Theatre on Hollywood Boulevard. It's interesting to note the date—December 8, 1941, the day after Pearl Harbor was attacked!

and was greeted by Bud's voice over a loudspeaker, shouting, "Is that you, neighbor?" (Bud called everyone "neighbor" since he claimed he could never remember names. "Hi ya, neighbor" became his trademark on radio.) Every Sunday it was open house at the Abbotts' and a group of Bud's pals from burlesque dropped by for a little reminiscing and a lot of card playing.

Lou constructed a theater in his house and built up an impressive film library. He also owned a fleet of five cars, including a bright red limousine that he was particularly fond of.

Bud preferred being chauffeured around town in a Cadillac that had genuine alligator upholstery.

Lou purchased an eighty-foot subchaser from the Navy and converted it into a yacht for weekend trips.

Abbott and Costello's friendly rivalry wasn't confined to household improvements. Bud bought a restaurant on Ventura Boulevard that specialized in Italian food. Many of the biggest stars in Hollywood dined there frequently.

Not to be outdone by his partner, Lou bought a nightclub—the Band Box—on Fairfax Avenue that featured a floor show. Bud once bragged to Lou that he had to stay up all night to count up the profits from his cafe. "That's nothing," replied Lou. "Out at my joint we don't even count the money any more. We just weigh it."

They were notoriously generous. They supported dozens of friends and acquaintances from the burlesque circuit. Whenever a grip working on one of their films had a birthday, the boys lavished expensive gifts on him. At Christmas everyone even remotely connected with the film received valuable presents from Bud and Lou.

Since their first engagement at the Steel Pier in Atlantic City was an important step in their careers, they played there at least once a year until 1946 when the pier was sold and, as a favor to the pier's manager Frank Elliott, they always took a minimal salary.

Together they raised fourteen thousand dollars to pay off the mortgage of St. Anthony's, the church Lou attended as a boy in Paterson. The team then contributed thousands more to help build a new church. In a New York *Times* interview, Lou spoke of the parish priest of St. Anthony's: "Funny thing, he tried to keep me from running off to Hollywood when I was a kid and now I'm there and I can help him get a new church."

During World War II the team made a nationwide tour, raising millions for war bonds. The proceeds of another tour went to the Emergency Relief Fund for soldiers' dependents.

Hollywood has always been famous for its nepotism. Abbott

and Costello refined this practice to an art. As soon as they settled on the Coast, they financed a mass migration of relatives from the East—sisters, brothers, brothers-in-law, cousins and nephews. Bud and Lou bought them all homes and got most of them jobs working on their films. Lou had a wonderful relationship with his parents and he had a beautiful home built for them on Ventura Boulevard.

Their gambling was legendary in Hollywood. They had always gambled backstage in burlesque, awaiting their turn on stage between strippers. Now that they were making big money, they could really do it right. A marathon card game was always in progress on the studio sound stage and sometimes they gambled away more money than they earned making the film. At the Costello mansion, there were round-the-clock card games. Many nights, the butler, who participated in the games, went home with several thousand dollars in winnings. Bud and Lou became the prey of professional gamblers who beat them for hundreds of thousands of dollars. When the team played Las Vegas, they usually lost twice the amount of their paycheck. Alex Gottlieb, who produced the best of the Abbott and Costello features, recalled one incident during the filming of PARDON MY SARONG.

> Every day on the set they played seven-card stud at forty dollars a card—and they were the worst poker players in the world. Anyone could beat them. Whenever I tried to interrupt the game to talk to Lou about the picture, he used to shout, "Sit down and play!" It got to a point where I was winning so much money from these two that I told them I wouldn't play with them any more. So I returned to my office and a few minutes later I received a call from the head of Universal, Nate Blumberg. He said, "Lou just called me and he won't finish the picture unless you play with him." There were still ten days of shooting left to go so I had to play with them to keep them happy. By the time we finished the picture I had won $15,000 from them.

On a quiet afternoon at Del Mar racetrack Lou bet four thousand dollars on a long shot. Because of the size of the bet, the odds on the horse went down, and the horse ultimately became the favorite. The horse lost but Costello was pleased with himself because he had almost single-handedly controlled the betting in the race!

They were terrible businessmen and squandered a great deal of money in unsuccessful ventures. For instance, Lou bought a stable

Bud and Lou with their sons: Bud Jr., who was adopted, and Lou Jr., as seen at Christmastime, 1942. Wide World photo.

Lou and his one-year-old son on November 1, 1943, just three days before Lou Jr. died.

of racehorses and trained them on a ranch he owned in Canoga Park. The horses gave him more headaches than trophies. Sid Fields, a longtime friend of Costello's, tells this anecdote.

> Lou bought a horse from Ireland named Bazooka, a great sprinter. One day we were at the studio and the horse was running at Bay Meadows in San Francisco. When Lou came to the studio, everybody yelled, "Hey, Lou–your horse is running today! We all bet on him!" Lou said, "Wait a minute. I haven't talked to my trainer yet." He got ahold of a racing form and he saw the race was a mile and a sixteenth. "My horse is a sprinter," Lou said. "What's he doing in this race?" He called his trainer in San Francisco and the trainer explained to him that he just put the horse in for a sharpener. "He can't win but he needs the workout," he told Lou. Well, it turned out that the race was run so slow, Bazooka won, paying eighty-two dollars. Everyone in the studio had it but Costello.

Another Sid Fields anecdote:

> Costello bought a mare but it always finished last, and he couldn't figure this out. One day another horse owner asked Lou how the mare was doing and he explained how the horse was always dead last. "When are you going to pump her up?" asked the owner. Lou said, "What do you mean, *pump her up?*" "Don't you know? That horse has a collapsed left lung. You have to pump up the lung so she can get air in it and breathe." Lou was furious. He called his trainer and yelled, "How can you claim a horse for me that has a collapsed lung!" The trainer didn't know anything about it. Then Lou got an idea. "We can make a killing with this horse!" he said. So he sent the trainer with the mare to New Jersey. When the trainer got to Jersey, Lou called him and told him to enter the horse in the last race on Saturday. "Pump her up–*and don't tell anybody!!* Do you hear me?" "I could hear you without the phone!" said the trainer. Saturday came and Lou bet four thousand dollars across the board. The mare never won a race so the odds were 20 to 1 in the New York papers and 20 to 1 in the scratch sheets. That night Lou sat by the radio and listened to the results. The mare won. As soon as he heard that, Lou switched off the radio, got a pencil and paper and started to figure out how much he won for four thousand at 20 to 1. When he got the newspaper the next morning, the horse paid

four dollars! Never won a race before! Lou called the trainer and yelled, "What happened? Didn't I tell you not to tell anybody!!" "I didn't tell anybody," the trainer said. "You must've told somebody!! Well . . ." said the trainer, "on the way to the track I stopped off at a little Italian restaurant and told the waiter to put a few dollars on the horse." Costello hollered into the phone, "When you tell one Italian in New Jersey–you tell Italy!!"

Besides gambling, Bud and Lou had another common interest: practical jokes. Producer Robert Arthur recalled that during the shooting of ABBOTT AND COSTELLO MEET FRANKENSTEIN, every morning Bud and Lou stopped off at a little bakery near the studio to buy a dozen cream pies. The owner of the bakery was very proud of the fact that Abbott and Costello enjoyed his pies so much. What he didn't know was that the boys were throwing them all over the set of the movie. Their producers and directors tolerated the most outlandish practical jokes because they kept Bud and Lou "up" during the long, dull stretches between scenes.

In 1943, they were riding the crest of their popularity. For the second year in a row they were voted the number one box office attraction. They had their own NBC radio series and it was always among the ten top-rated shows. Then in March of 1943 it looked as if the partnership might come to a tragic end. On March 3, his thirty-seventh birthday, Lou Costello collapsed from rheumatic heart disease. He had suffered from rheumatic fever as a child and now the disease flared up. It would continue to plague him for the remainder of his life. For several weeks Bud Abbott carried on with their radio show, hoping Lou would have a speedy recovery. A different guest star filled in for Lou each week. But when Lou's condition didn't improve, Bud gave up the series to await his partner, who had to be confined to a wheelchair. The doctors thought that Lou might never be able to work again. But he was such a determined man, he fought the disease and slowly began to gain back his strength. While he was recuperating, all of the biggest stars in Hollywood visited him to pay their respects, including Lou's childhood idol, Charlie Chaplin. At this time Bud and Lou drew up plans for a Rheumatic Fever Foundation to be established in Palm Springs. They planned a nationwide tour, turning over their salaries to the foundation. They would also donate the profits from a reissue of BUCK PRIVATES. However, another tragedy in Lou Costello's life curtailed their plans for the foundation.

A jaunty Bud Abbott arrives in Southampton for a 1950 tour of the British Isles with Costello.

In September, on his mother's birthday, Lou got out of bed and took his first steps in six months, and by November he was able to resume work. On Thursday afternoon, November 4, the team was busily rehearsing at NBC for their first radio show since Lou's illness. Three hours before the broadcast Lou was told that his baby son, Louis Francis, Jr., had somehow crawled from his playpen to the swimming pool, fell in and drowned. That morning Lou had bought a teddy bear for the baby. A week later would have seen his first birthday. Costello shut his eyes at the news and clutched Bud's sleeve. As the show's air time approached, Jimmy Durante, Red Skelton and Mickey Rooney offered to fill in for him. Lou was grateful but insisted on doing the show. No one in the studio audience was aware of the tragedy when Lou solemnly walked into the studio. The red light blinked on and he became the old Lou Costello. The team began one of their typical radio dialogues.

Lou: "HEYYYYYYY ABBOT-T-T-T-T! I just took a shower with my shirt, socks and underwear on."
Bud: "Now, why did you do that, Costello?"
Lou: "Do you know a better way of getting your laundry done?"

They continued the routine, which was filled with references to

Dedication ceremonies for the Lou Costello Jr. Youth Foundation in 1947. Lou's family seated left.

Lou's health. The studio audience could see that both Bud and Lou were upset. Lou's face was white and swollen. Several times during the show he fluffed his lines and lost his place. Lana Turner was the guest star and she couldn't suppress her own grief for Costello's loss and read her lines barely above a whisper. The band number began and Lou slumped into a chair, silently waiting for the next sketch. At the end of the show Bud, in a broken voice, apprised the audience of what had happened. This is what he said: "Now that our program is over I would like to pay tribute to my best friend and a man who has more courage than I have ever seen in the theater. The old expression, 'The show must go on,' was brought home to all of us. Just before our broadcast, Lou Costello was told that his baby had died. There is nothing more that I can say except that I know you all join me in expressing our deepest sympathy to a great trouper."

Lou never got over the loss of his son. After the tragedy, the dinner parties shifted to his mother's home. He brooded about it and eventually moved from the house to try to forget. Bud and Lou then devoted their energies to creating the Lou Costello Jr. Youth Foundation, a recreational area for underprivileged children to be built in the child's memory.

To raise the money needed to build it, Abbott and Costello

made a personal appearance tour of the country for twenty weeks at twenty-five thousand dollars a week. A three-week engagement at the Roxy Theatre in New York broke all attendance records. New York *Times* critic Bosley Crowther mentioned the stage show in a review of the accompanying movie: "With Bud Abbott and Lou Costello as the stars of its stage show the Roxy Theatre could be flashing the telephone directory on its screen and still draw the clamoring customers."

By the end of the tour they had raised half a million dollars and construction began on the foundation in the Boyle Heights district of Los Angeles. The three-acre recreational center opened May 3, 1947. "If they don't have ragged clothes we don't want 'em," was the only qualification needed for membership set by Lou Costello. The center included libraries, medical clinics, a huge gymnasium, wood and metal shops, a baseball diamond and a swimming pool. Four months after it had opened, ten thousand underprivileged children made use of the center. The team shared the costs on a 50-50 basis. At times it was a struggle to keep the center in existence. Its running costs were estimated at eighty thousand dollars a year. Abbott and Costello sank a good part of their earnings from movies and nightclubs into the center. It was eventually absorbed by the city of Los Angeles in the fifties.

Their phenomenal success in Hollywood earned Abbott and Costello millions and they were able to live in the style that they had always dreamed of. But all of their fame and wealth didn't really change either of them. Mentally, they had never left burlesque. They were still, after all, just Bud and Lou.

Mr. and Mrs. Costello attend a Hollywood premiere in 1948.

WHO'S ON FIRST

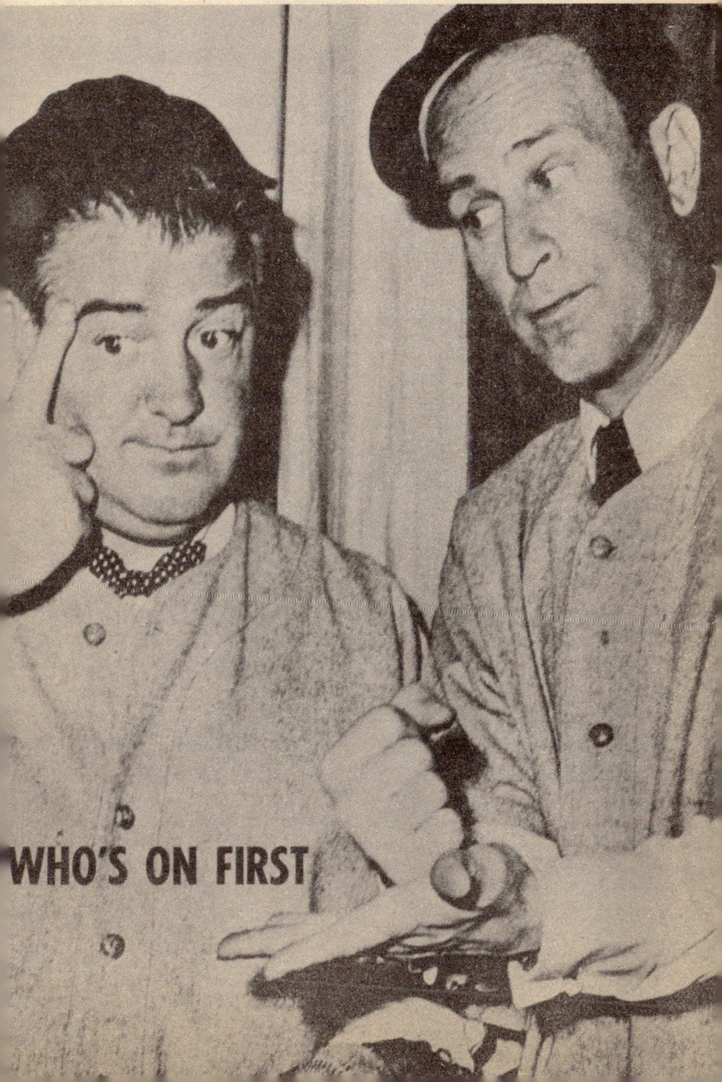

A book about Abbott and Costello wouldn't be complete without discussing "Who's on First," which is one of the most famous and funniest comedy routines of all time. This was a burlesque standard long before Abbott and Costello teamed up. Lately a number of people have been taking credit for creating "Who's on First," which is ridiculous since it is a derivative of several different gag routines. Possibly its earliest forerunner was "The Baker Scene," which dates back to the dawn of burlesque in the early 1900s. In this bit, the straight man announces to the comic that he just got a job working in a bakery. The comic asks, "What are you doing?"

S: "I'm loafing."
C: "I thought you said you were working."
S: "I am. They pay me to loaf."
C: "They *pay* you to loaf? How much do you get?"
S: "Seven dollars a week and double for overtime."
C: "For loafing??"
S: "Yes."
C: "Can I get a job loafing?"
S: "I don't know. You have to belong to the union."
C: "You gotta belong to a union to loaf?"
S: "Certainly, if you want to be recognized."
C: "I wouldn't care if they didn't recognize me. I wouldn't care if they didn't even *talk* to me! Say, I'd like to work in that bakery. Who's the boss?"
S: "Yes."
C: "Who's the guy you're working for?"
S: "That's exactly correct."
C: "I'm asking you what's the name of the boss."
S: "No, What's the name of the street."
C: "I didn't ask you that. I asked you who's the boss!"
S: "That's what I told you!"

The team of Bert Wheeler and Robert Woolsey performed a vaudeville routine that preceded "W.O.F.," in which Wheeler and Woolsey, studying a map, get into a furious argument over two towns named "Which" and "What."

Abbott and Costello themselves did a variation on "W.O.F." in their ninth film, WHO DONE IT? This time Bud tries to explain to Lou about "volts" and "watts," with predictable results.

Bud: "You know what volts are."
Lou: "They're what?"
Bud: "That's right. Volts are watts."
Lou: "Well go ahead and tell me."
Bud: "You just said it."
Lou: "I'm askin' you–what's volts?"
Bud: "That's right–watts are volts."
Lou: "What are you askin' *me* for??"

So it is clear that through the years "W.O.F." evolved from a number of routines, such as the aforementioned.

Bud and Lou performed "W.O.F." before they met in 1936. They spent the first two years of their collaboration polishing it in burlesque and vaudeville theaters all over the country. With John Grant's help, they expanded it, adding new bits of business. By the time they performed it on their first "Kate Smith Show" it was a flawless routine, the laughs building one on top of the other in rapid succession. The team had to change the closing gag for radio. The burlesque version ended with Costello yelling, "I don't give a damn!" and Abbott replying, "Oh, that's our shortstop!" On radio the line became "I don't care," which isn't nearly as funny as "I don't give a damn." Millions of listeners, unfamiliar with burlesque, were now hearing the routine for the first time and it quickly became identified with Abbott and Costello. Reportedly, President Roosevelt called Bud and Lou while they were featured on "The Kate Smith Show" to tell them how much he enjoyed it. Whenever they played a nightclub the audience invariably requested the baseball skit. It is also featured in three of their movies, most successfully in THE NAUGHTY NINETIES. Shorter versions pop up in ONE NIGHT IN THE TROPICS and WHO DONE IT? The team repeated it countless times on their NBC radio series–often on the closing show of each radio season. They naturally took advantage of the surefire skit when they made their TV debut on "The Colgate Comedy Hour," and once again on that show with Joe DiMaggio joining the act. It can be heard in an episode of their own television show titled "The Actors' Home," and in the mid-fifties they did the routine once again on The Tonight Show while Steve Allen was the host. "Who's on First" is filed in the archives of the Smithsonian Institution as Americana and a special gold record and a copy of the text have been on permanent display at the Baseball Hall of Fame in Cooperstown, New York, since 1956. For a number of years NBC

Abbott and Costello are crowned the top box office attractions of 1942 at the Waldorf-Astoria in New York.

ran a film clip of the team performing "W.O.F." after the final game of the World Series.

"Who's on First" is timeless, remaining as fresh and funny today as it ever was. New audiences are continually discovering the Abbott and Costello routine through television and numerous recordings that have preserved it.

Following page: Abbott and Costello tangle with French customs officials in a sketch from their only Broadway show, THE STREETS OF PARIS (1939).

ABBOTT AND COSTELLO ON BROADWAY

The Streets of Paris opened June 19, 1939, at the Broadhurst Theatre on West Forty-fourth Street. It was just meant to play through the summer but it was such a smash hit with audiences and critics alike that it ran for over a year. The lavish musical revue in two acts was co-produced by Olsen and Johnson and it bore considerably more than a passing resemblance to their own *Hellzapoppin'*. The revue was crammed with slapstick burlesque routines, acrobats, chorus girls, novelty acts and pistol shots galore. James McHugh and Al Dubin supplied the songs and six writers contributed the comedy sketches. Bobby Clark, making his second solo appearance after the death of his partner Paul McCullough, was billed as the star. The revue also introduced Carmen Miranda, the "Brazilian Bombshell," to American audiences. Other cast members included Luella Gear, French singer Jean Sablon, a comedian named Ben Dova whose specialty was a drunk routine, and one of the great vaudeville acts, Dr. "Think a Drink" Hoffman. But it was Abbott and Costello who stole the show. Every critic pointed out that the hilarity of *The Streets of Paris* was mostly due to these two ex-burlesquers. In a New York *Times* review, Brooks Atkinson described the team: "Abbott is the overbearing mastermind whose feverish, impatient guidance of the conversation produces the crisis. Costello is the short, fat he-who-gets-slapped. He is a moon-faced zany with wide, credulous eyes, a high voice and puffy hands that struggle in futile gestures. Both men work themselves into a state of excitement that is wonderful to behold."

Bud and Lou participated in four scenes titled "Customs," "On the Boulevard," "Rest Cure" and "That's Music."

In "Customs" the boys simply ran through one of their many patter routines, such as "Hole in the Wall." This starts with Abbott placing his rotund partner in a hypothetical situation. "Suppose you bore a hole in that wall over there," imagines Bud. When Lou goes along with this make-believe, Bud suddenly chastises him. "What right do you have to bore a hole in that wall!" This snowballs until Abbott has poor Costello ready to give himself up to the police for committing vandalism. This was the basis for many of their routines. Lou makes a perfectly innocent remark which Bud distorts until his partner believes he is guilty of a crime against mankind.

"On the Boulevard" was a new name for the "Lemon Bit." The

team performed this innumerable times and it can be viewed in their third film, IN THE NAVY.

The critics singled out "Rest Cure" as the highlight of *The Streets of Paris.* This riotous sketch brought down the house at every performance. John Grant adapted the sketch from "Crazy House." We find Costello checking into a sanitarium for some rest, and that's about the only thing he doesn't get during his stay. Upon his arrival the nurse warns him that he is in a hospital and must observe the rules. "We must have absolute quiet–silence," she whispers. The nurse then announces that the patient has arrived by screaming at the top of her lungs, "MR. LOU COSTELLO IS HERE!" Lou realizes he's in an insane asylum and tries to leave. He is stopped by the head doctor (Abbott), who places Lou in a room to get a good night's sleep. There Lou is annoyed by a parade of lunatics. Two men march into the room and one shouts, "Take it back!" The other replies, "I won't!" The first man shoots the second and drags the body out of the room. Then Lou is visited by a woman who mistakes him for a bed of roses and begins to drench his nightgown with a water pail. Another oddball wearing a turban asks Costello if he'd like his palm read. "Why not," says Lou and the swami paints Lou's hand red. A man walks into the room with one arm extended and his female companion pronounces, "He's a pump! Pump him!" Lou pumps the man's arm and gets a face full of water. Some of Costello's other guests include a firing squad armed with seltzer bottles and a gangster with an imaginary gun. Finally, a woman looks about the room and exclaims, "What lovely apples," and proceeds to pick invisible apples from an invisible tree. When she leaves, Lou tries shaking the "tree." A bushel of very real apples falls on him, knocking him out cold.

Lou Costello repeated "Crazy House" often for the next twenty years. A less successful version appears in the film RIDE 'EM COWBOY. The boys also did it on their first "Colgate Comedy Hour" and on their own TV series. After the team split up, Lou revived the sketch on the Steve Allen variety show and it was a big hit.

Abbott and Costello joined Bobby Clark in the final sketch of *Streets.* "That's Music." In this one, Clark played an American tourist and Bud and Lou were the proprietors of a French music store.

At one point during the show's run, Bud and Lou were holding down three jobs simultaneously. After their last scene in *Streets* they rushed over to the popular restaurant-nightclub the Versailles and did two shows. In addition to this they were regulars on the Kate Smith radio hour on CBS. The combined paychecks enabled Bud to rent a luxurious apartment on West Forty-fifth Street and buy a summer home in New Jersey. Lou and his family continued to live in Paterson.

When *The Streets of Paris* concluded its run at the Broadhurst, the legendary Mike Todd produced the show at the Hall of Music at the New York World's Fair. Todd condensed the show to a seventy-minute running time and it was a hit all over again. Bobby Clark and Carmen Miranda were no longer in the cast and Bud and Lou received top billing. Sharing the spotlight with the team was an old friend from burlesque, Gypsy Rose Lee. Costello got the opportunity to sing a duet with her titled "Is It Possible?" Brooks Atkinson remarked that Abbott and Costello were even funnier in the World's Fair version than they were in the original show.

ABBOTT AND COSTELLO ON RADIO

Abbott and Costello were Fred Allen's summer replacement on radio in 1940.

After their debut on "The Kate Smith Show" in 1938, Abbott and Costello continued to work in radio on a regular basis for thirteen years. For their first appearance with Kate Smith, the team was paid five hundred and fifty dollars. Their ten-minute stint on the show was a success but they discovered that their voices sounded alike on the air. Listeners wrote in, complaining that they couldn't tell who was asking and who was answering. To solve this problem, Lou adopted the shrill falsetto voice for which he became famous. It also fit perfectly with his tag lines, "I'm a ba-a-ad boy!" and "I'm only thwee-and-a-half years old." They were featured every week on the show for a year and a half and also filled in for the star while she was on vacation. By this time they were earning twelve hundred and fifty dollars a week. Bud and Lou then became frequent guests on "The Edgar Bergen and Charlie McCarthy Show," and in July of 1940 they were signed as Fred Allen's summer replacement. This was an important step for the team since Fred Allen had one of the highest-rated programs in the country. NBC was also grooming the fast-rising comedy duo for their own weekly variety show. They scored another big hit on the summer series, which was on Wednesday nights at nine o'clock, New York time. It was a half-hour of burlesque routines and music. Harry Von Zell was the announcer, Peter Van Steeden was the orchestra leader and actress Benay Venuta served as a foil for Bud and Lou. A feature on the summer show was a weekly rib session in which they invited an amateur inventor to explain some bizarre gadget that he was trying to market, such as a musical typewriter. Bud and Lou would then make wisecracks about the inventions and their creators.

Their own series, "The Abbott and Costello Program," premiered on NBC Thursday night, October 8, 1941, at seven o'clock. The half-hour show, sponsored by Camel cigarettes, remained in the top fifteen shows for six years. The comedians were aided by Ken Niles, who was the announcer, vocalist Connie Haines and the Leith Stevens Orchestra (later replaced by the Freddie Rich Orchestra). The special guest star on the premier episode was Veronica Lake, whose "peekaboo" hairdo was kidded by Costello throughout the show. *Variety,* reviewing this show, commented: "There was not a trace of highbrow anywhere in this program . . . It was all mirth-inducing but not, definitely not, subtle." If this reviewer was expecting subtlety, he wasn't familiar with Abbott and Costello. Their stock-in-trade, particularly in radio, was pure, unadulterated corn. The following are some typical jokes that the team did on their radio series.

Lou explains to his partner that he slept all night on a park bench.
Bud: "It's a wonder you didn't freeze to death."
Lou: "I had my radio with me. That keeps me warm."
Bud: "How can a radio keep you warm?"
Lou: "I tune in Gabriel Heatter!"

Bud: "Costello–I'll have you know that last night I had a date with Betty Hutton."
Lou: "You make a lovely couple–Hutton and nuttin'!"

Bud: "In our new picture *I'm* taking care of the love interest."
Lou: "Oh yeah? What do you know about makin' love, Abbott?"
Bud: "Why, yesterday at the studio, Hedy Lamarr and Lana Turner had a hair-pulling match over me."
Lou: "Yeah, but it was *your* hair they were pullin'!"

A policeman (Mel Blanc) tells Lou that he never misses the Abbott and Costello program.
Lou: "You don't?"
Mel: "No, I don't hear it and I don't miss it!"

Because of the constant demand for material in a weekly radio show, Abbott and Costello couldn't rely solely on their old routines. So they hired an army of gag writers to turn out new jokes. Some of their writers through the years were Eddie Forman, Sid Fields, Harry Crane, Hal Fimberg, Don Prindle, Martin Ragaway, Leonard Stern, Ed Cherkose, Parke Levy, Paul Conlon and, of course, John Grant. Lou's brother, Pat, was also a contributor. Many of these writers started out with Abbott and Costello and went on to be very successful in television. The quality of the jokes they wrote for the team is evidenced by the fact that other comedians are still using them today.

The work schedule in radio was rather casual compared to that in today's television. "The Abbott and Costello Program" was no exception. The writers wrote their respective jokes at home. They attended a meeting with the producer (Hollywood veteran Martin Gosch produced many of the shows) and went over the material. On the day that the show was broadcast, everyone gathered at the studio at NBC, which was located at the corner of Hollywood and

Vine. Bud, Lou, the writers and the producer sat at a long table and made changes in the script, adding and cutting jokes. They generally worked right up until air time.

The program originated from Hollywood but once a year the team headed east to do a few weeks of shows from New York.

The show opened with Costello's famous cry, "HEYYYYYYY ABBOT-T-T-T-T!" The team then launched into a routine, establishing the theme of the episode. In one of their dialogues, Lou wants to buy a house but he doesn't have enough money. Bud offers a solution.

Bud: "I'll get you a loan in the bank."
Lou: "Who wants to be alone with you in a bank?"
Bud: "I'm trying to tell you that you can get a lien against the house."
Lou: "Lean against the house? What's the matter with the joint–is it gonna fall down?"
Bud: "Talk sense, Costello. To get in the house you must go through escrow!"
Lou: "Why can't I go through Glendale?"

After their opening exchange, announcer Ken Niles was introduced. Apparently Niles was very thin, because he was constantly the target of "skinny" jokes. Costello would say, "Niles is so skinny, yesterday in a drugstore, he drank a glass of tomato juice—a lady looked at him and said, 'My, ain't it warm today!' " Announcers have always been the brunt of insults by comedians, but usually for their drinking. Johnny Carson still keeps up this grand old tradition with Ed McMahon.

Following this spot in the program, character actress Elvia Allman joined the discussion. Miss Allman was a fine straight woman and she worked with the team often. She played Mrs. Niles, the fictional wife of the announcer. She traded insults with Costello in an on-the-air feud that they kept up for quite some time.

Examples:

Lou: "Mrs. Niles, I'm going to buy you a lovely present, a nice red fire extinguisher that will last you a hundred years."
Allman: "But I don't expect to be here for a hundred years."
Lou: "That's all right. Where you're going you can take it with you!"

Allman: "Costello, the stork that brought you should have been

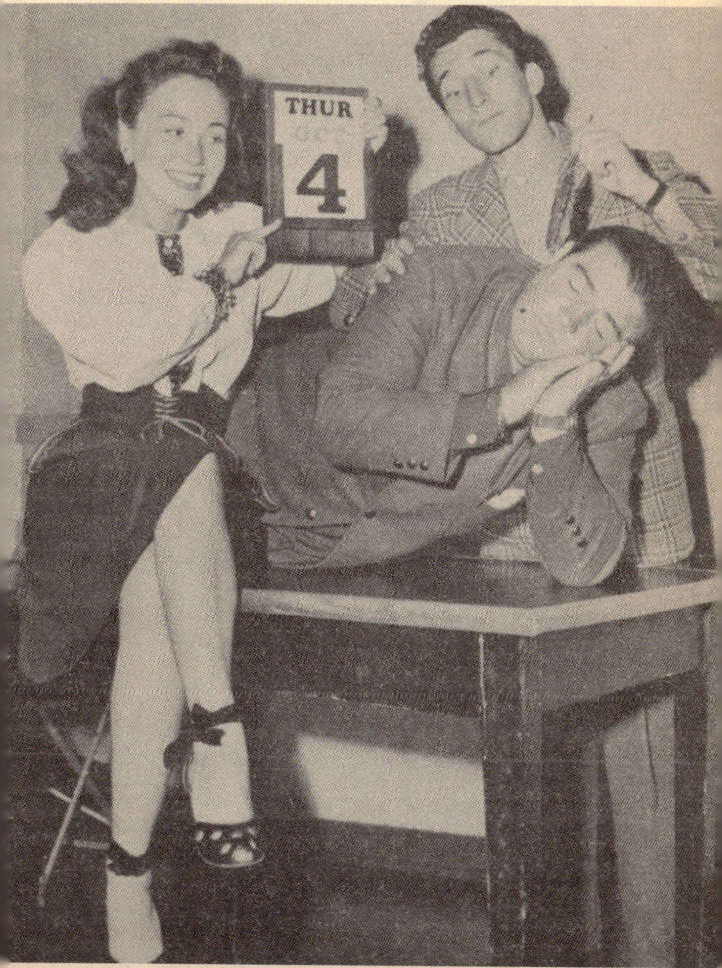

Publicity photo for Abbott and Costello's own radio series. Connie Haines and Freddie Rich are reminding Costello of the opening show of their fifth season (1945).

arrested for smuggling dope!"

An interesting fact about the radio series is that Lou Costello's character was the opposite of the character he portrayed on film. In the movies he was a pathetic child-man who was either scared or confused. On radio, however, he came off as sort of the Don Rickles of his day, insulting everyone on the show, including Abbott. Costello would never dream of insulting Abbott in any one of their films. Lou was hilarious on radio but these Rickles-type barbs didn't fit him. He lost the audience's sympathy, which was so important to his kind of comedy. This points out the basic weakness of Abbott and Costello. They never discussed characterization. If a joke was funny, they did it, and that was that. They also did quite a lot of mild double-entendre jokes on radio. This was unusual for Abbott and Costello, who even in their burlesque days never used blue material. And they were always careful not to include risqué gags in their movies. But due to the pressure of a weekly series, they didn't have time to be as fussy about material. Of course, these jokes are innocent by today's standards. The writers also created a girl-crazy bachelor image for Lou on radio that just wasn't him at all.

Abbott and Costello shied from topical references in movies and television, but they more than made up for it on radio. The program was at its peak during World War II, and there were constant references to gas rationing, oil shortages and the high price of meat. In one episode Costello is very excited because he claims that he's just been made a wealthy man. Abbott asks him what happened and Costello responds, "My uncle died and left me three pounds of hamburger!"

As good as Lou Costello was on radio, the medium was confining to him. Lou was a great ad-lib comedian. He didn't have this luxury on the radio series. These shows were done live and the actors read their lines from the script. So Lou was confined to the written page and the strict time limits of a half-hour show. Lou was also a visual comedian. You had to see him really to appreciate his comedic talents.

Bud and Lou were surrounded by an expert cast of regulars on their program. The brilliant Mel Blanc turned up as many different characters, utilizing his talent for voices as he did on "The Jack Benny Show."

Double-talk comic Al Kelly occasionally appeared as Bud and Lou's "head writer," Buford Clardy.

Sid Fields was featured on many of the programs, in addition to writing them.

Another regular was Artie Auerbach, a dialect comedian, wh played a character named "Mr. Kitzel."

Other featured performers were Milt Bronson and Frank Nel son. Costello also played several different characters, includin his own seven year old nephew, "Sebastian."

The list of guests that appeared on "The Abbott and Costell Program" reads like Who's Who in Hollywood. Here are jus some of the guest stars on the show during the 1943-44 season Cary Grant, Lana Turner, Hedy Lamarr, John Garfield, Georg Raft, Charles Laughton, Humphrey Bogart, Linda Darnell, Ala Ladd, George Brent, Bert Lahr (who substituted for Lou durin Lou's illness), Adolphe Menjou and Hedda Hopper.

The biggest stars in Hollywood appeared frequently on radi during the forties. It was a good way to plug their latest movies, a actors do today on TV talk shows. There was very little rehearsa involved. They just showed up and read their lines into a micro phone.

The second half of "The Abbott and Costello Program" was de voted to a song number by Connie Haines and the main sketc featuring the guest star. April 6, 1944, Cary Grant guested on on of the funniest shows. The premise of the show is that Costello ha bought his own radio station, Station I.O.U.

Cary: "Pardon me–is this Station I.O.U., the Voice of the Credi tors?"

Bud: "Costello, look who it is–Cary Grant!"

(APPLAUSE)

Bud: "Cary, this visit's a great surprise. What brings you over her to Costello's radio station?"

Cary: "Well, Bud, next Sunday is Easter–you can't get thos candy eggs, so I thought I'd come over here and pick up the rea thing!"

Lou: "YOU CAN PICK THAT ONE UP, GRANT–YO BROUGHT IT IN WITH YOU!"

Cary: "Oh, don't take offense, Lou–I was only kidding. I think you're a very funny fellow. In fact, everybody at our house gath- ers around the radio each Thursday night at seven o'clock!"

Lou: "Yeah???"

Cary: "Yes, and at seven-thirty we turn it on!"

Costello remembers meeting Cary's family: "I climbed up the tree and shook hands with his father!"

Cary says that his family recalls Costello, too. "That is, all but y grandmother."

ou: "Don't your grandmother remember me?"

ary: "No, but she remembers your jokes."

When Alan Ladd was a guest, the whole cast got together to oof daytime serials. Alan Ladd played the announcer and did a keoff on radio commercials.

add: "MEN! A new shaving cream has hit the market! It is called—REVERSO! REVERSO does away with shaving of any kind!—it makes the whiskers grow inside your mouth. All you have to do is BITE 'EM OFF! Remember, REVERSO! Spelled backwards it reads—OSREVER!—which makes it harder to remember!"

add then introduces an Abbott and Costello version of a typical rties soap opera, titled "Blossom Fink, Girl Street Cleaner."

add: "As we look in upon Blossom this morning, she and her husband are having breakfast."

lossom's husband then spends the entire episode trying to decide he should have coffee or milk with his breakfast.

add (IN FAST AND LOUD): "Tune in tomorrow!! Will John have milk or coffee!!"

The format remained pretty much the same until 1946. Then arilyn Maxwell and bandleader Skinnay Ennis replaced Connie aines and Freddie Rich. The following season found Abbott and ostello with a new network and a new time slot. They moved to BC. The show was then broadcast on Wednesday at nine 'clock. On the premiere of the ABC show, Lou made a reference o his former home, NBC. He called it "the network with fifteen residents." This series remained on the air until 1949. In addition o the variety series, the team hosted a Saturday morning kiddie how on ABC radio appropriately titled "The Abbott and Costello hildren's Show." This program, which featured a weekly talent ontest for children, was quite popular and lasted three seasons. The team then left radio to host TV's "Colgate Comedy Hour."

ABBOTT AND COSTELLO IN THE MOVIES

One Night in the Tropics

Bud Abbott and Lou Costello made their screen debut in a lavish musical (by Universal standards), ONE NIGHT IN THE TROPICS. It is not officially an Abbott and Costello film since Bud and Lou are supporting players, performing their famed routines as they had done in *The Streets of Paris.* They brought writer John Grant with them to Hollywood to integrate their material into the story, although Grant doesn't receive any screen credit. One of Grant's talents was an ability to take an old burlesque standard and make it seem new by switching it around and cleverly working it into the plot of a film. He was a brilliant comedy writer in his own right. He wrote most of the Abbott and Costello comedies and contributed, in no small way, to the team's incredible popularity.

ONE NIGHT IN THE TROPICS (originally titled CARIBBEAN HOLIDAY) is also notable for a lovely musical score composed by Jerome Kern. "Remind Me" and "You and Your Kiss," with lyrics by Dorothy Fields, are charming tunes. "Your Dream," with lyrics by Oscar Hammerstein, is also memorable. "The Farandola" provides the musical finale.

The story, based on the old novel *Love Insurance* by Earl Derr Biggers, centers on an eager insurance salesman, Jim Moore (Allan Jones), and his best friend, Steve Harper (Robert Cummings). Steve is worried that his girlfriend, Cynthia (Nancy Kelly), won't marry him. Jim gets the idea to insure Steve's wedding for a million dollars. That way, if Cynthia won't marry Steve, he stands to collect the million. Jim gets a tough nightclub owner, Roscoe (William Frawley), to finance the policy. When Cynthia sees Steve kissing another girl, Mickey (Peggy Moran), she gets furious. Cynthia and her aunt (Mary Boland) board an ocean liner heading for San Marcos, South America. Steve and Jim follow them to the mythical country. Roscoe, who doesn't intend to pay off on the policy, orders his employees, Abbott and Costello, to go to San Marcos and make sure Steve marries Cynthia. After a series of complications, Steve lands up marrying Mickey, Jim marries Cynthia and everybody lives happily ever after.

Abbott and Costello use their own names in TROPICS. The only other film in which they used their own names was their last for Universal, ABBOTT AND COSTELLO MEET THE MUMMY. TROPICS contains five of their most popular comedy

Bud and Lou make their screen debut in ONE NIGHT IN THE TROPICS. Pictured here doing "Who's On First".

routines, including an abbreviated version of "Who's on First."

We are introduced to Bud and Lou in Roscoe's nightclub. We don't see them at first, but merely hear their familiar voices off-screen. Perhaps this was Universal's way of introducing two radio comics to the filmgoing audience. The camera then pans to a roulette table where Bud and Lou are in the midst of one of their money-exchanging routines. A version of this turned up the following year in IN THE NAVY. (In this sequence Abbott also gives Costello his first screen slap.) Another typical Abbott and Costello gag:

Bud: "Stop smoking in here, Costello."
Lou: "Who's smoking?"
Bud: "You are."
Lou: "What makes you think I'm smoking?"
Bud: "You have a cigar in your mouth."
Lou: "I got my shoes on but I'm not walking."

In another routine from their vast repertoire, "Jonah and the Whale," Lou attempts to tell a joke that he claims he's written by himself. It concerns Jonah and the whale. Lou doesn't get very far since Bud constantly interrupts him with ridiculous questions like,

Villain William Frawley threatens Bud and Lou in ONE NIGHT IN THE TROPICS.

"What kind of a whale?" "How do I know what kind of a whale?" Lou yells. "Do you think I hang around with 'em? What do you think I do—belong to a whale gang!" Not only does Bud continue to interrupt Lou, but he reveals the punch line of the joke, embarrassing his partner.

When Bud fires Lou for bungling his job, Lou demands to be paid off. "I was supposed to get a dollar a day. I worked for you one year—that's three hundred and sixty-five dollars." Bud then cheats Lou out of his salary with a hilarious series of deductions. Bud tells him, "There's twenty-four hours in a day and you only worked eight hours a day. Then you only worked one-third of each day. Now one-third of three hundred and sixty-five is approximately one hundred and twenty-one dollars." Lou demands the money. Bud takes further deductions for weekends, vacations, lunch hours and holidays. Finally, Lou is left with a single dollar bill, which a waiter snatches from his hand, mistaking it for a tip. Lou, broke again, asks Bud if he can have his job back. Bud consents, "But not for the same money!"

The team also performed "Mustard," probably their most popular routine next to "Who's on First." Lou buys a hot dog but he doesn't want any mustard with it. He says that mustard makes him sick. Bud becomes indignant—explaining that thousands work in factories just to manufacture mustard and Lou's selfishness will not only result in mass unemployment for mustard workers but will send their children to orphan asylums. Lou can't comprehend this. He says, "Are you trying to tell me that those thousands of people are making one little jar of mustard just for me! Well, you can tell 'em not to make any more because I'm not gonna eat it!"

ONE NIGHT IN THE TROPICS received generally lukewarm reviews. Almost every critic pointed out that Abbott and Costello saved the film. Bosley Crowther of the New York *Times* commented, "Abbott and Costello stand out as logistical wizards amid the helter-skelter confusion of the story." The plot is silly and contrived but Allan Jones, Nancy Kelly and Robert Cummings are likable actors and they make it all work somehow.

The film was a resounding flop at the box office, and Bud and Lou rarely mentioned it again. They preferred to say that BUCK PRIVATES was their initial film. This is unfair to ONE NIGHT IN THE TROPICS, which is an engaging musical comedy.

Buck Privates

One day in 1940 a young screenwriter named Alex Gottlieb was summoned to the front office at Universal. "How would you like to be a producer?" Gottlieb was asked upon his arrival. "Sure," answered the screenwriter. The studio was looking for a producer-writer to make a series of B comedies starring a pair of low comics named Abbott and Costello. "You'll land up with A comedies," Gottlieb told the executives. "I saw them in *The Streets of Paris* in New York and they were a sensation." He recalled how sophisticated Park Avenue types roared at old burlesque routines as if they were just discovering them. The studio people were not as confident as Gottlieb because of the poor box office returns of the team's first film, ONE NIGHT IN THE TROPICS. But they decided to give them another chance and Gottlieb was assigned the task of being their producer. He later found out that seventeen other writers had turned the job down. They didn't want to be associated with low comics. Universal wanted their first film to be an army comedy, to cash in on America's new peacetime draft. They were eager to release it as soon as possible since Paramount was planning a similar film, CAUGHT IN THE DRAFT, to star Bob Hope. The film, titled BUCK PRIVATES, turned out to be Universal's biggest money-maker to that date, eventually grossing four million dollars and establishing the team as the third-ranking box office attraction of the year.

Gottlieb remembered his first meeting with Bud and Lou. Lou Costello said to Gottlieb, "I understand you're going to be our producer. I've had only one ambition all of my life—to be a movie star. You just tell me what to do. I'll do anything you say." Gottlieb told Lou what he had told the Universal executives and assured him that he would indeed be a movie star.

The studio wanted someone who could shoot the picture quickly and cheaply. A young director on the lot, Arthur Lubin, had directed some low-budget Westerns starring John Wayne. He had a reputation for being a good director and an economical one. Lubin told how he got the job directing BUCK PRIVATES: "The people at Universal came to me and asked me if I would direct Abbott and Costello. At that time there was a very popular dance team called the Abbott Dancers. I said, 'I don't know why you're selecting me to direct them. I don't know anything about dancing.' They said, 'No, they're a comedy team from New York.'" Lubin

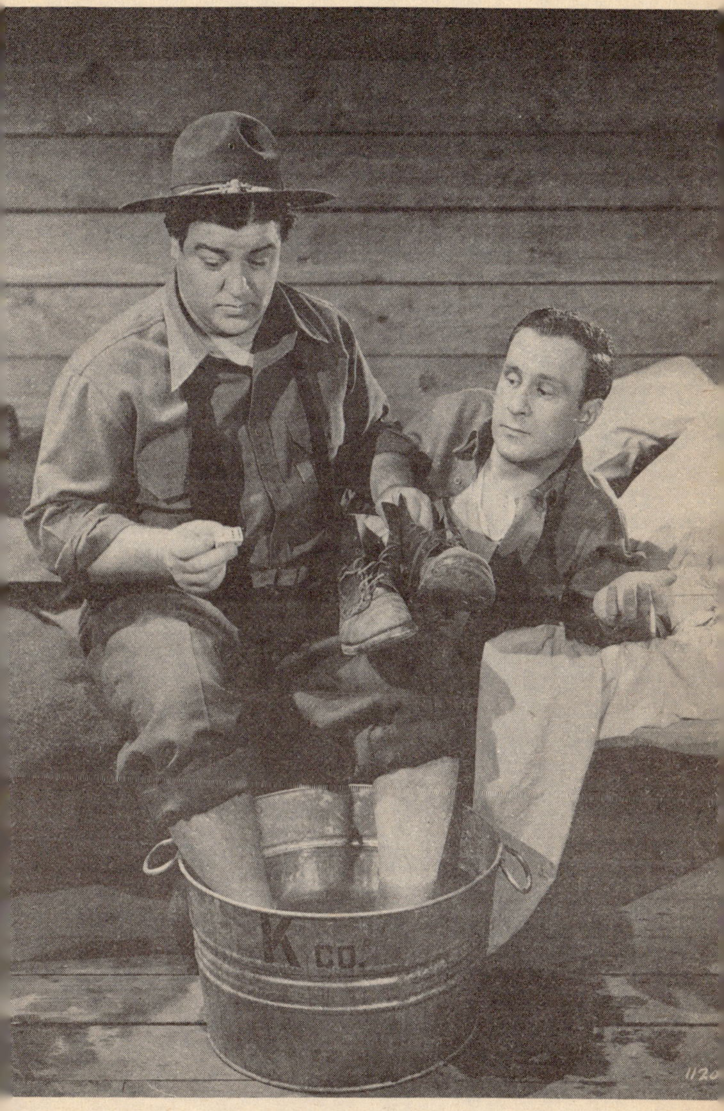
K CO.
1120

The two most popular teams in the forties—Abbott and Costello and the Andrews Sisters. From BUCK PRIVATES.

had never seen or heard of Abbott and Costello. He agreed to direct the picture and Bud Abbott threw a party so everyone could get acquainted. Lubin became good friends with Bud and Lou and their families.

Arthur T. Horman wrote the story line for BUCK PRIVATES and John Grant supplied the material for Abbott and Costello. When Arthur Lubin received the script from Grant, Lubin found it very puzzling. The story would go along nicely for a while and then it would suddenly say: "An Abbott and Costello routine here," or "The boys do the drill routine here." Since Bud and Lou knew all these burlesque bits by heart, Grant didn't bother to write out the dialogue. Lubin had to get the boys to act out the material for him, so he'd get the idea.

"I found it very difficult to direct them at first," said Lubin. "They were naïve as far as filmmaking was concerned. They played to the people on the set, instead of the camera. They were used to having a live audience, and missed getting laughs. But they learned quickly and we had a lot of fun on that picture."

Bud and Lou were fascinated with the business of making movies. If the call was for 9 A.M., they were on the set at eight. They both couldn't get over the wonders of the lights and cameras. This excitement and freshness is very evident in the film. In none

Lou confronts his ring opponent for the first time.

of their other films did the team perform with the same level of enthusiasm. After several subsequent films, the newness wore off for them and they became bored. It is painfully evident, in later years, that their hearts were no longer in their work.

In BUCK PRIVATES Bud and Lou are Slicker Smith and Herbie Brown, two street merchants who sell dollar neckties, worth at least two cents. Fleeing a tough cop (Nat Pendleton), the boys duck into an army recruiting center, thinking it's a movie house. Lou asks a corporal, "Hey, mister, what picture's playing?" The corporal says, "You're in the army now!" "Good," says Lou, "I never saw that picture." A sergeant asks Costello, "Draftee?" Costello naturally answers, "No, not a bit." The boys enlist, thinking they're signing up for a bank night raffle.

Universal decided that every Abbott and Costello film needed a romantic story line to bridge their comedy routines. BUCK PRIVATES suffers from a subplot that is laughable to today's audiences. A wealthy playboy, Randolph Parker III (Lee Bowman), gets drafted into the same regiment as his ex-chauffeur (Alan Curtis). Both men fight for the affection of a pretty army hostess, played by Jane Frazee. Parker the playboy learns that there is more to life than "sport roadsters and chorus girls" and the army transforms him into a hero by the last reel. The action takes place in Camp

Publicity still from BUCK PRIVATES. (Bud does not appear in this scene in the film.) With Shemp Howard.

Greely, an army base that could only exist in Hollywood. It has a recreation hall replete with a fifty-piece band and the Andrews Sisters. They put on a series of musical numbers for our boys that make Busby Berkeley look like the master of subtlety. From the looks of things, the country had a pretty jolly war ahead of it.

From the finished script it's easy to see how much was ad-libbed by Abbott and Costello. Lou ad-libbed all over the place. Halfway through a scene he would throw away the script and start to improvise. But Bud Abbott always brought Lou back on the track.

Lou's asides were often funnier than the scripted jokes. In the middle of the famous dice game scene, Lou suddenly said, for no apparent reason, "Startin' Tuesday I'm goin' out with girls." Bud simply said, "I don't blame you," and quickly went on with the routine. The dice game is a comedy tour de force. Costello stumbles into a crap game on board the troop train heading for army camp. Lou confides to Bud that he's never played the game before. Abbott agrees to let him play and Costello then surprises Abbott with his knowledge of gambling slang, such as "Fade that" and "Let it ride." "You sure you never played this game before?" Abbott asks suspiciously.

Since it was an army film, the team resurrected an old burlesque chestnut in which Bud teaches Lou close order drilling. Lou loved to try to confound his partner by tossing non sequiturs into a scene without warning. While doing the drill scene before the cameras, Lou turned to Bud and asked, "What time is it?" which wasn't in the script. Bud shouted back, "None of your business!"

The drill routine ran only two and a half minutes. When producer Gottlieb looked at a rough cut of BUCK PRIVATES he realized this was the funniest scene in the picture. He then screened all of the outtakes from the drill routine. Gottlieb saw that this discarded footage contained priceless bits of business improvised by Costello. No matter how many times he repeated a scene, Lou never did it the same way twice. So Gottlieb took some of this footage and added it to the completed scene. The result was a five-minute sequence instead of a two-and-a-half-minute one. When Lou saw this, he was amazed. They had taken a routine he had performed for years on stage, and with a few editing tricks made it twice as funny. He had no idea this could be done. Lou had tremendous respect for film after that.

Because of the fact that Lou never did a scene the same way twice, Lubin shot all of his scenes with two or three cameras simultaneously, just to make sure they didn't lose any of Lou's reactions. This became standard procedure on an Abbott and Costello movie.

John Grant managed to fit in Costello's first burlesque sketch, "Go Ahead and Sing." In this version Sergeant Nat Pendleton scolds Costello for playing the radio. As soon as Pendleton leaves, Bud tells Lou to "Go ahead and play the radio. You're an American citizen, aren't you?" Lou turns it back on and, of course, the sergeant returns and beats the daylights out of Lou. Pendleton asks Costello, "Why don't you be quiet like your buddy?" Bud, the instigator, has been sitting quietly, smoking a cigarette during all this.

Another highlight is a slapstick boxing match between Costello and a gorilla-like soldier. Nat Pendleton is the referee and he is clearly biased. When Lou gets knocked on the mat, Pendleton counts him out by twos. "What happened to one, three, five, seven and nine?" asks Lou. "I don't like those numbers, they're odd," Pendleton says. Costello yells, "Put 'em in! I like 'em!" Bud coaches Lou but he isn't much help.

Bud: "Now when you get in the ring . . . (illustrates punch) give him that old one-three . . . one-three . . ."
Lou: "What happens to 'two'?"
Bud: " 'Two' *you* get!"

Lou's lookalike brother, Pat, did some of Lou's stunt work in the boxing match.

The film's only lull is a lengthy war maneuvers sequence in which Lee Bowman and Alan Curtis blow up the rival army's blockhouse.

BUCK PRIVATES was shot in twenty days on the back lot. It cost less than two hundred thousand dollars to produce. Universal didn't think it was much and they quietly previewed it in Inglewood, California. It was immediately a smash. The audience laughed long and loud at these two fast-talking comedians. At this time, Universal was in grave financial trouble. They knew that if Abbott and Costello could make more comedies as funny as this one, they could save the studio. And they did. The day after the preview, Arthur Lubin was given a five-thousand-dollar bonus and told to get started on the next one right away. Four weeks later, they began shooting another film.

Even the critics liked BUCK PRIVATES. The New York *Times* described it as "one hour and a half of uproarious monkeyshines." The *Times* further stated that, "Army humor isn't apt to be subtle and neither are Abbott and Costello. Their antics have as much innuendo as a thousand-pound bomb but nearly as much explosive force." *Variety* predicted that the film would skyrocket Abbott and Costello to starring ranks as a comedy team. The reviewer also commented, "(The) picture is studded with several Abbott and Costello routines that are particularly effective for sustained laughs. Tops is a sequence in which Costello is a member of the awkward squad for special rifle drill. Running about five minutes, episode builds quickly for continuous hilarity—with dialogue drowned in the audience uproar."

Lou Costello was hailed as the funniest comedian since Chaplin. Chaplin himself said that Lou was "the best comic working in the business today." Metro-Goldwyn-Mayer signed Bud and Lou to make one film annually at that prestigious studio.

In retrospect, it is easy to see why they had such an impact. By 1941 the Marx Brothers had virtually disbanded, and Laurel and Hardy were clearly past their prime. The field was open for a new comedy team. Although Bud and Lou were not in the same league with Laurel and Hardy and the Marxes, their brand of knockabout comedy came as a welcome relief to audiences preoccupied with imminent war. The film also had the advantage of perfect timing. Released in February of 1941 (five months after the draft bill was passed), it was the first to deal with America's rookie army.

BUCK PRIVATES was the second film to feature the fabulous Andrews Sisters (Patty, Maxene, LaVerne). They were previously in something called ARGENTINE NIGHTS. In BUCK PRIVATES they introduced a lively song, written by Don Raye and Hughie Prince, called "Boogie Woogie Bugle Boy." It became the biggest song in the country. (Recently Bette Midler recorded the song and it became a million seller once again.) Two other songs from the film, the beautiful "I'll Be with You in Apple Blossom Time" and "You're a Lucky Fellow, Mr. Smith," also became hits. A specialty number performed by Costello, "When Private Brown Becomes a Captain," is quite good too. In fact, all the musical numbers are very well done and they're still enjoyable today. Patty Andrews has said that she loved working with Bud and Lou, particularly Lou. She described him as "the Peck's Bad Boy" of the Universal lot, since he was constantly playing practical jokes.

Bud Abbott and Lou Costello were suddenly the biggest celebrities in Hollywood. It had been a long, hard climb from vaudeville and seedy burlesque houses. Both men came from very poor backgrounds, and now they were earning ten thousand dollars a week. Bud and Lou didn't really know how to deal with this newfound wealth and success, and it would cause them many problems in the years to come. But in 1941, they were the reigning Kings of Comedy.

LaVerne Andrews, Lou, Patty Andrews, Lee Bowman and Jane Frazee.

With Lou's brother, Pat Costello, who did some of Lou's stunt-work in BUCK PRIVATES.

The boxing match from BUCK PRIVATES. With Al Billings and Nat Pendleton.

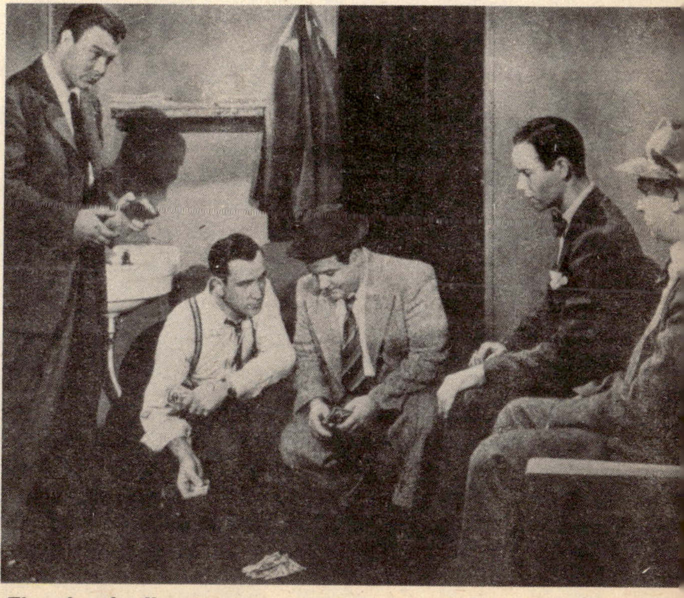

The classic dice game.

In The Navy

John Grant suggested that a ghost story would be ideal for Abbott and Costello's next effort. Grant could write the script quickly since he knew all the stock haunted house gags from burlesque. The result was HOLD THAT GHOST. This film was well into production when the huge box office returns started coming in from BUCK PRIVATES (in larger cities it ran second only to GONE WITH THE WIND). Universal decided to shelve HOLD THAT GHOST and release it later that year, following IN THE NAVY. They felt that IN THE NAVY was a more suitable follow-up to the army film. IN THE NAVY has slicker production values but it isn't as funny as BUCK PRIVATES. It still has many bright moments and the team gets to do two of their favorite routines. Again John Grant collaborated on the script with Arthur T. Horman, the latter supplying the straight story. Before the opening credits we see Bud and Lou, in sailor suits, fastening a signal flag to a line. They hoist the flag up a pole and the flag reads "Bud Abbott and Lou Costello in 'Buck Privates.' " Abbott looks up, does a take, and slaps Costello. They pull the line down, and raise the correct flags, reading: "Bud Abbott and Lou Costello and Dick Powell 'In the Navy.' " They were certainly not above exploiting the success of BUCK PRIVATES.

Lou Costello plays Pomeroy Watson, a navy baker who's never been to sea. Abbott is Smokey Adams, an electrician's mate. Dick Powell is Russ Raymond, America's singing heartthrob, who decides to leave the tinsel and glitter of show business and become a "plain simple gob" in the navy. Dick Powell was by far the best of the straight leads in the Abbott and Costello vehicles. The opening scene of IN THE NAVY (working title: HELLO SAILOR) takes us to a radio station in New York that's broadcasting the "Fluffso Soap Hour" starring Russ Raymond. Powell sings "Star Light, Star Bright," as the matronly women in the audience begin to swoon. At the end of the broadcast he jumps into his limousine, escaping a crowd of autograph hounds. The next day newspaper headlines announce, RUSS RAYMOND DISAPPEARS! The singing idol joins the navy, under his real name, Tommy Halstead. He gets stationed at the naval base in San Diego, along with Bud and Lou. Hot on his trail is girl reporter Dorothy Roberts (Claire Dodd), who's after the story for *Photo Facts* magazine. The Andrews Sisters also turn up at the San Diego base and sing a patriotic tune,

Lou with Shemp Howard and Dick Powell in team's third film, IN THE NAVY.

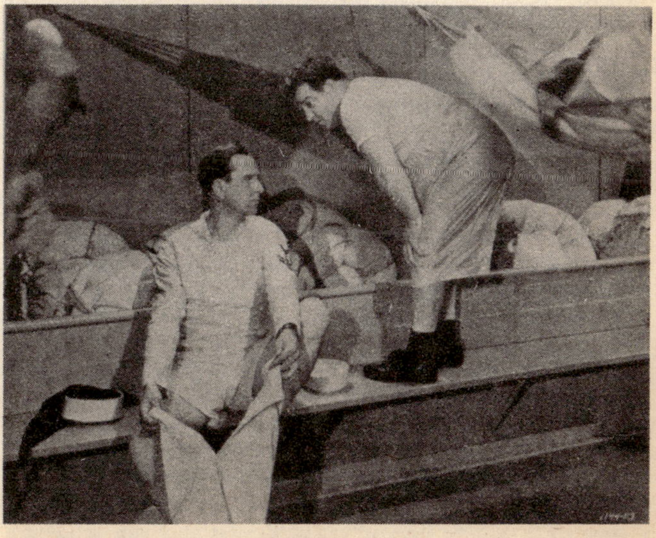

Costello has just thrown all of his clothes out the porthole. "I thought it was a little closet."

"We're Off to See the World." Bud and Lou then reprise the "Lemon Bit." In this bit Bud cons Lou with a variation on the old shell game. He places a lemon under one of three metal cups and wagers Lou that he can't find the lemon. Abbott then manipulates the cups so that the lemon falls through a hole in the table into a wire basket. Abbott keeps repeating this and it builds to a terrific pace as Costello is cheated out of all his money. Abbott also cons him with a series of zany business transactions. For instance, Bud asks his partner if he has two tens for a five. Lou complies, realizing too late that he's been taken again. Some of the bits of business involving exchanges of money are brilliant. Eventually Lou discovers the basket containing the missing lemons. "He's got a fruit stand under the table!" cries Costello. Lou pockets all the lemons while Bud isn't looking, and puts them under each cup. Abbott manipulates the cups and as the lemons fall through the hole in the table, Costello quickly replaces them with more lemons. This is performed at dazzling, breakneck speed. For the blackout, Lou suddenly produces a grapefruit from his coat and tries to squeeze it under the metal cup. The team had polished this bit for years until it was an expert blend of verbal and visual comedy.

Chief Petty Officer Dynamite Dugan (Dick Foran) places the boys in the brig after they get involved in a brawl. The boys are then assigned to duty on a battleship en route to Hawaii. Also on board is Dick Powell, alias Russ Raymond. The girl reporter stows away on the ship to get some candid pictures of the crooner. Bud and Lou take the opportunity to resurrect a couple of ancient gags. "Where do all the little bugs go this time of year?" Powell asks Costello. Lou: "Search me." Powell: "No thanks, I was just wondering." Lou sees a picture of a ship in his handbook and asks Bud about it. Abbott explains, "That's a hull of a ship." "You're tellin' me!" Lou observes. A song, "Oh for the Life of a Sailor" is performed by Dick Foran and Costello. The song is only fair, but it's a lot better than the original song that was planned–a number appropriately titled "Flotsam and Jetsam."

The boys then do the initiation routine, based on a burlesque standard called "Buzzing the Bee." Costello, anxious to join the Sons of Neptune club, must first be passed by the committee. The head of the committee (Shemp Howard) asks him what branch of the service he prefers–the air, the land or the water? Lou naturally answers, "Give me the water!" Five sailors are facing him. Each has a mouthful of water and they let him have it right in the face. Lou tries the gag on Bud but it backfires and once again Lou gets a faceful of water. Arthur Lubin, while directing this sequence, started to laugh uncontrollably. Lou spotted him and he too began to break up. Lubin left in the footage of Costello breaking up and it is the funniest thing in the movie. Another interesting point is that the censors requested Lubin not show on the screen the actual spitting of water into anyone's face. They considered this too offensive. How times have changed!

Butch and Buddy, the captain's two obnoxious nephews, delight in playing pranks on Costello. (Child actors Billy Lenhart and Kenneth Brown were also featured in a few other Universal pictures such as W. C. Fields' NEVER GIVE A SUCKER AN EVEN BREAK.) A sequence that was deleted from the finished film has Costello telling the two kids the story of Little Red Riding Hood but they keep interrupting him with inane questions. (This routine made it to the screen in ABBOTT AND COSTELLO IN HOLLYWOOD, with Lou telling the story to M-G-M child star Butch Jenkins.)

Dick Powell sings "We're in the Navy" during a band concert on deck. The song, meant to be a stirring tribute to the United States Navy, seems silly today. In fact, it must've seemed silly in 1941. The music in general is pretty bad compared to the inspired score of BUCK PRIVATES. The Andrews Sisters do a Hawaiian opus, "Hula-Ba-Luau" with lyrics like, "She'll be comin' around the ol' volcano when she comes, singin' 'Beat me, daddy, eight to

With Shemp Howard and Dick Foran.

Attending the Hollywood premiere of IN THE NAVY.

the bar'!"

Costello can't seem to get used to life on the open sea. He undresses for bed and throws all of his clothes out the porthole. When Bud asks him why he did that, he says, "I thought it was a little closet." Costello then tries to get a night's sleep in a hammock with hysterical results. Abbott can't believe that Lou has been in the navy for six years and never slept in a hammock. "Six years I was a baker–I always slept in a sink," he explains. His every attempt to climb into the hammock lands him flat on the floor. "How are you gonna sleep in a snood?" he protests. Costello does some zany improvisation–he plays the strings holding the hammock as if they were harp strings . . . he rides the hammock pretending to be a cowboy on a horse. "Whoa, boy!" he drawls.

In an ingenious routine, Lou, for once, gets the best of Bud by showing him that seven times thirteen is twenty-eight. Through multiplication, division and addition, he actually proves it, and it all seems quite logical. This classic does not appear in the shooting script. It was added to the film when it was realized that there was too much romantic plotting and not enough Abbott and Costello.

The elaborate finale has Costello, disguised as the captain to impress Patty Andrews, taking command of the battleship. He's dressed in an oversized Horatio Hornblower outfit, complete with cockade hat and dress sword. Patty is impressed with the captain's cabin. "You must enjoy your quarters," she says. "Money means nothing to me," he brags. He then shouts orders to the crew, by phone to the bridge, and the ship takes part in some wild maneuvers with hairpin turns. The admiral and a visiting senator are impressed with this incredible display (much of this footage was filmed at Pearl Harbor).

Throughout the filming of IN THE NAVY, Universal had received the cooperation of the United States Naval Department. When the film was completed, a print was sent to the Naval Department in Washington for their approval. They were furious. Their chief objection was the final maneuvers sequence, with Lou taking charge of the ship. They claimed that it made fools of the entire American fleet. They would not allow the film to be released. Naturally this caused quite a panic at Universal City. They had a surefire box office smash on their hands, but now they couldn't release it. Alex Gottlieb came up with an idea that resolved the whole matter. His idea was to shoot some new footage before and after the controversial maneuvers sequence, establishing that it was all a dream. Costello drinks a sleeping solution by mistake and dreams he's the captain. At the critical point in the dream, when the ship is about to collide with a flagship, Abbott wakes Costello from his slumber. They sent the film, with the new ending, back to Washington and the Naval Department approved it.

Bosley Crowther, in the New York *Times,* said, "Maybe they aren't quite as funny as they were in BUCK PRIVATES but even fair with Abbott and Costello is good enough for now."

Newsweek commented that Costello's comedy "is as broad as he is, and even closer to the ground."

The New Yorker review stated, "The Andrews Sisters, poor ladies, though they keep busy and bustle about a lot, don't actually stir up the commotion that Abbott and Costello, esteemed popular comedians, manage to work out of IN THE NAVY . . . Messrs. Abbott and Costello make the whole U.S. fleet just a lot of knick-knacks."

IN THE NAVY, released in July of 1941, racked up huge profits, outgrossing BUCK PRIVATES.

Hold That Ghost

HOLD THAT GHOST is the team's best film next to BUCK PRIVATES. It was originally titled OH CHARLIE. (This title refers to a running gag in the film. The corpse of a gangster, Charlie Smith, keeps turning up, causing Costello to yell, "Oh Charlie!") Unlike BUCK PRIVATES and IN THE NAVY, HOLD THAT GHOST didn't have any musical numbers. Universal decided it needed music so a few extraneous numbers were added before it was released as the third Abbott and Costello film of 1941.

It was the first film really to showcase Lou Costello's flair for pantomime. Lou was brilliant in this one. His frightened antics in a ramshackle haunted house left audiences convulsed. The more frightened Costello acted, the more the audience howled. The studio kept this in mind and put the team in a series of vehicles involving all sorts of ghosts and monsters. KEEP 'EM FLYING has a segment with Lou lost in an amusement park ghost house, although it has nothing to do with the rest of the film.

HOLD THAT GHOST opens at the Chez Glamour nightclub, in which Bud and Lou, as Chuck Murray and Ferdie Jones, have managed to get jobs as waiters. They quickly turn the place into a shambles and are fired by maître d' Mischa Auer. The entire nightclub scene does not appear in the script. It was added after the rest of the movie was completed to allow for two musical numbers. One was performed by the Andrews Sisters and the other was Ted Lewis' famous "Me and My Shadow." The nightclub scene is generally edited from TV versions of HOLD THAT GHOST.

The boys return to their old jobs in a filling station. Bud asks Lou, "Suppose someone comes in and asks for ethyl–what would you do?" Lou answers, "I'd tell them it's her day off." Moose Matson, public enemy number one, just happens to pull into the gas station. While Bud and Lou are tending to his car, the police arrive on the scene. This triggers a chase with the boys being forced to drive Matson's getaway car. Matson is killed and Bud and Lou find they're beneficiaries in his will. He has left his entire fortune "to those who stick by me when, in that final moment, the coppers dim my lights." Matson's "fortune" turns out to be the Foresters' Club, a deserted, weather-beaten tavern in the country. Marc Lawrence, as oily villain Charlie Smith, offers to drive them out to the place: "It will be a pleasure to take you boys for a ride."

The real fun begins when Bud and Lou are forced to spend the

In a good sequence, Bud and Joan lecture Lou on the silliness of common expressions such as "Water under the bridge" and "Never the twain shall meet".

night in the shuttered inn, along with a group of fellow travelers. The others include a girl (Evelyn Ankers), a doctor (Richard Carlson) and a zany radio actress (Joan Davis). The film benefits immensely from Joan Davis' performance. She was a truly gifted comedienne and she worked so well with Costello that it's a shame they never made another movie together. Joan plays Camille Brewster, an actress whose sole credit is that she does the scream which opens the "Tales of Terror" radio show. Midway through GHOST Joan and Lou perform a charming slapstick ballet to the "Blue Danube." As dancing partners, they lack the grace of Astaire and Rogers. (The rubber-limbed Miss Davis falls into a bucket of water; as she twirls about the dance floor, she continually smacks Costello in the head with her elbows.) The "ballet" culminates in a free-for-all as Joan and Lou childishly splash each other in a puddle of rainwater. This routine is only vaguely outlined in the finished script—most of the gags were devised by these two superb clowns during rehearsals. For some strange reason, this sequence was set up with the other cast members clearly visi-

Lou Costello and Joan Davis made a memorable combination in HOLD THAT GHOST.

ble in the background, watching the zany proceedings and somehow managing to keep a straight face.

The most memorable scene has Lou being terrified by a mysteriously moving candle. The candle only moves when Bud isn't in the room to see it. Every time it moves Lou screams for his partner.

Lou: "Oh Chuck! Chuck!"
Bud (Rushing in): "What is it?"
Lou: "What kept you?"
Bud: "I came as soon as you hollered 'Oh Chuck.' "
Lou: "From now on don't wait for me to say 'Oh Chuck.' Get in here on the 'Oh'!"

Olsen and Johnson paid homage to this sequence in their own mystery-comedy, GHOST CATCHERS, released in 1944. (GHOST CATCHERS also "borrowed" the clever animated titles from HOLD THAT GHOST.)

Another highlight is the scene in which Lou's room suddenly is transformed into a gambling casino. To Lou's bewilderment, the bed changes into a crap table, roulette wheels and slot machines appear and so forth. But when he runs and gets his partner, the room has returned to its original condition. Bud never sees what is getting Lou so frightened and he thinks Lou is crazy. They used this premise in several of their comedies, notably ABBOTT AND COSTELLO MEET FRANKENSTEIN.

When Charlie Smith disappears, Lou is forced to search the basement to find him. Lou's range of facial expressions in this sequence is hilarious.

Abbott tries to convince Costello that there's nothing to be frightened about. "That ghost is just a rumor," he assures him. "I don't care if he's the landlord!" Lou cries.

The culprits behind these mysterious happenings are members of Moose Matson's old gang. They try to scare the guests out of the tavern so they can find their boss's loot. Lou uncovers the hidden money and the crooks arrive to collect it. "I didn't work for Moose Matson for fifteen years so someone else can get the gravy," says one of the gangsters. Lou tells him, "We don't want the gravy. You can have it." And he hands him a dish from the dinner table. Lou grabs the satchel with the money and there's a very well-staged chase throughout the house. A funny gag tops off the chase. The gangsters make a hasty getaway when they hear the sound of a "police siren" wailing in the distance. It turns out to be merely Costello, who does an excellent impression of a siren. (Steve Allen recalls seeing the film when it was first released. He particularly enjoyed the siren gag and it gave him an idea. "Whenever I was driving on the freeway and I got behind a car that was crawling along, I'd roll down my window and make this siren-like sound. It

Joan Davis tries out her "radio scream" for Bud and Lou.

never failed to get the guy in front of me to increase his speed.")

Bud and Lou decide to turn the place into a health resort with the money. We then dissolve to opening day at the resort. They have hired Ted Lewis and the Andrews Sisters to perform. The finale is another good production number by the Andrews Sisters, "Aurora."

The ending that was originally filmed shows the duo happily running a posh sanitarium for the very rich. They have even employed Joan Davis as the staff dietician (Joan Davis does not appear in the last scene of the released film). For the blackout, Lou pulls a bell cord to ring for dinner, but instead the ubiquitous body of Charlie Smith falls out of a closet. But all of this was cut when Universal decided the film needed a musical finale.

The script of GHOST is chock full of gags and situations that don't appear in the film. For instance, it contains one of their routines in which Lou refers to a "bunch of cows." Abbott corrects him. "No, herd of cows." Costello says, "Certainly I heard of cows. Do you think I'm a dummy?" They performed this bit in a later film, RIDE 'EM COWBOY.

There is another scene in the script that was deleted from the finished film. It shows the duo stopping off at a roadside diner on the way to the inn. Lou asks the proprietor what's on the menu. He

With Ted Lewis.

Richard Carlson, Bud, Lou, Joan Davis, and Evelyn Ankers prepare to enter a mysterious room in HOLD THAT GHOST.

tells Lou, "I got a duck in the icebox." Lou quips, "Go ahead. We'll wait till you come back." Like most comedians, Abbott and Costello felt "protected" with a lot of material. They were afraid to do a scene unless it was insured with tried-and-true jokes. They were funny jokes but they were often out of context and made some of the films look disjointed. But most of the gags in HOLD THAT GHOST were integral to the setting and gave the film a progression.

The romantic leads in HOLD THAT GHOST, Richard Carlson and Evelyn Ankers, are very appealing. In most of their other films, Abbott and Costello got stuck with the most saccharine contract players on the Universal lot. I've always felt that their films are rarely revived in theaters because these romantic subplots are downright painful to endure and have marred some good comedies.

Arthur Lubin created a fine, eerie atmosphere in HOLD THAT GHOST. Although it's a comedy, it generates quite a bit of suspense. Two years later, Lubin really displayed his talent in this department by directing THE PHANTOM OF THE OPERA.

The film received a good set of reviews. *Newsweek* observed, "HOLD THAT GHOST is very low comedy with a very high percentage of rumbling, unabashed belly laughs. To students of the muscle-and-meringue school of comedy, and/or admirers of the comedy team, the new film will prove as funny as BUCK PRIVATES."

Keep 'Em Flying

By the end of 1941, there were four Abbott and Costello comedies in release and shooting was completed on another, RIDE 'EM COWBOY. Milton Berle joked in one of his monologues at the time, "Things are slow in Hollywood. Abbott and Costello haven't made a picture all day."

The team had already wreaked havoc on the army and navy, so it was only natural that they took on the air force. If KEEP 'EM FLYING bears any resemblance to BUCK PRIVATES and IN THE NAVY, it's strictly intentional. Universal had a winning formula and they weren't about to try anything new or daring. The formula consisted of a boy-girl subplot, a couple of songs and as many burlesque turns as John Grant could fit into the setting. It all pays off in KEEP 'EM FLYING (working title: UP IN THE AIR), which rates as one of their best.

The boys (this time out they're named Blackie and Heathcliffe) work in Gonigle's Carnival and Air Show, assisting a daredevil stunt pilot, Jinx Roberts (Dick Foran). When all three get fired by the carnival owner, they join the army air corps. To celebrate, they go to the Propeller Club, a lavish nightclub. Jinx falls for the club's sultry singer, Linda Joyce, who has just quit to join the USO hostess corps. Linda is played by Carol Bruce, a very beautiful and talented singer.

Bud and Lou arrive at the Cal-Aero training school the next morning and wait for Jinx in the USO building. They only have twenty-five cents between them so Bud explains that he'll order a turkey sandwich and share it with Lou. Lou isn't allowed to order anything. But when it's time to order, Bud keeps coaxing him into asking for something. "What do people go to a restaurant for?" Finally Lou gives in and asks for a sandwich, only to have Bud slap him in the face. This funny routine is compounded by twin waitresses (both played by Martha Raye). The boys, thinking there's only one waitress, are confused by her apparent split personality. One minute she seems to favor Abbott and the very next minute she's making eyes at Costello. Martha Raye gives a gem of a performance as the twins—Barbara, who's quiet and reserved, and Gloria, who's a total extrovert. Martha also gets a chance to belt out a good song, "Pig Foot Pete."

Meanwhile, Jinx Roberts is having difficulty adapting to army life. His conceited ways have aroused the ire of his superiors. His

In this scene, deleted from the finished film, Costello does his impression of a five-year-old boy, a routine he performed often on radio. With Dick Foran.

instructor, Craig Morrison (William Gargan), thinks that he's "the best flier that ever hit the blue," but his refusal to obey regulations may cost him his wings. Jinx can't seem to get off the ground with Linda, either. Linda is more concerned for her kid brother, Jim, a cadet who's afraid to make a solo flight.

Meanwhile Bud and Lou have gotten jobs as mechanics and proceed to do everything wrong. Bud orders his pal to taxi a plane off the field. Lou calls for a taxi. Lou asks Bud how many miles an hour a torpedo travels. Bud corrects him. "Not 'miles.' If you walked up to a sailor and you asked a sailor how fast that was going–he wouldn't say 'miles' to you. He'd say 'knots' to you." Lou indignantly yells, "And I'd say 'knots' right back to him! After all, if the guy don't want to talk . . ."

The film falters momentarily with its big musical number, "Keep 'Em Flying." During this corny number we see scores of cadets happily singing the title tune at 6 A.M. as they shower, get dressed in their uniforms and perform calisthenics. These cadets seem more qualified to be chorus boys than pilots. But things liven up in a good chase, with Costello in hot pursuit of a runaway torpedo. The bomb scoops him up and carries him away. The explosive narrowly misses cadets, planes and buildings while Lou and then Bud ride the thing bareback.

Trying to order lunch from waitress Martha Raye.

Lou takes his date, Martha Raye, to the carnival. He suggests that they go through the tunnel of love. "We could have a lot of fun in there. We'd get in a boat all by ourselves, and when we got to a place where it was dark and nobody could see us. . ." Martha excitedly asks, "Then what would we do?" Costello, blushing, says, "We could take our shoes off and put our feet in the water."

The tunnel of love provides the setting for a pleasant song, "The Boy with the Wistful Eyes," sung by Carol Bruce and Martha Raye. This song became very popular in 1941. The Andrews Sisters are missing from KEEP 'EM FLYING but the musical interludes are, for the most part, well done.

The film's high point has the duo piloting a dilapidated biplane. Lou, unaware that the plane has left the ground, steps out to get his jacket. Standing on the wing, he does a doubletake as he realizes he's thousands of feet in the air. Costello dangles from the wing as the plane alternately soars and plummets through the air. Somehow they manage to land the plane, although it's lost all four wheels during the flight. Costello then scurries out of the wreckage and begins kissing the ground. The scene is certainly one of the best of its kind. The thrilling aerial stunts are punctuated by Costello's frightened reactions.

Jinx takes Linda's brother Jim up in a plane, to try to cure the young cadet of his fear of flying. Jinx then parachutes out, leaving Jim alone so he'll have to learn to solo. Talk about trial by fire! But the kid panics and can't handle the plane. Jinx rushes to the control tower to talk him down. In an unintentionally funny moment, he gets on the radio and urges, "Stick to that ship, kid!" Jim attempts to land the plane. It hits the ground heavily and tips over on its nose. The young cadet shakily climbs out of the cockpit and Jinx reassures him, "You know what they say, kid. Any landing you can walk away from is a good landing"–and Jim promptly collapses. This is almost a parody of clichéd flying ace movies. Jinx gets washed out of the air corps, and for good reason. He's about to leave with his cronies, Bud and Lou, when an emergency arises. Craig Morrison, attempting a jump, gets his parachute caught on the plane's fuselage and he dangles helplessly in the air. Jinx saves Morrison's life in a daring rescue. (This whole thing looks silly because of the use of obvious studio models and rear projection.) Jinx becomes the hero of the day, gets reinstated in the air corps and wins the girl.

Beautiful Carol Bruce was a highlight of KEEP 'EM FLYING.

Bud and Lou conferring with director Arthur Lubin on the set of KEEP 'EM FLYING.

Lou Costello and Martha Raye in the tunnel of love sequence from KEEP 'EM FLYING.

Blackie (Bud) and Heathcliffe (Lou) entertain at a USO show in this deleted sequence from KEEP 'EM FLYING.

The boys have somehow managed a safe landing via parachute in KEEP 'EM FLYING.

Bud and Lou, airborne again, are having more problems. They are forced to bail out because of engine trouble. Bud jumps first, followed by Lou. Lou lands directly on top of Bud's parachute. He walks around on it, resembling a child in the snow as his legs disappear in the billowing silk of the parachute. Bud, suspended underneath, yells at him to get off. Lou cuts a hole in the chute so he can hear what his partner is saying. He tumbles down, landing on Bud, and they go plummeting through space. "Quick!" Bud hollers. "The ring!" Lou says, "Fine time to talk of marriage!" Bud pulls the ring on Costello's chute and they both float safely to the ground. This is anticlimactic in comparison to the previous aerial gags.

For the film's closing gag, Lou informs Bud that he'll never set foot off the ground again. Immediately the backwash of a plane catches his parachute and carries it and Costello skyward once again.

Lou Costello's range of talents is fully evident in the movie. Early on we get a glimpse of his acting ability when Lou pleads with the major of the academy to give him a job. In a patriotic speech, he says that there must be something for a little guy like him to do "in the biggest team we ever had." This speech could've easily been mawkish but Costello manages to make it touching. This was his first fling at any kind of straight acting and audiences responded favorably. Still he was given only a few opportunities to display this talent during his years at Universal.

Arthur Lubin filmed an interesting scene which was deleted because the film ran too long. It shows the boys and Martha Raye at a roller-skating rink. Costello takes a series of spectacular falls and then finds himself as the end man on a crack-the-whip line. Abbott and Costello, never ones to waste comedy material, used many of the gags from this unused scene in a later film HIT THE ICE.

Another scissored sequence from KEEP 'EM FLYING has Bud and Lou performing a magic act in a USO show. During the course of the act, Lou reveals all of Bud's tricks. This routine turns up in LOST IN A HAREM.

The newspaper critics generally liked KEEP 'EM FLYING but they all agreed that it wasn't as funny as the boys' initial service comedy, BUCK PRIVATES. The reviewers also soundly trounced the Carol Bruce–Dick Foran subplot–and rightly so–and hoped that in the future Bud and Lou might have the screen all to themselves. No such luck.

Ride 'Em Cowboy

RIDE 'EM COWBOY was filmed before KEEP 'EM FLYING but Universal held up its release until February of 1942. It was one of their funnier outings and continued their string of box office smashes. It can hardly be termed a satire on Western movies since the Western setting is merely used as a backdrop for their routines. They were more successful in spoofing the genre in a later film, THE WISTFUL WIDOW OF WAGON GAP. There are some typical nonsequitur gags.

Bud: "Did you ever ride a jackass?"
Lou: "No."
Bud: "Well, you oughta get on to yourself."

The boys are cast as hot dog vendors at a Long Island charity rodeo. The rodeo's feature attraction is Bronco Bob Mitchell (Dick Foran again), an author of best-seller Western novels and range songs, who has never been west of the Hudson River. Gossip columnist Martin Manning (Charles Lane) has written an exposé on Bronco Bob. A fellow reporter asks Manning, "How about all those books he wrote, *I Caught Cattle Rustlers, I Caught Horse Thieves* . . ." Manning interrupts, "Well, I caught him where it hurts. Read my column today." Bob, eager to salvage his reputation as a cowboy hero, rides a horse for the first time in his life. He nearly succeeds with his ruse until a steer escapes and Bob is thrown from the horse. Anne Shaw (Anne Gwynne), a student rider in the show, manages to bulldog the steer. She is injured and must bow out of the riding championship, losing the cash prize of ten thousand dollars. Anne heads home to her father's dude ranch in Arizona. Bob boards the same train so he can apologize to her. Bud and Lou, who have hidden from their boss in the cattle car, are also en route to Arizona. On the train they participate in a poker game with some tough cowboys. In a routine reminiscent of the dice game in BUCK PRIVATES, Lou claims he's never played poker before but he manages to win every hand. Some of the puns are amusing. One of the gamblers asks, "Where's your ante?" Costello answers, "She's home with my uncle. I didn't know he knew anything about my relatives." Bud orders him to raise or call. "Call who?" Lou asks. Bud: "The man who made the bet." Lou yells, "Hey, you!" Abbott tells his partner to feed the kitty and Costello says, "Get me some milk." By the time the train

Peanut vendors Abbott and Costello hide from their boss at a rodeo in RIDE 'EM COWBOY.

arrives out west, Lou has not only won all the cowboys' money, but their clothes as well. At the train depot Anne is greeted by her father (Samuel S. Hinds) and the ranch foreman, Alabam (Johnny Mack Brown). Lou tangles with a racketeering Indian chief, Jake Rainwater, played by Douglas Dumbrille. (This was a different kind of part for Dumbrille, who was usually cast as a suave heavy. Dumbrille lent his villainous talents to three Abbott and Costello comedies.)

Costello accidentally shoots an arrow through the tepee of the Indian chief's plump sister, Moonbeam. That, in the language of the tribe, is a proposal of marriage. Lou narrowly escapes but the chief assures his sister, "We'll have a bow-and-arrow wedding."

At the dude ranch, the Lazy-S, the boys apply for jobs. Before they start work, they do some clowning at the swimming pool. Costello, in a bathing suit that must have been left over from the Civil War, does a few pratfalls on the high diving board. The only reason this scene was included was to show off a group of Universal starlets in swimsuits.

Costello's attempts to milk a cow are priceless. Abbott tells him to put the pail under the cow's udder. Costello is confused. "The cow's udder *what?*"

Practical jokers place a life-size dummy, dressed up to resemble

Bud and Lou are wallflowers at a square dance in RIDE 'EM COWBOY.

the Indian chief, in Costello's room. Lou returns to the bunkhouse and is terrified to find the dummy sitting in his chair. Abbott convinces his pal that it's only a wooden figure. Of course, the real Indian chief shows up, hides the dummy and takes its place. What follows is essentially the "moving candle" gag used in HOLD THAT GHOST. The dummy seems suddenly to come to life but only when Bud, as usual, is not in the room to see it.

Bud tells Lou to go to bed and forget all about Indians. In a dream, Lou imagines himself as a patient in a sanitarium where everyone is an Indian. This is a variation of "Crazy House." Since it was nearly impossible to fit this sketch into the film's setting, it was decided to make it a dream sequence, with only mildly amusing results.

In the meantime, Bronco Bob has been taking ridin' and ropin' lessons from Anne so he can enter the state rodeo, while the town baddie, Ace Anderson, is staking his bankroll on the defeat of the Lazy-S team.

On the day of the rodeo, Anderson kidnaps Bob and Alabam so the Lazy-S is certain to lose. Bud and Lou, in an old jalopy, drive through the desert to get help. The Indians join in the climactic chase, which is one of the craziest in screen history. The jalopy drives under water, onto a railroad track and into a cave. It crashes

The "Crazy House" sketch from burlesque gets a Western look in RIDE 'EM COWBOY. With Dick Foran, Anne Gwynne and Johnny Mack Brown.

Martha Raye visits the boys on the set of RIDE 'EM COWBOY.

through the side of a house and comes out the other side, pushing an iron bed, in which a cowboy is sleeping. At one point a bear takes the wheel of the car. When Bud tells Lou to throw out the brake, Lou does so–literally.

Bob and Alabam escape from the outlaws and Alabam is wounded in a gunfight with Anderson. "Hey, you're hurt!" Bronco Bob observes brilliantly. "Never mind that," winces Alabam. "Let's get to the rodeo!" They arrive at the rodeo just in time and Bob wins the championship single-handed.

The musical finale features a parade of cowboys and cowgirls singing the rousing title tune. The film features more music than usual. "I'll Remember April," sung by Dick Foran, has a haunting melody and beautiful lyrics (written by Don Raye and Gene de Paul). This is probably the best song that ever came out of an Abbott and Costello film. Unfortunately, the television version never includes the song. But a couple of badly dated tunes, "Wake Up, Jacob" and "Rockin' and Reelin'," performed by the Merry Macs, are usually left intact. A very young Ella Fitzgerald is also on hand to sing "A-Tisket A-Tasket."

The release of RIDE 'EM COWBOY ended director Arthur Lubin's association with Abbott and Costello. "They were becoming difficult to work with," Lubin said. "They were bored. They arrived on the set later and later each day. One day Bud was ill and couldn't come to the studio, the next day Lou was ill. And for the first time they were beginning to complain about the scripts." So Lubin bowed out after making five of their comedies, although he remained friends with them, and continued to see them often. He is very grateful for all that they did for his career. "I learned everything about timing from them," he said. It is too bad that he never worked with the team again because the quality of their films, with notable exceptions, went downhill after he left. Lubin directed many more features for Universal and for the second time in his career, he helped to save the studio. In the 1950s, due to the advent of television, Universal was again foundering. Lubin made a low-budget feature titled FRANCIS dealing with the exploits of a talking mule. It was a huge success and Lubin directed a series of these comedies, earning millions for the studio.

Rio Rita

RIO RITA, their first for Metro-Goldwyn-Mayer, is generally considered an inferior remake of the Ziegfeld operetta and the 1929 RKO film version. But the fact is that Abbott and Costello's RIO RITA is an altogether better show. The comedy routines are much funnier (Wheeler and Woolsey starred in the original stage show and movie). Even the musical interludes are more entertaining. Fortunately only two songs remain from the original score–the title tune and "The Ranger's Song" ("shootin' pals, hootin' pals," etc.). Harold Arlen and E. Y. Harburg wrote a new song for the Abbott and Costello version, "Long Before You Came Along," which is pleasant. Bud and Lou wander in and out of the silly plot, performing their routines, as did Wheeler and Woolsey thirteen years before. Just one comedy scene survived the transition. In the scene Costello, upon drinking some potent tequila, imagines he's seeing a girl taking off her clothes. Abbott grabs the bottle, shouting, "Give me a drink of that!"

It must have been a treat for Lou Costello to return to M-G-M a full-fledged movie star, after working as a carpenter and a stunt man at that studio in the twenties. M-G-M allotted a sizable budget for this Pandro S. Berman production. The "Ranger's Song" number, sung by a chorus of Texans galloping along the Rio Grande, is pure cornball but the production values are quite lavish by Abbott and Costello standards.

The studio also gave the boys a pretty good director, S. Sylvan Simon. Simon directed some of the Red Skelton comedies, such as WHISTLING IN THE DARK, its two sequels and the marvelous FULLER BRUSH MAN. Simon's forte was action-comedy employing imaginative special effects. And he put his talents to good use in RIO RITA.

Practically nothing remains of the plot of the original show. And that's no great loss. Writers Gladys Lehman and Richard Connell ("Special material for Abbott and Costello" is credited to John Grant) updated the story by substituting Nazi spies for Mexican bandits. Bud and Lou, traveling under the names Doc and Wishy, somehow have ended up working in a pet shop in Texas. The pet shop scene is merely included to give the comedians a chance to toss off some clever puns. Bud inquires about the breed of a dog in Lou's care. "Spitz?" he asks. "No, but it drools a little," his partner responds. A customer named Mrs. Pike calls the

Trapped on an auto turntable overlooking a bottomless cavern in team's first M-G-M comedy, RIO RITA.

shop and wants them to pick up her dog, which happens to be a Pekingese.

Bud: "Wishy, go over and get a Peke at Mrs. Pike's."
Lou: "Why can't I take a good look?"
Bud: "I want you to get me Pike's Peke!"
Lou: "Pikes Peak? What do you think I am? A mountain climber?"

Our heroes, longing to return to their native New York, stow away in the trunk of a car which they believe is heading in that direction. The car's owner is none other than radio crooner Ricardo Montera (John Carroll). He is actually on his way to the Hotel Vista del Rio to visit his childhood sweetheart, Rita Winslow (Kathryn Grayson). Ricardo arrives at Rita's hotel and leaves his car with a mechanic for some repair work. A good special-effects sequence follows. Bud and Lou are trapped on the car, which has been raised on a hydraulic lift, dangerously suspended over a canyon. The boys then take a frantic ride on the turntable, which suddenly goes berserk and begins to spin wildly in the air. This gets the film off to a lively start.

After escaping this near-calamity the boys wander onto the

ranch. They spot a crate of apples and Bud orders Lou to climb through the window to get it. "Why me?" Lou wants to know. "You wouldn't want anybody to catch me stealing, would you?" Abbott sensibly argues. The apples turn out to be fakes and they throw them away. Concealed inside the artificial fruit are short-wave radios used by the Nazi spies to receive messages. The "apples" are eaten up by some donkeys and a stray dog. In a hysterical scene, Lou encounters the dog that's swallowed the radio. He is surprised, to say the least, when the dog tells him the score of the latest Dodgers game. The comedians really milked this swallowed-radio gag. Later in the film the voice of Hitler is heard coming out of the mouth of a donkey.

When the two hungry men come across a table laden with food, they think it's a mirage. Lou quickly realizes it's for real and begins to devour a roast chicken. The team then does an old chestnut, "Ten Dollars You're Not There." Bud bets his share of the food that he can prove Costello is not where he thinks he is. And he *does* prove it through the process of elimination.

Rita feels sorry for the boys and decides to hire them as house detectives.

Singer Kathryn Grayson, then twenty years old, was just starting her career at Metro. She sings beautifully in the film, if a bit

With Arthur Space and Peter Whitney.

too often.

The newly appointed house detectives learn that the ranch is crawling with fifth columnists. The hotel manager, Craindall (Tom Conway), is the leader. Tom Conway was a notch above the usual villains in the team's films. Character actor Peter Whitney is also very good as a slow-thinking henchman. The spies plan a national broadcast during the big fiesta which will distribute orders through code. Needless to say, Bud and Lou thwart the spies.

RIO RITA's most memorable scene has Costello trapped inside a monstrous washing machine. Hiding in a laundry hamper to escape the spies, Costello is dumped down a chute. He finds himself inside the huge glass-encased machine. Abbott comes to the rescue but isn't much help. He steps on the button that activates the washing machine. An avalanche of soapsuds buries his chubby partner. Abbott does more harm than good as he tries to locate the button that shuts off the machine. The machine then whirls out of control, as the auto turntable did earlier. It stops abruptly and Lou is flung across the basement, crashing through a wall. This sequence is genuinely funny until Costello's predicament becomes a little too painful to be humorous. Robert Youngson included the washing machine gag in his compilation film M-G-M'S BIG PARADE OF COMEDY, and it was easily the highlight of *that* film.

A scene deleted from RIO RITA shows Bud and Lou participating in an unusual contest at the fiesta. Costello must close his eyes and guess which one of a group of pretty señoritas kissed him. Bud tries to help out his pal with some clues but fails. The team eventually did this bit with Sid Fields on their TV series.

The film is not as funny as their Universal releases but it is such a fast-moving comedy that you don't really notice that the formula is starting to wear a little thin. It is too bad that the pair's career at Metro was such a brief one. They only made three films at the studio, RIO RITA being the best of them. These films are not totally satisfying but at least they *look* good. They were handsomely mounted and photographed and the casts were better than what Universal had to offer.

The New York *Times* found RIO RITA to be "a likable, funny extravaganza."

The *Hollywood Reporter* said that "Abbott and Costello are even more hysterical in M-G-M's RIO RITA than they have ever been before. They have the best comedy material they've had to date."

Lou is in hot water again—literally, in this scene from RIO RITA.

Costello finds himself in still another predicament in RIO RITA.

Pardon My Sarong

Back at Universal the team made this great spoof of all those Dorothy Lamour South Sea epics. Even the title, PARDON MY SARONG, lampoons the silly titles of the films of that genre. Erle C. Kenton replaced Arthur Lubin at the directorial chores, and did a good job. PARDON MY SARONG is certainly their best release of 1942. The film moves at a terrific pace, with many bright lines and situations. The whole thing is topped off with their most elaborate and funniest chase. Once again the film is flawed by boring musical numbers. It is often frustrating to watch the Abbott and Costello comedies on television because the local stations, almost inevitably, edit out many of the comedy segments to fit in commercials. But for some strange reason they leave in the music, which should be cut instead.

An early scene in SARONG usually doesn't make it to the TV screen. It shows Bud and Lou conning a filling station attendant (Irving Bacon) out of paying for their gas. Bud tells Lou to give him the old "baseball story," an account of a game that is so exciting it is supposed to make the attendant forget all about the money. But Costello is unaware that the attendant has already been duped by his old ruse. Costello proceeds to tell the story to his victim but it appears that he knows more about it than Costello. "You sure you didn't hear the game?" Lou questions.

The plot of the picture is completely absurd. True Boardman, who wrote SARONG (with a great comedy writer, Nat Perrin), offered an explanation why the plot doesn't always make much sense. Boardman would carefully work out a plot sequence of about twelve pages. He then submitted the pages to John Grant, who would make changes. When Boardman got it back, the plot sequence was reduced to about three pages, the rest containing gags and routines devised by Grant. This was standard procedure in writing an Abbott and Costello script.

Anyway, Bud and Lou play Algernon Shaw and Wellington Phlug, two Chicago bus drivers who hijack their vehicle to take playboy Tommy Layton (Robert Paige) to California to enter a yacht race. The owner of the bus company (Charles Lane) hires a detective (William Demarest) to track them down. It is a shame that William Demarest, one of Hollywood's great character actors, appears only briefly in the film. Detective Demarest finds the boys in a West Coast nightclub (the nightclub scene is dragged in mere-

Costello is disguised as a magician to elude detective William Demarest in PARDON MY SARONG.

ly to showcase the four Ink Spots singing "If I Don't Care"). The boys try to elude the detective by disguising themselves as magicians. The perpetually exasperated Demarest is in good form during this encounter. He apprehends the duo and forces them to drive the bus back to Chicago. Abbott orders Costello to back up the bus, but finishes the statement by saying, "Go ahead." Costello wants him to make up his mind. Bud tells him, "Go ahead and back up!" Costello is so bewildered that he drives the bus right into the Pacific Ocean. They escape the detective by hitching a ride on Tommy Layton's yacht. Also on board is Joan Marshall (Virginia Bruce), the sister of a rival yachtsman. Robert Paige and Virginia Bruce supply the romantic story line.

Costello proves that he's less than an able seaman when the boat almost founders in a hurricane. He gets a chance to do some pantomime as he desperately tries to shave during the storm. The rocking of the boat causes the mirror to move back and forth on a shelf, with Costello following after it. When the storm subsides they find they are way off course, in uncharted waters. The party is stranded for days as supplies dwindle. Costello does another wonderful act of pantomime as he prepares to eat the last remaining food on board—a tiny, shriveled pea. With knife and fork in hand, he joyfully carves the pea as if it were a Thanksgiving turkey. This is followed by a strange sequence in which Abbott gives Costello a pistol and tells him to shoot himself so there will be one less mouth to feed. Naturally Lou pulls the trigger and misses. This is too grisly to be funny and it takes the film a little while to recover from it. Abbott seems unusually cruel to his partner in this film, prompting one of the cast members to ask him, "What are you so mean to that little fellow for?" Luckily, they manage to find an exotic island paradise with the usual assortment of giggling native girls (among them the young Marie McDonald). The natives pronounce Costello the hero of the island when he inadvertently rings the huge bell in the village. Legend has it that whoever rings the bell will save the islanders from the evil spirit that resides in the volcano. He must also marry the chief's lovely daughter, Luana (Nan Wynn). Another inhabitant of the island is the mysterious Dr. Varnoff (Lionel Atwill). He plans to do away with Bud and Lou, who are interfering with his work—which is stealing diamonds from the natives.

Luana takes her future bridegroom Costello to the "tree of truth." She tells him that if he tells a lie under this tree something will happen to him. "Well, I got nothin' to worry about," Lou boasts. "I never tell any lies." Immediately a coconut falls on his head. Every time he lies he gets conked with another coconut. Ab-

Stranded at sea with Virginia Bruce in PARDON MY SARONG.

bott suggests that he tell Luana a story. Lou starts to tell her the story about the traveling salesman and the farmer's daughter. Bud interrupts him, explaining that's not a proper story for a young girl. But the native girl is curious and asks Costello what the salesman wanted. "He wanted a glass of milk," Costello says, and he is clobbered with a shower of coconuts.

The action grinds to a halt with two intolerable production numbers involving scores of extras in native costumes. The choreography is more Radio City Music Hall than Polynesian. The songs are summed up by their titles, "Vingo-Jingo" and "Lovely Luana." The quality of the music in this picture might explain why their next effort—WHO DONE IT?—has no music in it at all.

One of the islanders, Whaba (Leif Erickson), threatens to kill Costello if he marries Luana. Costello loses his temper and calls him a "stinker." The towering native has never heard this word and asks what it means. Abbott quickly explains to him that a stinker is a great man. "You bet your life me stinker!" the native stupidly brags. "My whole family's stinkers!" Costello adds, "Yeah, but you're the biggest stinker of them all." "Thank you!" shouts the native, bowing to such praise.

In another stock gag situation Costello realizes that his drink has been poisoned and tries a number of ways to get rid of it. This routine, in different versions, turns up in several of their movies. Lou's moment of truth comes when Chief Kolua (Samuel S. Hinds) sends him to do battle with the evil spirit that haunts the volcano. Five men before him have gone to the volcano, never to return. Just as he is about to leave Abbott takes him aside and pays him the dollar he owes him. "A fine time you pick to pay me!" Lou complains. The chief gives him a huge diamond to take along with him and assures him that no harm will come to him as long as he has it. For the rousing finale Costello is pursued all over the island by Varnoff's gang (including movie tough guy Jack La Rue), who are after the valuable jewel. Abbott joins the chase and he and Lou pose as statues in a temple to elude the villains. Jack La Rue chases Costello up a long flight of stairs. The two stop long enough for a breather and some amiable chitchat, and then continue the pursuit. Lou, up in a tree, uses his suspenders as a slingshot to hurl coconuts at the bad guys below. The nonsensical antics include Lou riding a zebra bareback and confronting some lions. It is never explained what zebras and lions are doing on an island in the Pacific. Outlandish sound effects punctuate the sight gags. Varnoff kidnaps Joan and escapes in a motorboat. Lou follows by hitching a ride on a friendly seal. He then balances on a surfboard that's being towed by the motorboat. A swordfish

At the wedding feast, Whaba (Leif Erickson) warns Costello not to marry Luana (Nan Wynn).

With Marie McDonald and Nan Wynn.

comes up behind him, saws the surfboard in half and Lou now has makeshift skis. He also takes a ride on the outboard motor, which has fallen off the boat. Bud and Lou capture Varnoff and his gang and depart from the island after a job well done. If this all resembles a silent movie, it's because director Erle Kenton was a veteran of silent comedy and he contributed some of the gags in the chase.

Bosley Crowther of the New York *Times* said that an uncharted tropical isle was the perfect locale for Abbott and Costello. "For here," said Crowther, "amid a swarm of hula dancers and Lionel Atwill's invidious pirate gang, these two burlesque Quixotes can fire their gags and generally roughhouse around without placing anything in peril, with the possible exception of their customers' sides."

Kate Cameron, in a New York *Daily News* review, made this excellent comment: "Most of the material in the new Universal comedy has been used by the boys before, but Lou Costello has the knack of making every little trick of business and expression seem spontaneous."

Who Done It?

In the brilliant satire THE SENATOR WAS INDISCREET, directed by George S. Kaufman, there's a line describing an inept senator who's running for President: "He has about as much a chance of being elected as Abbott and Costello." Maybe Bud and Lou couldn't be elected to the presidency, but in 1942 they were the most popular movie stars in the country. With the release of WHO DONE IT?, they ranked as the top box office attractions of the year, beating out such stalwarts as Clark Gable and Mickey Rooney.

WHO DONE IT? is an exciting mystery-comedy, almost as good as HOLD THAT GHOST. There are no cumbersome musical numbers to slow up the action and the boy-girl subplot is less intrusive, allotting more footage to the comedians. Abbott and Costello are in practically every scene. Abbott and Costello devotees didn't like the idea of their favorite comedy team taking a back seat to music and romance, so Universal finally gave the team carte blanche. Lou Costello is in top form, improvising like mad. The team is ably supported by a better than average cast. Patric Knowles and Louise Allbritton are very attractive in straight roles. Knowles was a fine actor and one of the few leading men in the Abbott and Costello movies that you could care about. The rest of the cast includes William Bendix, William Gargan, Mary Wickes, Thomas Gomez, Jerome Cowan and Don Porter.

The boys, named Chick Larkin and Mervyn Milgrim, are soda jerks in a New York radio station. There are some neat bits of business as they work behind the counter. Lou wears a gas mask to serve a Limburger cheese sandwich. An obnoxious elevator boy bets Costello a nickel that he can drink orange juice faster than Lou can make it. The kid loses the bet but gets to drink five glasses for a nickel.

Bud and Lou are hoping to acquire jobs as radio mystery writers. They've written a script for a crime show about two sleuths, titled "Muck and Myer." For some reason they can't get anyone interested in the idea. Lou meets Juliet (Mary Wickes), who is secretary to the head of the network, Colonel Andrews (Thomas Gomez). Bud tells Lou that if he makes a play for Juliet, she'll get them jobs as radio writers. Costello flirts with the secretary but she just isn't interested in his advances. Mary Wickes, one of Hollywood's finest character comediennes, is excellent as the wisecracking secretary. Her tall, lanky appearance is in perfect contrast to Costello. Their "love scenes" together are charming.

English professor Jim Turner (Patric Knowles) has been hired to write scripts for the "Murder at Midnight" program. Jim quits when he discovers that the show's producer is an old flame of his, Jane Little (Louise Allbritton). Meanwhile, Colonel Andrews uncovers a Nazi plot at the radio network. Spies have been using a news broadcast to send coded messages to tip Nazi agents of Allied shipping. The network executive plans to make a public announcement prior to the broadcast of "Murder at Midnight." Andrews is just about to make the speech on the air when he suffers an apparent heart attack. But it is soon discovered that he's been murdered. He was electrocuted by a wire fastened to his chair. The killer's methods parallel the plot of the mystery episode, titled *The Steel Chair Murder Case*. Jim decides to stay and catch the culprit. Among the suspects are the show's writer (Jerome Cowan) and Dr. Marek (Ludwig Stossel), who diagnosed that the Colonel succumbed to a heart attack. Bud and Lou, seeing this as an opportunity to solve a real crime, pretend to be detectives. Costello is amusing as he interrogates the suspects ("Where were you on the night of January 16?"). The real detectives, Moran and Brannigan (William Gargan and William Bendix) arrive on the scene and they don't appear to be much brighter than Bud and Lou. The detectives are convinced that the boys are the murderers. The remainder of the film is one big chase. The boys are pursued all over the radio station by the two investigators. They're also being pursued by the killer (seen only in silhouette). The killer is after a piece of incriminating evidence in Lou's possession–a rubber glove found at the scene of the crime. Lou ducks into a closet and discovers the dead body of Dr. Marek. The doctor has been murdered because he knew about the spy operation. The boys also find time to tangle with a runaway elevator and a temperamental water fountain that keeps squirting Lou in the face. In the funniest segment, Lou hides in a record storage room to elude the police. He accidentally presses a switch and a recording of a gangster program starts to play. Costello thinks there are real gunmen in the room. When he hears the recorded gunshots, he believes he's been mortally wounded and does a classic death scene. He leans against another switch and an announcer's voice is heard, asking, "Do you have halitosis?" "What difference does it matter now?" gasps Costello.

The chase progresses and Bud and Lou hide backstage at a variety show. Lou unintentionally takes part in a riotous acrobatic act. (The name of the act is "The Flying Bordellos"!) The little man

They're witnesses to a murder in WHO DONE IT

panics as the acrobats balance him in the air. The boys then escape the police by climbing onto the back of a truck that's leaving the station. The truck driver switches on his radio and it's announced that Costello just won the "Wheel of Fortune" jackpot of ten thousand dollars. But he must contact the station in five minutes to collect the prize. They jump off the truck and run into a drugstore to make the phone call. What follows is a famous sketch, "Alexander 2222." Costello tries desperately to call that number but the nasal-voiced operator keeps telling him that the line is busy. While he waits, a group of oddballs parades into the phone booth, making crazy, long-distance calls with no difficulty. One guy asks the operator for the Consolidated Coffee Company in Brazil. He's immediately connected with Brazil and has a ridiculous conversation with his friend, Joe. He asks, "How's the coffee business? Oh, just a grind, eh?" Lou tries again to call the radio station but the operator mechanically tells him that the line is busy. Two other people place calls to Nome, Alaska, and Moscow,

On the Universal backlot with WHO DONE IT? co-stars Mary Wickes and Louise Allbritton.

Russia, as the frustrated Costello looks on. He finally gives up and the boys decide to sneak back into the radio station to get the cash prize. They also win a radio, and when they turn it on they hear themselves performing "Who's on First," and quickly turn it off in disgust. "Every time you hear those two guys it's 'Who's on first, what's on second!' " moans Costello.

When Brannigan catches him, Lou tricks the dim-witted cop into demonstrating how to put on handcuffs. Lou handcuffs Brannigan's hands behind his back. Lou refuses to unlock the cuffs and there's an amusing vignette as Costello bullies the helpless detective. Costello runs to get his partner and while he's gone Brannigan is freed by Juliet. He pretends that he's still bound while Bud and Lou insult him and slap him in the face. The boys are surprised to discover the detective isn't handcuffed. (This routine was revived on the team's TV series with Gordon Jones playing the befuddled cop.)

Jim searches Colonel Andrews' office, finding the Nazi code that the Colonel was trying to decipher. He writes a special script for "Murder at Midnight" to be broadcast that evening, hoping it will trap the killer. The show commences with all the suspects, including Bud and Lou, on stage. The actors re-create the events leading up to the death of the network executive. Halfway through the broadcast, the murderer (Don Porter) is revealed. He escapes and the police search the building. Bud and Lou race to the roof of the skyscraper, figuring the killer will never find them there. Of course, the killer is also hiding on the roof. Costello falls off the skyscraper and lands on a flagpole. He then dangles from the flag-

Lou clings to a flagpole atop a skyscraper in WHO DONE IT?

Lou thinks he's trapped the murderer but it turns out to be Bud. With William Gargan and William Bendix.

pole à la Harold Lloyd. He also balances on a ledge, fifty stories above the ground. Meanwhile, Bud diverts the killer as Lou climbs back up the side of the building. A convenient neon sign on the roof, reading VOTE FOR TOWNSEND PHELPS gives Lou an idea. He hurls stones at the sign, breaking the light bulbs until it spells out SEND HELP. Bud and Lou are chased about the rooftop. Costello hangs from high-tension wires and thousands of volts go through his body. He falls off the wires, hitting the killer below and knocking him out. The police spot Lou's warning and apprehend the killer. Lou thinks that he has recovered from the electric shock until he picks up a light bulb and it begins to glow in his hand.

Reviewing WHO DONE IT?, the New York *Herald Tribune* wrote, ". . . it gives full scope to the antics of the stars . . . I would still like to see Costello in a film which would exploit his fine sense of comedy, rather than his ability to make gags, double takes and slapstick stand up in a production."

WHO DONE IT? should have proved to Universal that the team could easily carry a feature film without the aid of music and romance. But the studio continued to weigh down their films with silly songs and boy-girl nonsense.

The final sequence of one of their funnier Universal comedies, WHO DONE IT? With Mary Wickes.

It Ain't Hay

IT AIN'T HAY is very loosely based on a Damon Runyon short story, "Princess O'Hara." Early in this delightful comedy, we see a couple of racetrack touts standing on Broadway. One of the touts asks his cohort why he always carries an umbrella—even when the sun is shining. "How should I know?" he replies. "I'm a Damon Runyon character!"

Although the film is another showcase for Abbott and Costello's time-honored routines, it manages to capture the flavor of Runyon's Broadway fables. One of the reasons for this is a supporting cast of familiar character actors such as Eugene Pallette, Cecil Kellaway, Shemp Howard, James Flavin, Eddie Quillan, Jack Norton, Richard Lane and Samuel S. Hinds. Erle C. Kenton did another good directorial job, keeping the music and romantic plotting to a minimum.

Costello is Wilbur Hoolihan, a New York cabbie, and Abbott is his unemployed pal, Grover Mockridge. They befriend King O'Hara (Cecil Kellaway) and his young daughter, Princess (Patsy O'Connor). O'Hara is a carriage driver in Central Park and his horse, Finnegan, is his pride and joy. Costello enjoys feeding candy to the horse. Abbott chides Costello: "You'll spoil the horse's appetite. Now he won't eat his fodder." This leads to a typical exchange. The baffled Costello want to know how the horse can eat his fodder. "They're going to hang his fodder on his nose," Bud explains, confusing Lou even more.

The story's love interest is provided by bandleader Leighton Noble, as a GI trying to put on a big show for our boys, and dancer Grace McDonald as his girl friend.

Bud and Lou, broke and hungry as usual, have a big lunch in a cafeteria, although they can't pay for it. Blustery Eugene Pallette is Mr. Warner, an efficiency expert who is starting his first day on the job at the cafeteria. Warner has hired three musclemen to take care of "the next guy who can't pay his bill." Bud rushes out of the restaurant to borrow some money, forcing Lou to keep ordering food until he gets back. Warner's henchmen watch as Costello nervously devours a plate of spaghetti, also eating his necktie in the process. Lou manages to escape without paying and Warner is fired. Eugene Pallette is the film's running gag. Because of Costello, he gets fired from several jobs throughout the story.

The boys learn that Finnegan the horse is ill after eating Lou's candy and they rush to the stable to tend to the sick horse. Some good footage is devoted to Costello's attempts at curing the animal. He devises a unique way of getting Finnegan to swallow a horse pill. He places the pill in a rubber hose and he prepares to blow it into the horse's mouth. Suddenly Lou does a terrific double take. "The horse blew first!" he gasps after swallowing the giant pill. In another exchange, Abbott tells Costello that a horse's "forelegs" are in front. Lou demands to know, "What's those things in the back, crutches?" Finnegan temporarily recovers and this is followed by an overblown musical number featuring hundreds of extras singing in tribute to the carriage horse. However, the next scene is quite poignant. We see Lou happily on his way to visit the horse the following morning. He arrives at the stable and learns that Finnegan has died during the night. He is heartbroken. All of the people in the neighborhood blame the little man for the death of the horse and a child calls him "a murderer." In this scene Lou Costello again showed what a fine dramatic actor he could be when given the chance.

The movie then focuses on the duo's efforts to find a new horse for the O'Haras. There are several clever gag situations. In one, they have a double-talk discussion about "mudders." Lou is perplexed when Bud tells him that in horse racing sometimes a he is a better mudder than a she. Lou wants to know how you can tell if a horse is a mudder. "By looking at its feet," Bud informs him. "Ain't we livin' in a wonderful age!" Lou exclaims. The team really got a lot of mileage out of this routine. They repeated it in THE NOOSE HANGS HIGH and several times on radio and television.

The boys visit a gambling parlor in hopes of raising cash to buy a horse. The fast-talking bookie (Richard Lane) knows a couple of easy marks when he sees them. "Try your luck on the ponies, boys?" he asks. Lou corrects him: "No, we wanna play the big horses." Costello is bilked of all his money in a series of phony horse races, staged in a back room, complete with an announcer and sound effects. Costello, who has lost practically all of his money, is assured that in the last race, only one horse is running. But when the race begins, the announcer shouts, "They're off in a bunch!" Bud and Lou turn the tables on the crooks and make off with the winnings. But Lou squanders the money when a Broadway con man "sells" him a policeman's horse. Three gamblers, Umbrella Sam, Harry the Horse and Chauncey the Eye (Shemp Howard, Eddie Quillan and Dave Hacker) inform the boys that there's a nag ready for carting away at the Empire racetrack. The boys, believing they're doing the owner a favor, appropriate the

With Matt Willis, Mike Mazurki, Sammy Stein, Eugene Pallette and Patsy O'Connor in IT AIN'T HAY (1943).

The boys hide champion racehorse Teabiscuit in their bed in IT AIN'T HAY.

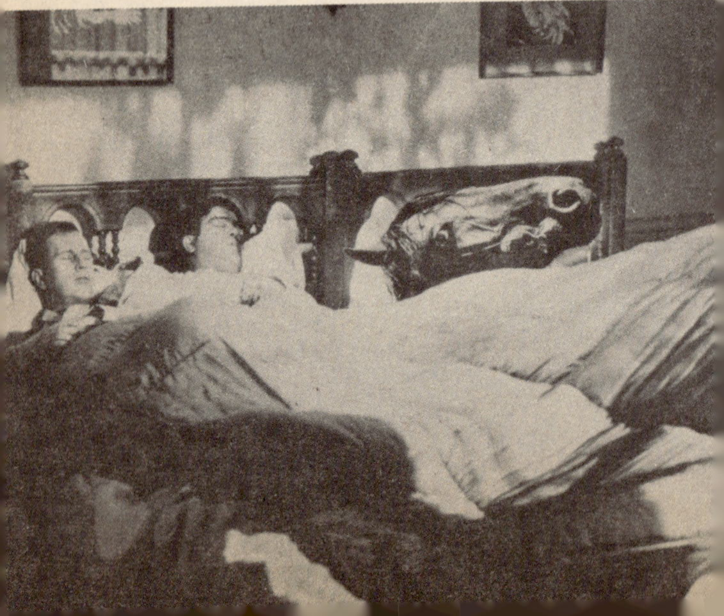

horse. But they unwittingly steal its stablemate, the famous racehorse Teabiscuit. King O'Hara, pleased with his new horse, drives a fare to Saratoga (his passenger is Hollywood's perennial drunk, Jack Norton). Bud and Lou discover what they've done and rush to the spa to retrieve the stolen thoroughbred. They hide Teabiscuit in their hotel room (pillows are attached to its feet so no one will hear hoofbeats in the corridor). A sight gag is used that originated in the Marx Brothers' DUCK SOUP. It is nighttime and the camera pans the floor of the hotel room. First we see Bud's shoes, then Lou's, and then two horseshoes. The camera pans over to the bed, in which the boys are sound asleep, along with the racehorse. The zany scenes in the hotel, as they try to conceal Teabiscuit from the management, work quite well. The hotel staff is confused when Lou calls room service and orders a bale of hay. Lou figures out a way to disguise the champion racehorse–he puts a pair of huge dark glasses on its nose. Colonel Brainard, Teabiscuit's owner, enters his horse in the big race "for sentimental reasons" even though the horse is missing. The odds on Teabiscuit are 100 to 1 when Costello shows up at the track, riding the thoroughbred. Although the climactic race is lively, it suffers in comparison with so many other scenes of this type, particularly the finale of A DAY AT THE RACES. The race in IT AIN'T HAY has all the clichés, including the unscrupulous jockey who resorts to foul play in order to win. But some of the gags are effective. Costello, in the lead, loses his cap, and he turns around and rides the other way to retrieve it. Costello's saddle slips and he spends part of the race riding *under* the horse. After several detours he is back in the lead, heading for the finish line. He suddenly stops so that he can watch the odds go up on the tote board and loses the race. But it turns out that Costello inadvertently switched horses with another jockey, and Teabiscuit wins after all. This was the same ending used in A DAY AT THE RACES. Bud has placed the only bet on Teabiscuit, winning thousands of dollars. The horse is returned to its rightful owner, and everyone lives happily ever after. There's a funny inside joke toward the end of the movie. Mr. Warner (Eugene Pallette) knocks on their door and Bud says, "It's Warner!" Lou quips, "It won't do any good. We're signed up with Universal."

The musical score is dreary. One song, "Sunbeam Serenade," fares better than the others. The finale is a typical overarranged number titled "Hang Your Troubles on a Rainbow." It is saved by a comical dance routine with Costello and the Step Brothers. The closing gag has Lou shrieking in delight as he finds a discarded billfold. He then takes the rubber band off the billfold and throws away all the money. "Good rubber!" he exclaims, clutching onto the rubber band, in a rather weak joke referring to the wartime rubber shortage.

Child singer Patsy O'Connor is very likable in the early footage and then is shunted to the background. Evidently Universal introduced her in the movie hoping she would join the studio's roster of child stars, including Deanna Durbin, Gloria Jean and Peggy Ryan. Straight leads Grace McDonald and Leighton Noble have practically nothing to do in the film, which is just as well. Eugene Pallette's bullfrog voice and exasperated expressions are, as always, delightful.

Variety gave the film a good review, saying, "Direction by Erle Kenton unfolds at a lively pace, spotlighting the Abbott and Costello routines for maximum audience reaction." The New York *Times* critic was less enthusiastic: "Costello's woebegone, roly-poly countenance is still worth a chuckle all by itself, but for the most part the boys–or is it their scriptwriters?–are beginning to repeat themselves." But the *Times* had to admit that the film had several hilarious moments.

Costello creates an ingenious disguise for Teabiscuit.

Hit The Ice

HIT THE ICE was the team's first encounter with director Charles Lamont, who was responsible for their worst films. HIT THE ICE is certainly a great deal better than the Abbott and Costello films he directed in the fifties, such as ABBOTT AND COSTELLO GO TO MARS and COMIN' ROUND THE MOUNTAIN, which hastened the team's decline. Lamont directed many of the Educational comedies in the twenties and thirties before joining Universal.

True Boardman, who wrote the story for HIT THE ICE, recalled the original concept. The film (at first titled OH DOCTOR) was to be the story of a chronic hypochondriac, played by Lou Costello. (One of the gags devised by Boardman had the worried Costello wearing a conductor's changemaker that dispensed pills.) But after a number of rewrites and story conferences it evolved into the tale of a gangster who feigns illness to establish an alibi while he commits a crime.

Our heroes are Flash Fulton and Tubby McCoy, two sidewalk photographers. They bump into an old childhood chum, Bill Burns (Patric Knowles), who is now a leading physician. (It's never explained how Knowles developed a British accent while growing up in the same neighborhood as Bud and Lou.) Dr. Burns invites his two friends to tag along on an emergency call. A downtown building is on fire and the boys see it as a chance to get some great pictures. They take a wild ambulance ride with Costello hanging out of the back of the vehicle on a stretcher. At the burning building, Lou tries to take a picture by standing on the end of an extension ladder. The ladder is raised hundreds of feet into the air, with Costello still standing on it. He falls off and is rushed to a nearby hospital. Lou, lying dazed on a hospital cart, is mistaken for another patient and a nurse proudly announces that he has just given birth to a baby.

Three holdup men are hiding in the hospital. They are played by three of the movies' best heavies, Sheldon Leonard, Marc Lawrence and Joe Sawyer. The leader, Silky Fellowsby (Leonard), has checked into the hospital, claiming to be a very sick man. His plan is to establish an alibi while he and his cohorts rob a bank across the street. Silky mistakes Bud and Lou for a couple of gunmen, "the boys from Detroit," when they unwittingly give the password. The boys think they've been hired to take pictures of Silky

Sidewalk photographer Costello uses a trash can for a dark-room in HIT THE ICE. With Patric Knowles.

and his gang as they exit from the bank, whereas the gangsters think they are hiring them to cover their escape. In a very funny exchange Bud and Lou boast that they make a living by "shooting" people. The gangsters rob the bank and return to the hospital, leaving the hapless photographers at the scene of the crime. They investigate the bank, where they do a predictable play on the word "teller." "Tell her what?" Lou wants to know. They are horrified to discover that there's been a robbery and escape just as the police arrive. The boys are accused of the crime so they set out to clear themselves by capturing the robbers. A neat vignette has Lou packing for the trip. Bud decides that they shouldn't run away since they're innocent. So Lou begins to unpack. Bud changes his mind, saying it's best that they get out of town. This is repeated a number of times–Costello packing and unpacking since his pal can't make up his mind.

Silky leaves New York and goes to Sun Valley "for his health," with Dr. Burns and a suspicious nurse (Elyse Knox) accompanying him. Bud and Lou sneak onto the transcontinental train headed for the ski resort. When they arrive at Sun Valley they are hired as waiters in a hotel. Costello takes more pratfalls than usual–on an ice-skating rink, and into a swimming pool. Vocalist Ginny Simms sings a couple of songs that aren't bad, "Slap-Happy

Costello thinks he can outsmart bankrobber Joe Sawyer in HIT THE ICE. With Marc Lawrence and Sheldon Leonard.

Polka" and "I'm Like a Fish out of Water."

Lou is in love with the singer and eager to impress her. Bud gets an idea. He hides behind a piano with a phonograph and plays a recording of piano music while Lou mimics the action. The girl is impressed by Lou's talent until Bud falls asleep and forgets to shut off the phonograph. Lou's pantomime provides the film with its biggest laughs. (He plays the keyboard with his feet and elbows.) The team reactivated the piano routine on one of their TV episodes, "The Music Lovers." This version managed to be even funnier, courtesy of some really wild ad libs on the part of Lou Costello.

Abbott and Costello head for the robbers' mountain hideout to retrieve the stolen loot. Their means of transportation is a dogsled pulled by some mangy-looking mongrels. By the time they reach the cabin, *Costello* is pulling the sled, on which the dogs are resting comfortably. After a fight with the robbers, the boys grab the money and escape on skis. Silky's gang pursues them in a chase brightened by a couple of clever sight gags. A bear hitches a ride on the back of Lou's skis. "You've got a bear behind!" Bud warns his pal. Lou skis into a coal mine and comes out wearing a miner's cap and holding a pick. He crashes through a cabin and makes a hasty exit, only this time he's riding on a fast-moving rocking

A bear hitchhikes on Costello's skis in the big chase sequence of HIT THE ICE.

Director Charles Lamont discusses the skating rink sequence with Abbott and Costello and Patric Knowles.

They arrive at the gangsters' mountain cabin.

chair. Costello manages to eliminate his opposition one by one. The remaining gangster battles with Costello. They tumble down the mountainside, forming into a gigantic snowball. The snowball rolls menacingly toward Abbott, who's skiing in front of it. Silky and his gang are arrested by state troopers and the boys are cleared. In the last scene Lou, in full-dress suit and top hat, is awaiting Ginny Simms, at the train depot. The little man mistakenly believes that she is going to marry him. But he soon discovers she's marrying a bandleader instead. "If I ever fall in love with another girl I hope they hang me," he laments. As the train pulls out, he spots a pretty girl on board who smiles at him through the window. Just then, the mail hook catches him by the collar, yanking him off the platform for an unexpected train ride.

In a review of HIT THE ICE, the New York *Times* complained that "the element of originality is virtually nonexistent."

Variety, however, liked the film, saying it was "packed with solid laugh entertainment."

A *Hollywood Reporter* review stated, "There appears to be a choicer selection of gags in HIT THE ICE than ever before."

Shortly after completing this film, Lou Costello was stricken with rheumatic heart disease.

Abbott and Costello seem to be enjoying themselves on the set of their eleventh film, HIT THE ICE.

In Society

IN SOCIETY, released in August of 1944, was the team's first screen offering in eighteen months. One would never know that Lou Costello had been ill since his performance is so energetic. The film began Abbott and Costello's long association with Jean Yarbrough and Sid Fields. Jean Yarbrough is a fine comedy director. He directed five of their features and he produced and directed their TV series. Yarbrough began his Hollywood career in 1921. He became friendly with Harold Lloyd and Lloyd got him a job as Hal Roach's chauffeur. He talked his employer into letting him work as a prop man at the Roach studios and then quickly graduated to assistant director. His first full-fledged directorial assignment was making the Leon Errol shorts at RKO in the thirties. Since then Yarbrough was steadily employed, directing countless features and TV episodes. He recalled that working with Bud and Lou was a great experience. IN SOCIETY is the best of the Abbott and Costello comedies that Yarbrough made.

If IN SOCIETY resembles a filmed burlesque show at times, it might be because Sid Fields, a burlesque veteran, served as a gagman on the picture. Fields wrote and performed many of the classic burlesque scenes. He wrote a version of the famous "Slowly I Turned" routine that has been performed by comedians throughout the years. Bud and Lou were well aware of Fields' talent and they brought him out to "punch up" the script. He remained in Hollywood and is probably most famous for playing the cantankerous landlord on the team's TV series. Fields remembered Bud and Lou's generosity. When he first came out to Hollywood, Bud Abbott gave Fields his guesthouse at his home in Encino. He tells of another example of their generosity: "Whenever an old-time burlesquer was in town, Bud and Lou would ask him, 'What's your pet scene?' Every comic in burlesque had a pet scene. The comic might say, 'Floogle Street.' Then the boys would call their producer and say, 'You know what this picture needs? It needs a scene like "Floogle Street." The guy who does it is in town. We might be able to get him.' The producer would ask, 'How much does he get? Our budget only allows five hundred dollars.' They'd yell, 'Five hundred! This is his masterpiece! Give him a thousand!'" Since Abbott and Costello were the top money-makers at the studio, they generally got what they wanted. A thousand dollars was a great deal of money to comics who were used to earning

Millionaires for a day.

two hundred and fifty a week, tops. Bud and Lou never forgot their beginnings. Their old cronies popped up in practically all of their movies and TV shows. One of their cronies was Murray Leonard. Leonard appears in IN SOCIETY as a crooked chauffeur and can be seen in quite a few of the comedies (notably LOST IN A HAREM). He was a top straight man in burlesque, half of the comedy team of Leonard and Marshall. Murray Leonard later made some hilarious contributions to the Abbott and Costello TV series in a wide variety of zany roles.

Besides contributing gags to IN SOCIETY, Sid Fields was signed to perform one of his routines, "The Language Scene," which was deleted from the finished movie. In the scene Fields tries to give Costello a grammar lesson that is doomed from the start. Fields is appalled at Costello's mangling of the English language. He tries to offer an example. He asks, "Didn't you see that movie with Irene Dunne? Didn't you see what Irene Dunne did?" "What Irene done did!" exclaims Costello. "This guy talks worse than me!" "Can you name the consonants?" Fields questions.

"Yes, sir," Lou replies. "North America, South America, and Paterson, New Jersey." After several futile attempts at teaching Lou proper grammar, Fields explodes with a barrage of rapid-fire, polysyllabic insults, none of which Lou is able to comprehend. Four years later Costello and Fields performed a similar routine in MEXICAN HAYRIDE.

The boys play Eddie Harrington and Albert Mansfield, two ambitious plumbers ("We stand behind every bathtub we sell!"). Their plumbing shop is financed by a crook named Drexel (Thomas Gomez). Wealthy Mr. Van Cleve (Thurston Hall) hires the plumbers to fix a leaky faucet at his home. Elsie Hammerdingle (Marion Hutton, sister of Betty Hutton), a lady cabdriver, offers to drive the boys out to the Long Island estate. Before they get started they take time to do another version of "Go Ahead and Sing." This time a tough cop warns Lou not to blow the car horn. As soon as the cop leaves, Abbott orders Costello to go ahead and blow the horn, and so forth. Bud, Lou and Elsie the cabdriver arrive at the Van Cleve mansion in the midst of a costume party in honor of Peter Evans (Kirby Grant). Bud and Lou wreak havoc on the plumbing system and Mr. Van Cleve soon discovers that his bedroom is submerged in three feet of water. He opens the bathroom door and the two plumbers appear, floating across the room in a bathtub. At the costume party, Peter Evans notices Elsie in her cabbie uniform, and mistakes her for a guest. He invites her to spend the weekend at the country estate belonging to Mrs. Winthrop (Margaret Irving). In mailing the plumbers a letter of com-

Lou's daughters on the set of IN SOCIETY.

Bud takes a ride in the sidecar of Lou's motor scooter during a break in the filming of IN SOCIETY.

plaint the next day Mrs. Van Cleve inadvertently encloses her invitation to the same society weekend. Bud and Lou are delighted to receive the invitation and they set out for the Winthrop estate. En route they perform a hilarious rendition of "Floogle Street" (called Bagel Street here). Lou has promised a friend that he'll deliver some straw hats to the Susquehanna Hat Company on Bagel Street. Lou stops strangers on the street to ask for directions and they all go berserk at the mention of the words "Bagel Street." The funniest stranger they encounter is played by a man named Milt Bronson, who was another friend of the team's from their burlesque days. Bronson showed his flair for comedy in this scene, playing an antagonistic fellow who berates Costello, although the latter can't get a single word in. "Go ahead," dares Bronson, "say something nasty about my brother. Say something like he shouldn't get a parole." The routine is performed exactly right, capturing the lunacy of burlesque comedy.

The two plumbers arrive at Mrs. Winthrop's estate and begin to cause all sorts of confusion. No one can figure out who they are. They have a funny encounter with the butler, Pipps (Arthur Treacher, of course). When Lou rescues a drowning man (Don Barclay) from a swimming pool, Lou is scolded by Bud. "You had no business going out there," Abbott argues with his usual logic. "Don't you know there's lifeguards? They've got families. Those families depend on the salaries that those lifeguards earn. And you, as soon as their backs are turned . . . you do the work for nothing!"

Some good footage is devoted to a fox hunt with Costello riding a runaway horse. The villainous Drexel arrives at the estate and tries to force the boys to steal a costly oil painting. When they refuse, Drexel steals the painting himself. Mrs. Winthrop learns that the boys are plumbers, and accuses them of the robbery. Drexel escapes and Bud and Lou give chase in a fire engine. Lou hangs from the ladder as the fire engine careens down the highway. This truly spectacular sequence was originally the finale of W. C. Fields' NEVER GIVE A SUCKER AN EVEN BREAK, released in 1941. Jean Yarbrough said that the chase footage was included in the Abbott and Costello film simply to save the studio money.

This is one of the pair's most consistently funny efforts. The slapstick is well timed and performed (particularly the early sequence in which the boys flood the Van Cleve mansion). In many of their comedies they ignore the setting as they perform their stock routines. But in IN SOCIETY they take full advantage of it, kidding the superrich.

Marion Hutton and Kirby Grant are an innocuous pair of

straight leads. Their romantic interludes are trite and have dated the film. The music is so-so, except for one tune sung by Miss Hutton, "My Dreams Are Getting Better All the Time."

IN SOCIETY was another big success and proved that the comedy pair still had the old magic at the box office, despite a long absence.

Lou, puffing on his ubiquitous cigar, was waiting to have his pants pressed when this photograph was taken.

Lost in a Harem

This Arabian Nights spoof was Abbott and Costello's second film for M-G-M. They were fortunate to have experienced comedy director Charles Riesner who had been Chaplin's assistant director on several films. The script, filled with many imaginative gags, was written by John Grant, Harry Ruskin and Harry Crane. Crane recalls that he worked on the script of HAREM by himself, submitting scenes that were revised by Grant.

The film opens in the mythical city of Port Inferno. The narrator tells us, "Strange plots are hatched here which will affect the lives and destinies of two strange persons!" The "strange persons" are, of course, Bud and Lou who play a couple of vaudevillians stranded in Port Inferno. Blond singer Hazel Moon (Marilyn Maxwell) gets them jobs at the Cafe of All Nations, where they perform a disastrous magic act that ends in a riot in the nightclub. Hazel and the boys are carted off to jail. In jail Lou tangles with a derelict (wonderfully played by Murray Leonard). We are then treated to "Slowly I Turned." "I haven't always been a derelict, like you," he tells Costello. He recounts the sad tale of his wife leaving him for another man and how he tracked them to "the banks of the Pokomoko!" Every time he hears these words, he goes into a frenzy, beating Costello. Lou screams for his partner to help him. "What are you interrupting the man for?" scolds the unsympathetic Abbott.

Bud, Lou and Hazel escape from jail with the assistance of a young prince, Ramo (John Conte). Ramo wants them to help him dethrone his uncle Nimativ (Douglas Dumbrille) so he can regain the kingdom of Barabeeha. Nimativ is the most evil despot in Arabia. When he catches a trespasser in the palace, he orders his guards, "Seize him! Take him to the dungeon . . . the damp one!" The wicked sultan possesses two cat's eyes rings that have hypnotic powers. He has even hypnotized the entire Jimmy Dorsey band to play for him! This time he's gone too far! It is Ramo's plan that the boys steal his rings while Hazel diverts him. The ruler has a weakness for blondes. The boys spend the night in Ramo's camp before setting out on their mission. There's an unintentionally funny musical number, "Sons of the Desert," sung by Ramo's followers. Lou has some fine moments as he tries to sleep in a tent crowded with restless Arabs. The tribal chief's long, flowing beard keeps blowing in his face . . . he keeps getting jabbed with the

Veteran director Charles Riesner tells Douglass Dumbrille and Abbott and Costello how he wants the scene played during rehearsals for LOST IN A HAREM.

chief's sword. Bud and Lou arrive at Barabeeha the following morning and Lou spots a lovely girl in native costume in front of a shop. He looks at her and she suddenly slaps him in the face for no apparent reason. She returns to the shop, and the camera pulls back showing a sign that says, MIND READER. The twosome devises strategy for overthrowing the despot.

Bud: "You'll have to go in and outwit him."
Lou: "Why should I go out wit him? I'm afraid of that man!"

They gain entry to the palace by convincing the giant guard that they're talent scouts from Hollywood and promise to get him into the movies. In a funny segment Nimativ uses his magic rings to hypnotize Bud and Lou into thinking they are termites. The pair hungrily devours every bit of furniture in sight. Nimativ has also hypnotized Hazel. He prepares to marry the blonde, making her wife number thirty-eight. Ramo frees the boys from the hypnotic trance and this is soon followed by HAREM's best scene. Captured again, the boys have been thrown into the palace dungeon. They find they are sharing the cell with the same crazed derelict as before. Their delirious cellmate confides that he knows a secret passage that will take them out of the dungeon. "Follow me," he

The fellow with the beard is Adia Kuznetzoff(!) who played the role of a desert patriarch in LOST IN A HAREM.

whispers. He then walks in a circle followed by Bud and Lou. He stops at the point he originally started from, imagining he's outside. Lou protests that they're still in the dungeon. "Keep quiet," Bud says. "You're attracting a crowd of people." Bud also seems to be losing his sanity. Lou tells their cellmate that he thinks he's crazy. "I have a brother who's crazy–but I'm all right," claims the cellmate. "Who told you?" Lou asks. "My brother," he answers. The derelict takes them to the imaginary home of his friend, "Mike." Costello and Murray Leonard then put on a wonderful display of pantomime. Lou sits down at a phantom piano and when he runs his fingers across the keyboard, an arpeggio is heard. Costello is handed an imaginary punch bowl, which he promptly drops, causing a loud crashing noise. The derelict says that his friend Mike is furious at Costello. "It was an accident, Mike," he pleads. The lunatic takes out an invisible gun and shoots Mike to protect Costello. When he sees what he has done, he runs away in horror. Costello re-enacts the lunatic's deliriums. Lou pulls out an imaginary knife, lunges, and a shot is heard. "I shot him with a knife!" exclaims Costello. Even James Agee, never an Abbott and Costello fan, liked this sequence. Years later Abbott and Costello repeated it on their TV series with Murray Leonard.

The boys escape from the dungeon and try to prevent the wed-

Douglass Dumbrille hypnotizes Bud, Lou, and Marilyn Maxwell.

ding between the sultan and Hazel. They sneak into the harem, where Costello disguises himself as one of Nimativ's wives. Costello does some hilarious female impersonating as the ruler's scatterbrained wife. Oddly, it was decided to include the famous mirror routine from vaudeville which the Marx Brothers made a classic in DUCK SOUP. Abbott, disguised as the ruler, takes the place of a broken mirror. Abbott and Douglas Dumbrille perform the routine, with Abbott mimicking Dumbrille's every movement. The boys hypnotize the evil sultan with his own rings. Ramo gets the girl, the rings and the throne and the boys depart for America. They climb into an Arabian taxicab and Lou just happens to say the word "Pokomoko." The driver turns out to be the derelict and the boys quickly jump out.

LOST IN A HAREM has such a great spirit of comic insanity that one can easily overlook its flaws. The scenes with Costello and Murray Leonard are enough to make the film memorable. Marilyn Maxwell looks terrific and John Conte manages to deliver some incredibly hokey dialogue with a straight face.

In what could hardly be termed a rave, the New York *Times'* Bosley Crowther wrote, "Apparently the people at Metro had nothing more to offer the boys than the set left over from KISMET and their very warmest regards. For LOST IN A HAREM is just another Abbott and Costello lark—amusing when those pals are in there pitching, but dull in the stretches when they're not."

Abbott and Costello, in an attempt to enter evil sheik Douglass Dumbrille's palace, convince the giant guard (Lockhard Martin) that they are Hollywood scouts. (Lockhard Martin later played the robot, Gort, in the classic science-fiction film THE DAY THE EARTH STOOD STILL.)

Here Come the Co-eds

It is difficult to think of a screen comedian who hasn't made a film with a college campus setting. The classroom and the athletic field have always provided ideal backdrops for comedy. One might wonder why it took Abbott and Costello so long to get around to making a college picture. HERE COME THE CO-EDS is their fourteenth film. It is an above-average vehicle with two of the comedians' most memorable scenes. John Grant produced this one and Jean Yarbrough directed.

Bud plays Slats McCarthy, the publicity man for the Miramar Dance Hall, in which Lou, as Oliver Quackenbush, works as an escort. The film gets off to a good start with some slapstick nonsense. A nearsighted husband (Richard Lane) mistakes Costello for another fellow who's been having an affair with his wife. In a fit of jealousy the husband beats the innocent Costello to a pulp. He then puts on his glasses and realizing his error, apologizes. This happens several times, each time the husband thrashing Costello and then apologizing. The subplot is introduced when Bud's sister, Molly (Martha O'Driscoll), receives a scholarship to staid Bixby College for women. Molly is a dancer and Bud figures she'll get some publicity by enrolling in the exclusive college. Our heroes tag along and are hired as school janitors. Molly falls for handsome Dean Benson (Donald Cook), who is trying to rid the school of its archaic traditions. The stuffy chairman of the college board of trustees, Jonathan Kirkland (Charles Dingle), is outraged by all the lurid publicity since Molly's arrival. He threatens to shut down the school by foreclosing the mortgage unless Molly is expelled. Universal contractee Peggy Ryan appears as Patty, a co-ed. She does a good song number with Costello, "Let's Play House." Costello remarks, "I feel just like Donald O'Connor," referring to all those campus musicals Peggy Ryan made with O'Connor. Lon Chaney, Jr., plays Johnson, the head caretaker, who bullies the boys. Director Jean Yarbrough recalled that Chaney enjoyed working with Abbott and Costello. He co-starred with the team again, as the Wolfman, in ABBOTT AND COSTELLO MEET FRANKENSTEIN. One crazy scene in CO-EDS has Lou swallowing some dice. Abbott then has an impromptu dice game with Chaney by spinning Lou around and then checking the results by X-raying Costello!

Midway through the film Costello does a neat bit of business.

Janitor Lou and co-eds Martha O'Driscoll and Peggy Ryan eavesdrop on a conversation in the dean's office. HERE COME THE CO-EDS.

After he finishes raking some leaves, he checks to make sure no one is watching. Then he peels back the lawn, as if it were a carpet, and sweeps the leaves under.

The team also repeats their standard "Jonah and the Whale" story that was in ONE NIGHT IN THE TROPICS. But a hysterical wrestling match constitutes the film's best moments. Costello's opponent is Chaney, who's disguised as the Masked Marvel. The referee explains that he wants a clean match, no dirty tricks. The referee then demonstrates several illegal punches on Costello. The bout gets under way and Chaney throws Costello all over the mat. Patty informs Lou that there's a phone call for him. "Tell 'em I'm all tied up!" he hollers while trapped in one of Chaney's strangleholds. Yarbrough went to a wrestling arena on Hollywood Boulevard and hired two professional wrestlers for the scene. The wrestlers doubled for Lon Chaney and Costello, with the latter two only appearing in close-ups.

In the other high point, Lou Costello revives a classic gag originated by Billy Bevan in a Mack Sennett silent. Bud takes Lou to a restaurant where Lou is served a seemingly innocent bowl of oyster stew. But he soon discovers that the oyster is very much alive and well. It bites his finger and squirts him in the face. He tries several methods of catching the elusive oyster. He attaches a pin to his necktie and lowers his tie as if it were a fishing line. The oyster grabs the tie, pulling Lou's face down into the bowl of stew. Abbott, as usual, doesn't see what's going on since he's completely absorbed in the newspaper. He can't understand why his pal is causing such a commotion. The "oyster" routine was also performed by Curly Howard in a Three Stooges short titled DUTIFUL BUT DUMB (1942). A slightly different version of the routine, with a frog replacing the oyster, turns up in another Abbott and Costello comedy, THE WISTFUL WIDOW OF WAGON GAP.

A basketball game between the Bixby team and a rival team will decide the fate of the college. The Bixby students have bet a thousand dollars at 20 to 1 to raise the mortgage money. A local racketeer, Honest Dan (Joe Kirk), rigs the game by hiring some Amazonian girl basketball stars to play for the rival team. Costello dons a wig, disguising himself as one of the Bixby players. This leads to a nonsensical game with Costello taking his usual number of pratfalls. A conk on the head causes Lou to get temporary amnesia. This gives Bud an idea. Bud convinces Lou that he's Daisy Dimple, the world's greatest girl basketball player. Lou, believing he's the basketball star, springs into action. He makes a series of spectacular shots to the amazement of his professional opponents.

Peggy Ryan and Bud try to revive Lou, who's been knocked unconscious during a basketball game in HERE COME THE CO-EDS.

Lou is naturally reluctant to wrestle with the Masked Marvel (Lon Chaney, Jr.).

(Costello was an avid basketball player, and as a youth he was a state champion. Yarbrough said that he made all of the trick shots by himself, never missing the basket.) Costello manages to tie the score when another conk on the head brings him back to normal. He accidentally dunks the ball into the opposing team's basket, causing Bixby to lose the game. This segment is incredibly contrived but there's some fun as Costello camps it up as a female player.

Donald Cook, Abbott and Costello, Lon Chaney, Jr., Joe Kirk and Charles Dingle argue about the outcome of the basketball game.

Lou is scorned by the students for losing the big game but he quickly redeems himself. He overhears Honest Dan discussing how he rigged the game and Lou runs away with the gambling winnings. This triggers another frenetic chase. Apparently the writers were running out of ideas for chase scenes. The finale of CO-EDS is one of their oddest. The boys, escaping the crooks, spot an automobile towing a sailboat on a trailer. They quickly jump onto the sailboat. The boat breaks loose from the car, weaving in and out of traffic while Costello dangles from the sail. He falls off the boat into an open manhole. The boat continues careening down a busy street when Costello appears from another manhole and climbs back on. This chase is well-staged but isn't as funny as the finales of the earlier films. The crooks are carted off to jail, Bixby officially wins the big game and Costello becomes the campus hero. The film's musical interludes are provided by Phil Spitalny and his Hour of Charm All-Girl Orchestra featuring Evelyn and Her Magic Violin!

CO-EDS received some enthusiastic notices. As *Variety* put it: "HERE COME THE CO-EDS is smartly gagged, smoothly paced, and even the familiar routines are given new twists."

The Naughty Nineties

THE NAUGHTY NINETIES, the pair's first costume picture, is noteworthy because they perform their venerable "Who's on First" routine. The biggest problem Jean Yarbrough had during production was keeping the studio technicians from laughing out loud while the boys ran through the baseball skit. (No matter how many times you hear "Who's on First," it's still funny.) After many takes, Yarbrough finally gave up, so if you listen closely the next time this film plays on TV, you can hear the cameramen and grips laughing in the background! The rest of the film is just standard but there are intermittent moments of fun.

Bud plays Dexter Broadhurst, a ham actor who performs on Captain Sam's showboat, *The River Queen.* Lou is Sebastian Dinwiddie, Bud's assistant. Kindly Captain Sam (Henry Travers) is proud of the wholesome family entertainment featured on his showboat. When the boat docks at St. Louis, Bud and Lou try to rescue Captain Sam from a poker game with three card sharks (Lois Collier, Alan Curtis, Joe Sawyer). But they are too late and the gamblers win a controlling interest in *The River Queen.* The gamblers move onto the riverboat and begin to take charge. To Captain Sam's horror they set up a crooked gambling operation on board. Abbott and Costello try to rid the showboat of the villains. Between skirmishes with the villains, the boys do a couple of funny routines. In one, Lou auditions for the big musical show. He attempts to sing a chorus of "My Bonnie Lies over the Ocean." Behind him, Bud is busily shouting orders to the stage crew. Indicating a painted backdrop, Bud yells, "Take it up!" Lou thinks he's talking to *him* and sings an octave higher. Then Bud shouts, "Lower it!" Lou complies by singing in a deep baritone. This keeps up until Lou falls off the stage into the orchestra pit.

Another good episode has Bud trying to perform a serious drama while stagehand Lou disrupts the proceedings and finally brings the scenery tumbling down around the actors.

In a less effective scene Costello is served a hamburger for lunch, and is convinced that it is cat meat. This is more distasteful than humorous.

One problem with THE NAUGHTY NINETIES is that there are many repetitions of timeworn gags. An example is a scene in which Bud falls overboard and hollers to Lou to throw him a lifesaver. Lou opens a package of candy Life Savers and throws

Performing "Who's on First" in their fifteenth film, THE NAUGHTY NINETIES (1945).

him one. This gag appears in the classic Marx Brothers comedy HORSE FEATHERS.

They reactivate the "mirror" routine. This time Lou takes the place of villain Joe Sawyer's mirror and mimics Sawyer as the latter tries to shave.

Another gag in THE NAUGHTY NINETIES can be seen in several other comedies. Lou is in the kitchen frosting a cake. He accidentally mistakes a pot holder for one of the layers and applies frosting to it. The "cake" is then served to the gambling patrons, and everyone starts coughing up feathers. This gag turned up in two Three Stooges shorts.

The reason that some of the gags are familiar might be because veteran gag writer Felix Adler contributed some of the comedy sequences.

A violent brawl provides the film's climax. Our heroes are chased all over the riverboat by Joe Sawyer and an assortment of other bad guys. Bud and Lou, armed with wooden clubs, pick off the opposition one at a time and deposit them in the river.

Captain Sam gets back his beloved *River Queen* thanks to Bud and Lou. The film ends with a stage production of *Uncle Tom's Cabin* in which Costello plays Little Eva!

Most of the critics dismissed this film as being minor Abbott and Costello, with the New York *Times* calling it "a musty archive of old gags and acts that they have played before."

Abbott and Costello in Hollywood

S. Sylvan Simon directed this film, which was the first to include Abbott and Costello's names in the title. Writers Nat Perrin and Lou Breslow devised some excellent gags. For instance, Costello hides in the M-G-M wardrobe department to elude the studio police. He finds himself on the end of a line of extras dressed as hoboes for a movie. An assistant director inspects the "bums" one by one, complaining to each that they're not sufficiently ragged-looking. However when he comes to Costello, who's not in costume, the director says, "You're perfect!" Two sketches in this film are among the best the team ever did, and the final chase, with Lou trapped on a runaway roller coaster car, is effective. Ralph Blane and Hugh Martin wrote the music and one song, "Midway," is pretty good.

As the film opens, we find Bud gainfully employed as a barber in a posh Hollywood salon. He supplements his salary by giving barbering lessons to shoeshine boy Costello. Abbott allows Costello to practice on one of his customers. Lou's victim is Rags Ragland, who miraculously escapes with his life after Lou gives him a shave. Claire Warren (Frances Rafferty), a former manicurist at the salon, has landed the lead in a big-budget movie musical. Her co-star is a fading matinee idol, Gregory LeMaise (Carleton G. Young), who has a reputation for being a Casanova offscreen as well. Bud and Lou are called to the office of the biggest agent in Hollywood, Norman Royce (Warner Anderson). Royce handles all the stars, including Claire and LeMaise. While they're giving him a haircut and a shoeshine, the boys hear Royce making big money by simply lifting up the telephone. This encourages them to quit their jobs and become Hollywood agents. A young singer, Jeff Parker (Robert Stanton), auditions in the office and impresses Royce with his talent. Just then, Gregory LeMaise barges in to announce that he wants Claire fired from the picture since she didn't respond to his advances. He tells the agent that he refuses to appear in the picture with her. Royce quickly replaces LeMaise with Jeff. Jeff is naturally thrilled until LeMaise reconsiders and agrees to do the picture after all. Bud and Lou appoint themselves Jeff's agents and promise the young singer that they'll get him the lead in the musical.

The boys attempt to talk the head of the studio, Mr. Kavanaugh (Donald MacBride), into hiring Jeff. They hardly make a good

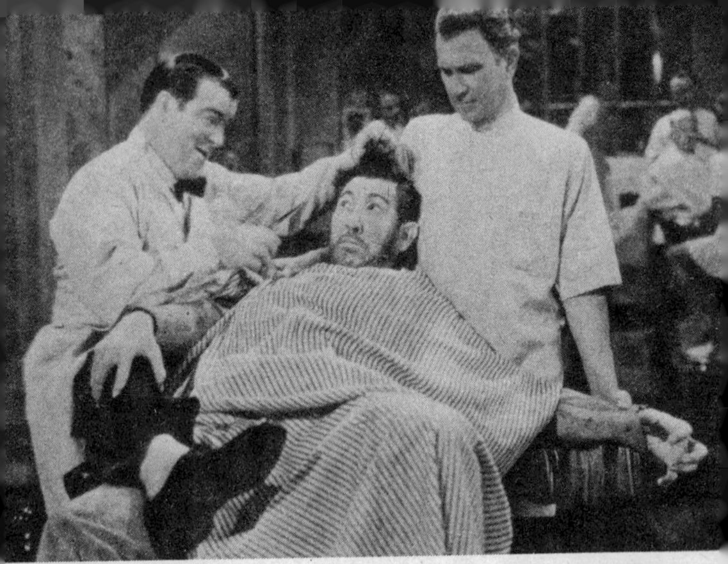

An old friend of Abbott and Costello's from burlesque, Rags Ragland, gets a haircut from Lou in ABBOTT AND COSTELLO IN HOLLYWOOD.

first impression with the movie mogul. When they arrive at the front gate, they crash into Kavanaugh's limousine, causing them to be barred from the lot. They sneak into the studio and the security guards search for the two trespassers.

In the course of his misadventures on the M-G-M backlot, Lou takes over a class of child actors and disrupts the filming of a love scene between Lucille Ball and Preston Foster. Lou also poses as a prop dummy on the set of a Western. He is continually dragged up a long flight of stairs and takes a beating from the movie's heavy, Mike Mazurki.

The film hits its best moments when Lou suffers a chronic case of insomnia. Bud gives Lou earplugs to help him sleep and asks Lou how they work. Lou, wearing the earplugs, can't hear his partner and this leads to a funny, fast-moving scene. The "earplugs" routine is featured in the compilation film, THAT'S ENTERTAINMENT, PART TWO.

Bud concocts a plan to get rid of Gregory LeMaise so Jeff can take his part. Lou must provoke LeMaise into a fight. When LeMaise strikes Lou, Bud will take a photograph of it. They'll have the actor arrested and the publicity will result in LeMaise's suspension from the studio. The boys reach the actor's beach house just as he is departing on his yacht. They jump on board and Lou

With guest stars Lucille Ball, Preston Foster and director Robert Z. Leonard.

begins to argue with him. A fight ensues and Costello falls overboard. LeMaise circles the harbor but there is no sign of Costello. Bud fears that his little pal has drowned. Abbott, devastated at the loss of his partner, wanders into a waterfront bar. He confesses to the bartender how badly he treated Lou and how he always took advantage of him. Lou, soaking wet, walks into the bar, unbeknown to Bud. Lou listens to Bud's tearful soliloquy and is touched to hear how much he really cared about him. In fact, Costello gets so caught up in this flood of sentiment that he joins Bud for a good cry. Bud turns around and is amazed to see that Lou is alive and well. Then Bud, back to his old self, slaps Costello in the face for getting him so worried. This scene is expertly acted by both Abbott and Costello and is quite touching. Almost identical scenes appear in AFRICA SCREAMS and ABBOTT AND COSTELLO IN THE FOREIGN LEGION.

Bud keeps Lou in hiding and spreads the word that LeMaise killed the little fellow. LeMaise takes it on the lam, forcing the studio to give the lead to Jeff. Lou must stay hidden until the big finale of the musical is filmed. The finale is an elaborate dance number on a carnival midway.

Lou, disguised with a beard and a turban, walks into a cafe near the studio. He has a drink with LeMaise, unaware it's the actor

Shoeshine boy Costello is as efficient as ever in the team's last M-G-M comedy, ABBOTT AND COSTELLO IN HOLLYWOOD. With Warner Anderson.

since he is also wearing a disguise. They suddenly discover each other's identity and Lou is chased onto the movie sound stage. The chase leads to a roller coaster constructed for the finale that's in progress. Lou struggles with LeMaise in and out of the roller coaster cars. Costello is pushed out and he falls hundreds of feet, landing on a flagpole. The flagpole breaks and he falls back into the roller coaster car. LeMaise releases Lou's car from the others and Lou takes a wild ride in the detached car. The car begins to break apart piece by piece until Costello is left balancing on the axle! The finale is completed and the movie becomes a smash hit, making Jeff and Claire stars.

In the last scene we see Bud and Lou, now big-shot Hollywood agents, in their plush office. Costello demonstrates how easy it is to be an agent. He dials a huge French-style telephone, a drawer opens at the base and money flies out.

"The running gags are drowned by gales of mirth before they're half finished," said the New York *Times.* "Among the real rib-tickling sketches in this film the two high spots are Costello's schooling in the tonsorial art and his desperate battle to overcome insomnia. During these interludes, his brilliant pantomimic talents are brought into full play."

The box office returns for ABBOTT AND COSTELLO IN HOLLYWOOD were disappointing and Metro-Goldwyn-Mayer dropped the team's option to do a film a year. Universal was now cutting down on their number of releases. The following year, 1946, saw only two of their comedies playing in theaters.

Little Giant

LITTLE GIANT is an interesting failure. Universal tried something new with the team in order to bolster box office receipts. It was decided to dispense with the usual burlesque turns in favor of a straight story. Bud and Lou weren't sure if audiences would accept them in essentially dramatic roles, so they incorporated one of their stock routines into the story—Lou once again proving to Bud that seven times thirteen equals twenty-eight. Otherwise, the team plays it straight. They only have a few scenes together since Lou commands most of the footage. Lou has some fine dramatic moments, particularly in a scene near the end of the film in which he discovers that he's been the victim of a cruel practical joke. Bud gives a fine performance in a dual role. The only problem is that the film just isn't funny. Director William A. Seiter, who directed the classic Laurel and Hardy feature SONS OF THE DESERT, did the best he could with a contrived and only sporadically amusing script.

Costello plays Benny Miller, a country bumpkin who lives with his mother on their farm in Cucamonga. His dream has always been to be a successful salesman one day. He has just graduated from a record correspondence school in salesmanship. He plays the final record and a chorus sings the school song as Lou proudly clutches his diploma. Lou says goodbye to his mother (Mary Gordon) and his childhood sweetheart, Martha (Elena Verdugo), and sets out for Los Angeles to seek his fortune. In L.A. he calls upon his Uncle Clarence (George Cleveland), who is a bookkeeper for the Hercules Vacuum Cleaner Company, hoping his uncle will get him a position with the firm. However, there is a company policy forbidding the hiring of relatives. Bud plays the sales manager, John Morrison. He mistakes Costello for a male model who is to portray Hercules in an ad campaign and orders the confused Costello to take off his clothes so he can see his physique. Before Lou can explain who he is, he has stripped down to his underwear. When the real Hercules shows up it is evident that an embarrassing error has been made. The sales manager is afraid that word of this might get out, which would make him the laughingstock of the company. Morrison can't be too careful since he has been juggling accounts, stealing thousands from the firm. He is also secretly married to Hazel (Jacqueline De Wit), the advertising manager. Hazel suggests that they give Costello a job to keep him quiet

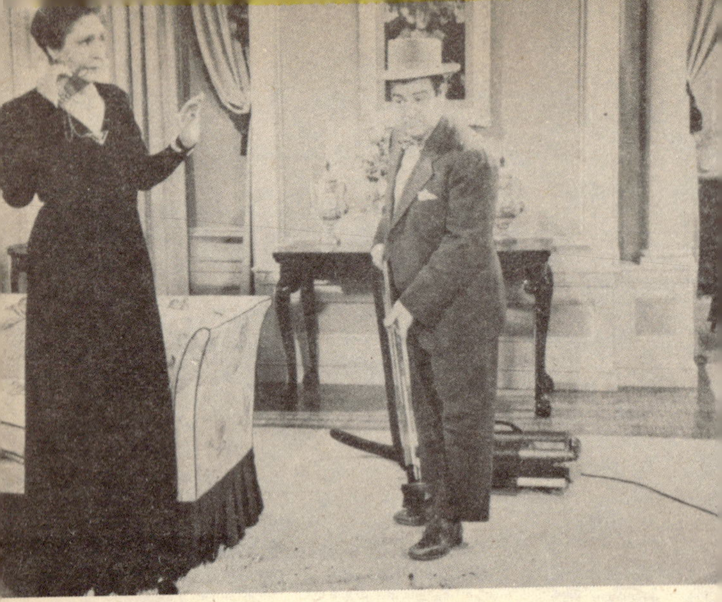

Lou demonstrates the Hercules vacuum cleaner for Margaret Dumont in LITTLE GIANT.

With Florence Lake in a deleted sequence from LITTLE GIANT.

about the incident so he is sent to the Stockton branch to sell vacuums.

Costello takes the train to Stockton, nearly causing a panic in the sleeping car. (Donald MacBride is the harried conductor.) Abbott also plays the head of the branch office in Stockton, Tom Chandler. At first Lou is puzzled by his strong resemblance to Morrison. Bud, as Chandler, explains that the two men are cousins. Morrison devised the rule that forbids the hiring of relatives in order to get rid of Chandler, who should rightfully be the district sales manager.

Lou is possibly the worst salesman in the company's history. He pays a visit to a wealthy dowager (Margaret Dumont) and, in demonstrating how the vacuum works, covers the entire living room, and Miss Dumont, with soot.

A sequence that was deleted from LITTLE GIANT shows Costello arriving at a farmhouse to sell his wares. The lady of the house tries vainly to tell something to Lou, but Lou, the persistent salesman, won't give her a chance. He proceeds to litter her floor with all sorts of debris, boasting that the vacuum cleaner will pick it up easily. The housewife finally manages to tell Costello that her house doesn't have any electricity. This funny sketch turned up years later in an episode of the Abbott and Costello TV show, appropriately titled "The Vacuum Cleaner Salesman."

Chandler realizes that Lou must be fired before he causes any more damage, so he assigns the task to his secretary, Ruby (Brenda Joyce). Ruby takes Lou to the local saloon to break the news over a few drinks. The other salesmen are gathered in the bar and they play a practical joke on their co-worker. They convince the gullible Costello that he has the ability to read minds. They each concentrate on an object in the room, and Lou is supposed to guess which one it is. Whatever object he chooses, the salesmen tell him he's correct. Lou believes that he's psychic, unaware that the salesmen are laughing behind his back. This restores his confidence and Ruby doesn't have the heart to tell him that he has lost his job.

The following day Lou starts his door-to-door rounds, impressing his customers with his new self-confidence. Before long, Costello has sold a dozen vacuums, single-handedly maintaining the quota for the entire office. Word of this "boy wonder" gets back to Morrison at the home office, which results in Lou being made the salesman of the year. He returns to Los Angeles for the award ceremony. Morrison is worried that Lou might know about his crooked dealings since he can reportedly read minds. He dispatches Hazel to find out how much Costello knows. Hazel brings

Lou to her apartment and tries to give him a sedative. She takes the drug by mistake and passes out. Lou, smoking a cigar for the first time, gets dizzy and passes out also. Morrison and Lou's sweetheart, Martha, walk in and find Hazel and Lou asleep in the twin beds. Morrison is furious and Martha breaks off her engagement to Costello. Morrison learns that Lou's telepathic abilities are phony and arranges to have Ruby attend the award ceremony to reveal that it was all a practical joke. When Lou overhears the audience laughing at him, he returns to his mother's farm.

Back at the farm he is greeted by Chandler and Mr. Van Loon, president of the company. They happily inform him that Morrison has been fired and Chandler is the new sales manager. They appoint Lou to a representative job in Cucamonga. Lou and Martha are then able to get married.

LITTLE GIANT pretty much falls flat in every department. The film's funniest sequence–Lou Costello's desperate battle to undress in a cramped Pullman berth–is lifted from Laurel and Hardy. And as if that wasn't bad enough–Abbott and Costello have even kidnapped Margaret Dumont from the Marx Brothers!

Left to right: Brenda Joyce, Bud, Elena Verdugo, Lou, George Cleveland, Pierre Watkins, and Mary Gordon in the final scene of LITTLE GIANT.

The Time of their Lives

Of all the Abbott and Costello comedies, THE TIME OF THEIR LIVES is the most interesting. It has a sustained plot and the humor is derived from characterizations and situations, rather than Bud and Lou's stock routines. Once again the team was "split up." They share only a few scenes as they had done in LITTLE GIANT. But it works much better in this film. Lou, as a misplaced ghost, gives the performance of his career. Bud, playing a neurotic psychiatrist, showed that he was capable of being a fine character actor. This was director Charles Barton's first assignment for the team and he created a marvelously atmospheric film. The chilling séance scene is an example of his talent. Barton directed eight of their later comedies, including three of their all-time best.

THE TIME OF THEIR LIVES (originally titled THE GHOST STEPS OUT) opens during the American Revolution. The year is 1780 and the setting is Kings Point, New York. Lou is Horatio Prim, a patriotic tinker. At the beginning of the film we see him riding his horse, Lancelot, to the home of one of his best customers, wealthy landowner Tom Danbury (Jess Barker). The tinker plans to elope with one of Danbury's housemaids, Nora (Anne Gillis). However, he has spent all of the money they were going to use for the elopement–a pound and fourteen shillings–to buy food for some poor families. "What happened to your pence?" asks Nora. "I lost 'em in a card game," replies Lou. Lou tries to redeem himself by showing Nora a letter of commendation he has just received from George Washington, praising him for his work. The conniving butler of the house, Cuthbert Greenway (Abbott), is a rival for the hand of the pretty servant girl, and is eager to get Costello out of the way. He lures Costello into the barn to repair the lock on an old trunk belonging to the master of the house. Lou asks the butler if he'll put a good word in for him with Danbury. "If you can open the trunk–I'll put you in very good," promises Abbott, and he locks Costello in the trunk.

Tom Danbury is secretly a friend and accomplice of Benedict Arnold's. He kidnaps Nora when she overhears him plotting to betray the Continental cause. She is holding Costello's letter from George Washington. Danbury takes it away from her and conceals it in the secret compartment of a clock. His fiancée, the lovely Melody Allen (Marjorie Reynolds), learns what has happened and prepares to warn the revolutionary army of the traitorous

Lou and Marjorie Reynolds are eighteenth-century ghosts who set out to haunt a house in THE TIME OF THEIR LIVES.

plot. She frees Costello from the trunk and convinces him to accompany her. The patriots have already learned of Danbury's involvement with Benedict Arnold and they surround the estate. As Lou and Melody ride away, they are seen by the American troops. The troops give chase and shoot them both, believing they are the traitors. (This scene is startling, considering that they have been shot and killed.) The two bodies are then cast into an old well. An army major curses their souls to roam Danbury Manor "to the crack of doom," unless some evidence proves they were not traitors. He nails a hastily fashioned sign on the well, reading, "Here were buried two traitors." Lou and Melody materialize, unaware they are now ghosts. Lou, taking a drink from the well, doesn't notice that the water is squirting out of his chest where he was shot. "That's funny," he says. "I'm still thirsty." He tries to pat Melody on the back but his hand passes right through her body. The two spirits see the ghastly sight of their own bodies lying dead at the bottom of the well and realize that they are the traitors referred to on the sign. Costello remembers the curse placed on their souls by the major. He attempts to escape from Danbury Manor but some supernatural force imprisons him. He sadly watches as the butler rides off with his horse, Lancelot. The patriots set fire to the mansion and cart away all the furniture.

The scene dissolves to modern times. The year is 1946. After a hundred and sixty-six years the two ghosts are resolved to their fate. They have been living all this time atop the oak tree next to the well. A young man, Sheldon Gage (John Shelton), has gone to great expense to restore the Danbury mansion and decorate it with its original furnishings. He arrives to spend the night at the house, along with his fiancée, June Prescott (Lynne Baggett), and her Aunt Millie (Binnie Barnes). They are "greeted" at the door by the mysterious housekeeper, Emily (Gale Sondergaard). "Pardon me, but didn't I see you in *Rebecca?*" Millie inquires. Sheldon's psychiatrist, Ralph Greenway (Abbott), is also spending the night. He believes that a home in the country will do wonders for his patient's nerves. The psychiatrist is a descendant of the butler, Cuthbert Greenway. Lou believes that the doctor *is* Cuthbert. Melody asks how he could still be alive. "They say only the good die young," answers Lou. Costello overhears Sheldon saying that he will open the house to the public. The two spirits don't care for the idea of being annoyed by tourists so they decide to haunt the house at the stroke of midnight.

Costello hasn't quite mastered the art of going through walls and when he tries he gets stuck midway. After that, he resorts to the conventional method of opening doors. Inside the house, the

Bud Abbott's best performance: as the neurotic Doctor Greenway.

Discussing a scene with Marjorie Reynolds and director Charles Barton.

ghosts are intrigued with the modern-day conveniences such as the telephone, radio and electric light, which they attribute to Ben Franklin, "who's always inventing things." Costello uses his invisibility to play practical jokes on Abbott. The ghosts play the harpsichord, terrifying Bud. Lou trips Abbott, kicks him and whistles in his stethoscope. "Why do they always pick on me?" Bud demands to know. (Lou also seems to be getting even with Bud for all the slapping around he took in their other films.)

The spirits learn that the original furniture is in the house and they tear the place apart to find Lou's letter from George Washington. The letter will vindicate them and they'll be free to leave earth. Searching the cellar, Costello tampers with the generator, causing the lights in the house to blink on and off. Melody, investigating one of the bedrooms, takes time to try on an evening gown. She descends the staircase wearing the gown but the frightened Millie sees only the gown, apparently walking by itself.

The psychic housekeeper, Emily, suggests a séance to try to communicate with the restless ghosts. The séance is played completely straight, save for Millie's wisecracks (she refers to it as a "ghost-to-ghost broadcast"). This scene is very suspenseful, more so than scenes of this type in serious films dealing with the occult. The mortals ask questions of the spirits to determine their identities. Costello responds by rapping on the table, once for "no" and twice for "yes." They quickly learn that the spirits are Horatio Prim and Melody Allen. In the film's eeriest moment, the spirit of Tom Danbury "possesses" the body of Emily. Through Emily, Danbury gives a clue to the whereabouts of the letter from George Washington. Sheldon figures out that the clue refers to a clock. Lou and Melody are sure it must be the clock in the study since that is where Nora was abducted. As luck would have it, the clock is not the original, but a reproduction. The original resides in a museum in Manhattan. Bud volunteers to get the clock since he feels guilty about his ancestor who he admits was a scoundrel. The next morning Bud goes to the museum and steals the clock by hiding it under his coat. He returns to the estate but before he can find

With John Shelton, Marjorie Reynolds and Binnie Barnes in THE TIME OF THEIR LIVES.

the combination to open the clock, the police arrest him. The invisible Costello takes over the police car and drives it crazily all over the grounds, with Bud in the back seat. This chase sequence wasn't necessary. It's not particularly funny and it spoils the mood established in the film. But by this time moviegoers expected a chase in an Abbott and Costello comedy.

Sheldon uncovers the letter from George Washington and reads the letter aloud, which refers to Lou as a true patriot. The two spirits are then free to go to Heaven. At the Pearly Gates Lou is greeted by Nora. Lou wants her to let him in but Nora points to a sign on the gates proclaiming: CLOSED FOR WASHINGTON'S BIRTHDAY.

The critics weren't impressed with THE TIME OF THEIR LIVES. It was shrugged off as another in a long series of comedy-fantasies that Hollywood had been grinding out in the forties. The New York *Times* observed, "There is some frantic and uproariously funny slapstick in this mad patchwork of vocal and visual gags, but all the good stuff could have been compressed into a neat two-reeler." This critic missed the point altogether.

Abbott and Costello showed that they could get laughs individually, without relying on each other. In fact, they never even speak to each other in the film, except briefly at the beginning. Bud is fun to watch as the psychiatrist who thinks he might need a psychiatrist. "Be calm, be reasonable," he tells himself after each encounter with the mischievous ghosts. As for Lou Costello's acting ability, witness the scene in which he confesses to Nora that he's given away all their money, or the scene in which he says goodbye to Melody.

Binnie Barnes is responsible for a good share of the laughs in her usual role of a wisecracking relative, and Gale Sondergaard is coolly sinister as the housekeeper.

The special-effects people really outdid themselves on this film. The double exposure tricks are as old as Hollywood itself, but they have seldom been used as effectively as they are here. One gag is especially clever. We see Costello and Melody running on a collision course. Since they are ghosts, they pass right through each other, the result of which is they're wearing each other's clothes.

Sadly, this was the team's last venture at character comedy. They returned to their standard smart guy–dumb guy relationship for the remainder of the films . . . although their characterizations in their next, BUCK PRIVATES COME HOME, have more dimension than usual.

Buck Privates Come Home

BUCK PRIVATES COME HOME is a Hollywood rarity. It is a sequel that is, at times, as good as the original film. It doesn't evoke as many big laughs as BUCK PRIVATES did, but this is compensated for by more plot than usual and some moments of genuine pathos. Lou Costello's scenes with a six-year-old war orphan are reminiscent of Chaplin's THE KID. (Costello said in an interview that Chaplin had planned to direct him in a remake of THE KID.) For the second time director Charles Barton was at the helm and he did an outstanding job. The chase ending, with Lou at the wheel of a midget racing car, is really something to see.

The film opens, appropriately enough, with the "drill routine" footage from the original BUCK PRIVATES. The war in Europe ends but the war between Abbott and Costello and Sergeant Collins (Nat Pendleton) continues. On board the troop transport heading back to the States, Costello, in the space of a few minutes, hits Collins with a mop and a gooey cake. Bud has risen to the rank of corporal, but Lou is still a private, which comes as no surprise. The only surprise is that Costello actually participated in the war and the Allies still won. Lou brags that during the war he was where the bullets were the thickest–"underneath the ammunition truck."

Lou has smuggled a six-year-old French child, Evey (Beverly Simmons), on board. Evey is an orphan and Lou plans to adopt her when they reach the States. When Sergeant Collins finds the child, Evey is held for the immigration authorities by a beautiful nurse, Sylvia Hunter (Joan Shawlee). Lou has also smuggled a souvenir from the war–a German booby trap. He triggers the time bomb by mistake and then tries to get rid of it, finally throwing it overboard. The bomb explodes, causing a minor tidal wave that nearly drowns the captain (Don Porter).

The transport arrives at New York Harbor and all of the soldiers merrily sing "Going Home" as they leave the ship. All of the soldiers, that is, except Costello, who is brokenhearted that he can't adopt Evey. The scene then shifts to the Fort Dix separation center. Costello complains how they rush you into war–"and when it's time for you to get out, everybody takes their time."

The boys, now civilians, return to their former occupation–selling neckties in Times Square. There's a good bit in which Abbott tries to hypnotize his shill Costello into buying some of the ties.

Meanwhile, Evey escapes from the immigration authorities and runs to Times Square to search for her two foster-uncles. She locates them just as Collins, back on the police force, is about to arrest them. The boys, with Evey's help, make a clean getaway. They disguise Evey as a boy since she is the object of a search by the immigration department. Lou learns that he must be married and have a steady income in order to adopt Evey. Evey remembers the nurse that took care of her and suggests that she might make a suitable wife for Costello. All three show up at Sylvia's apartment. Sylvia already has a boy friend, Bill (Tom Brown), a racing car designer and driver. Bill's racer is held in hock by a local garage for lack of eight thousand dollars in charges. If he can't raise the money he won't be able to enter the Gold Cup Stakes, in which his car is sure to win the first prize of twenty thousand dollars. The boys offer to help Bill raise the necessary cash, and Sylvia allows them to spend the night in the apartment. Costello, unable to find a place to sleep, climbs out on the fire escape. He fashions a hammock by pinning a blanket to the clothesline. When Bud asks him if he's asleep, Costello, lying in the hammock, replies, "No, but I'm about to fall off!" The following morning a housewife in a building across the yard begins to pull in the line to collect her laundry. Costello awakes and finds himself suspended five stories above the ground. The housewife's jealous husband looks out the window and concludes that his wife is carrying on an affair with Lou. A riotous tug-of-war follows, with the husband pulling on one end of the clothesline, Abbott pulling the other, and Costello in the middle. The husband threatens to cut the line and Abbott dares him to do it. The husband accepts the dare and cuts the line. Lou goes sailing downward, crashing through the window of an apartment below. The apartment just happens to belong to Sergeant Collins. Collins, clad only in his underwear, chases Lou onto the street. The police captain (Donald MacBride) see Collins and reprimands him for being out of uniform. The clothesline gag, recalling the best of silent comedy, is one of the film's high points.

The pair spends the next day trying to round up some cash to pay off Bill's debts. A visit to the bank for a loan proves disastrous. Lou has brought along a model of Bill's midget racer to impress the bank president. As Lou demonstrates how the model car operates, it begins to backfire loudly, reverberating through the bank like gunshots. Through the glass door of the banker's office, the guards see Lou's silhouette holding the model. It appears that he is spraying the room with a machine gun. The customers run out of the bank in terror. The guards descend on the office, and the boys quickly find themselves on the street, minus the loan.

In BUCK PRIVATES COME HOME, Abbott and Costello disguise Evey (Beverly Simmons) as a boy to elude immigration authorities.

Beverly Simmons and Joan Shawlee (formerly Joan Fulton) in BUCK PRIVATES COME HOME.

Bud and some fellow soldiers are heading home on a troop transport in this scene from BUCK PRIVATES COME HOME. (The soldier to Bud's right is Jimmie Dodd who gained prominence in the '50s as the world's oldest mouseketeer on "The Mickey Mouse Club".)

In a rare stroke of genius, Lou solves the crisis. He suggests that they borrow the money from all their old army buddies, who will be eager to invest in Bill's racing car. Bud agrees that it's a good idea. "I'm glad I thought of it," says Bud. They gather all the boys from their old outfit and Bill explains his ideas to them. The ex-GIs are more than happy to contribute. Bud and Lou then try to find a suitable home for Evey and themselves. A crooked real estate agent (Joe Kirk) sells them a seemingly beautiful suburban home. As soon as Lou hands over the money, a truck hauls away the house, which turns out to be just a false front. Behind it sits an old broken-down bus. Undaunted, the boys set up housekeeping in the bus. Bill and Sylvia help them to decorate it. On the day they're ready to move in, Collins shows up to take custody of Evey. Lou quickly renders the cop unconscious and they escape once again. The immigration officials and the police captain arrive at the bus to find a dazed Collins its only occupant. The captain suspends the cop from the force.

Anxious to get his job back, Collins stakes out the garage where Bill's racer is held. He plans to catch Bud and Lou, with the assistance of some strong-arm friends. The boys wait for them to fall asleep, and then they sneak into the garage to claim the racer. Collins wakes up and a brawl ensues. In the confusion, Bill is able to

Abbott and Costello run into trouble when Sergeant Collins (Nat Pendleton) and his buddies ambush them in a garage. With Tom Brown.

tow away the car. The boys jump on back and ride off, leaving the cop behind.

The day of the big race arrives. If Bill wins he and Sylvia will be able to get married and adopt Evey. The police, led by Collins, rush into the stadium, arrest Bud and Bill and take custody of Evey. Costello puts on goggles and a helmet to disguise himself and climbs into Bill's racer. Before he knows what is happening, the car is being towed onto the track. He accidentally jams the accelerator and takes the lead in the race. The car swerves out of control and crashes right through the stadium, heading for the open road. The police commandeer a limousine owned by an auto magnate, Mr. Appleby (Russell Hicks), and follow Lou. The pursuit leads to an airport, where Lou nearly collides with an airplane. He then speeds through the congested streets of Manhattan. The midget racer is small enough to allow him to drive *under* trucks. He crashes through a billboard, and the billboard now serves as "wings" for the car. The car soars through the air, finally crashing through the wall of a movie theater. Appleby has witnessed these incredible feats. He is so impressed he orders twenty of the cars and two hundred engines. Now Bill and Sylvia can adopt Evey. The police captain arranges to have Bud and Lou join the force, to the horror of Sergeant Collins. For the film's blackout we see the boys, now policemen, marching proudly in dress parade, giving Lou the opportunity to take another pratfall.

A curious sequence, deleted from the finished print of BUCK PRIVATES COME HOME, has Costello playing Romeo in a stage production of *Romeo and Juliet!*

An advantage that this sequel has over the original BUCK PRIVATES is an exceptional cast of supporting players, including Joan Shawlee, Tom Brown, Donald MacBride. Don Porter and Beverly Simmons, who is very affecting as the orphan girl. Nat Pendleton, as the ill-fated Sergeant Collins, tops his earlier performance in BUCK PRIVATES. Pendleton had been a popular character actor in the thirties, lending his talents to scores of comedies, but by the time he was cast in this film he was fifty-two and his screen career had virtually come to an end. BUCK PRIVATES COME HOME was his last film of any consequence. Nevertheless, Nat Pendleton was extremely talented and the perfect foil for comedians such as the Marx Brothers and Abbott and Costello.

BUCK PRIVATES COME HOME received an excellent review from the New York *Times:* "It doesn't make much sense—in fact, it doesn't make any sense at all—but the new Abbott and Costello comedy which opened at the Winter Garden is a lot of fun. BUCK PRIVATES COME HOME finds the roly-poly one and his straight man in the very best of form."

Variety echoed the sentiment, calling the film "frantic fun, climaxing in a hilarious chase that is socko . . . chase has Costello taking off in a midget racing car with police after him and builds to hysterical peaks of audience gasps."

The Wistful Widow of Wagon Gap

THE WISTFUL WIDOW OF WAGON GAP has a wonderful plot, based on an actual law that existed in Montana. The law required the surviving partner in a gun duel to pay off all debts of the deceased and to assume care of the family. Writers William Bowers and D. D. Beauchamp wrote a story treatment with this in mind. In William Froug's book *The Screenwriter Looks at the Screenwriter,* William Bowers said that the story was written for James Stewart. The idea was to have Stewart passing through a frontier town, shooting a man in self-defense and then having to support the boisterous widow, played by Marjorie Main. Universal bought the story but decided to make it a vehicle for Abbott and Costello. It turned out to be a good Abbott and Costello movie, offering the team a chance to lampoon just about every Western cliché.

The film opens with a subtitle that sets the mood: "Montana–In the Days When Men Were Men–with Two Exceptions." Duke Egan and Chester Wooley are the names adopted by the comedy duo this time. They're a couple of salesmen who stop at the town of Wagon Gap to sell their wares. No sooner do they arrive than Costello is accused of shooting the town drunk, Fred Hawkins. A trial is held in the saloon. Costello suspects that it's not a fair trial since all of the members of the jury are holding ropes. The town good guy, Jim Simpson (William Ching), saves the boys by pointing out the Montana law. Costello is informed that he must support Widow Hawkins (Miss Main) and pay off her late husband's debts, of which there are many. Bud is appointed to make sure that Lou fulfills his obligations. The two salesmen arrive at the Hawkins farm and Lou apologizes to the widow for shooting her husband. "Think nothing of it," says the widow. "He just wasn't any good. All he ever did was drink and gamble." Apparently that's not all he did because his seven children suddenly appear to greet their new guardian. At dinner one of the kids puts a frog in Costello's soup, which leads to a funny segment. Costello tries to switch soup bowls with Bud but Lou still lands up with the frog. The *Hollywood Reporter* called this scene "a low comedy masterpiece–in itself worth the price of admission." Besides his chores at the farm, the exhausted Costello must work nights in the saloon to settle Hawkins' accounts.

The fun really begins when Costello is appointed sheriff of the

Upon arrival in Wagon Gap, Duke (Bud) and Chester (Lou) are accused of murdering the town drunk. THE WISTFUL WIDOW OF WAGON GAP. With George Cleveland and Glenn Strange.

lawless town. He is chosen for the job since no one dares to shoot him in the fear of inheriting the Hawkins clan. As an added precaution, he carries a photograph of the widow and kids to discourage gunslingers. Costello strides around town flaunting his newly acquired power. There's a great takeoff on a typical Western movie cliché. Tough sheriff Costello saunters into the saloon and immediately the piano music stops and a hush falls over the room. "You don't have to stop talkin' on account of me!" Costello shouts to the patrons. The commotion in the saloon resumes and then Lou yells "SHADDAP!", quieting the room once again. There's also some fun as the Abbott and Costello roles are briefly reversed, with Lou giving the orders for a change. He stands up to his partner and tells him, "You've been bossing me around long enough! Now the worm has turned and every dog has his day!"

In no time the little sheriff has restored law and order to Wagon Gap. Costello pokes fun at another Western cliché. We see him slowly marching down a deserted street to face the gunslingers. There's even the typically pompous music identified with scenes of this type. Costello finishes his "High Noon" walk by taking a terrific pratfall.

Word gets around town that the widow's farm will be the site of the new railroad, and that stands to make her rich. It is then open season for Costello. Every cowboy in town wants to shoot him and inherit the widow's money. A stagecoach robbery and a barroom brawl are dragged into the plot with only middling results. Finally the town's leading villain, Jake Frame (Gordon Jones), confesses that he shot Hawkins and Bud and Lou are free to head for California.

THE WISTFUL WIDOW OF WAGON GAP, despite its weaknesses, is great fun. Marjorie Main helps to bolster the film and character actors like George Cleveland, Gordon Jones, Dewey Robinson and Glenn Strange lend fine support. Bud and Lou were up to their old nepotism again. Lou's father served as associate producer, and Bud's nephew, Norman Abbott was the dialogue director. Norman Abbott is now one of Hollywood's top producer-directors. His credits include the Jack Benny TV series, several of Benny's later specials, and "Sanford and Son."

Bud and Marjorie Main in THE WISTFUL WIDOW OF WAGON GAP.

The Noose Hangs High

THE NOOSE HANGS HIGH was the pair's first venture at independent production. It is a mild little comedy they made at the Eagle-Lion studios. Filming THE NOOSE HANGS HIGH was a happy experience for Lou Costello. His third daughter, Christine, was born two days before production started.

This time Bud and Lou portray two hapless window washers who are hired by gangster Joseph Calleia to collect a debt of twenty thousand dollars. They get the money but mail it by mistake to a girl (Cathy Downs), who proceeds to spend all of it. The gangster gives Bud and Lou twenty-four hours to find the girl and get back the money.

The team repeats no fewer than five routines that were in previous films, including "Mustard" and "Hole in the Wall." They also manage to fit two other burlesque scenes into the story. In one, Costello gets his tooth pulled by a nearsighted dentist (Murray Leonard), and in the other, Bud and Lou try to get arrested but they even bungle that. Another former burlesque star, Leon Errol, provides the film with its best moments. Errol plays Julius Caesar McBride, a compulsive gambler who never loses. Leon Errol had a great rapport with Costello and a scene in which the two comics play a game of billiards is the high point.

The team then returned to their home studio, Universal, to begin work on one of their most memorable movies

SPEEDY
SERVICE

Leon Errol, Lou, Cathy Downs, and Bud await the outcome of a horse race.

With Jack Overman, Joseph Calleia, and Mike Mazurki.

Abbott and Costello Meet Frankenstein

Critics never dare use the word "satire" in connection with Bud Abbott and Lou Costello. But the fact is that ABBOTT AND COSTELLO MEET FRANKENSTEIN is the best satire on horror movies ever made. One of the film's chief assets is that the horror sequences are played completely straight, leaving the comedy to the comedians. The whole thing might have been a disaster in the hands of a less talented producer and director. One can envision the Frankenstein monster doing double takes or Count Dracula tossing off bad one-liners. Fortunately producer Robert Arthur and Director Charles Barton knew better. They fashioned a film that adroitly blends the elements of humor and horror. The production is enhanced by stunning visual effects. Charles Van Enger's photography is first-rate and so is Frank Skinner's eerie musical score. The sets are superb. The set of Dracula's castle is the best of its kind since Tod Browning's original DRACULA. Producer Arthur really made the most of a budget of about eight hundred thousand dollars. He remembers how the film came about. One day at Universal he and a couple of writers were pondering the perennial question at the studio–what to do next with Abbott and Costello? It occurred to Arthur that since the studio owned the copyright to the Frankenstein story, why not have Bud and Lou pitted against the monster? But they needed an idea that would make it at least somewhat logical for the duo to "meet Frankenstein." Arthur went home, thought about it and came up with the idea that the monster has gotten too intelligent. A simpler, more pliable brain must be found for Dr. Frankenstein's creation. And who has a simpler, more pliable brain than Costello? One of the other writers suggested that Dracula could be in possession of the monster. The studio owned the rights to the Dracula character too. "And why not have the Wolfman to warn the boys?" another writer spoke up. The Wolfman was also a resident at Universal City. So with this framework, a script was written by John Grant, Robert Lees and Frederic Rinaldo. Robert Arthur then went about the task of casting the film. Bela Lugosi was signed to re-create his role of Count Dracula, Lon Chaney, Jr., was naturally cast as the Wolfman and Glenn Strange was brought in to play the monster (Strange had played the part in two previous epics. HOUSE OF DRACULA and HOUSE OF FRANKENSTEIN).

"Don't be afraid," Dracula (Bela Lugosi) assures the monster (Glenn Strange), "He won't hurt you."

This film was to rejuvenate Abbott and Costello's box office popularity. Curiously enough, Lou Costello didn't want to make the film. He read the script and didn't think it was funny. Producer Arthur talked him into it and Costello turned in one of his funniest performances in years.

Our heroes play Chick Young and Wilbur Grey, a couple of shipping clerks in Florida. Two huge crates arrive to be delivered to McDougal's House of Horrors, a wax museum. Bud and Lou are unaware that the crates contain the bodies of Dracula and the monster. Lou receives a mysterious phone call from Lawrence Talbot (Chaney) in London. Talbot warns Lou not to open the crates. While he's talking to Costello a full moon appears, transforming Talbot into the Wolfman. He begins to growl and Costello politely asks him to get his dog away from the telephone. Lou is then greeted by his girl friend, beautiful Sandra Mornay (Lenore Aubert), who is inexplicably in love with him. We later learn that she is an accomplice of Count Dracula and has volunteered to "donate" Lou's brain to the monster. That night the boys deliver the crates to the wax museum in the midst of a howling storm. Lou unpacks one of the crates, revealing Dracula's coffin. The vampire rises from his crypt and quickly puts Lou in a trance. Dracula then revives the Frankenstein monster, which is frightened at the sight

The Wolfman (Lon Chaney, Jr.) prepares to attack an unsuspecting Costello.

of Costello. Dracula assures the creature, "Don't be afraid–he won't hurt you." Both creatures escape just as the museum owner, McDougal (Frank Ferguson), arrives. He is furious when he sees that the crates are empty, and holds the boys responsible for the disappearance of his exhibits. Bud and Lou spend the rest of the night in jail.

The following day they are bailed out by an attractive blonde, Joan Raymond (Jane Randolph), who also seems to be enamored of Lou. Bud can't fathom his partner's newly acquired sex appeal. Joan is secretly an insurance investigator hired to uncover the missing exhibits. Meanwhile, Lawrence Talbot rents a room in Bud and Lou's apartment house. He tries to convince them of Dracula's plan to revive the monster. Lou believes Talbot since he's seen Dracula and the monster in action. Bud, as usual, hasn't seen a thing so far. It never occurs to Bud to turn around and see what all the commotion is about. He thinks that Talbot is even crazier than Lou. At one point in the film Talbot confesses to Costello, "In half an hour the moon will rise and I'll turn into a wolf." "You and twenty million other guys," quips Lou. Lou locks Talbot in his room at the latter's request. Talbot then changes into the Wolfman. When Costello walks back into the room to return a suitcase, he barely misses being attacked. Lon Chaney's transformation scenes are very effective and Lugosi's transformations into the bat are also imaginatively accomplished through animation.

That night on the way to a masquerade ball, Bud and Lou stop at Dracula's castle to pick up Sandra. Dracula is posing as a kindly research scientist to cover his devious experiments. His handsome and honest assistant Dr. Stevens (Charles Bradstreet) is oblivious of Dracula's real intent. Stevens isn't the brightest fellow in the world. The castle is crammed with all sorts of weird electrical gadgets and the operating tables are equipped with straps to hold down the "patients." Yet Doc Stevens doesn't catch on to anything until the last reel. Lou has invited Joan Raymond to join them. After Sandra discovers that Joan is a detective, she feigns a headache so she won't have to attend the party. Dracula insists that Sandra stay with Costello and when she refuses to obey him, the Count settles the argument by biting her on the neck. While all of this is going on, Bud and Lou explore the castle to see if Talbot is telling the truth. They stumble onto a secret passageway leading to a cavern. Lou finds the lair of the monster quite unintentionally. In an uproariously funny sequence, Lou decides to sit down and rest, unaware that he's sitting on the monster's lap. The monster's hand moves forward and Lou is surprised to notice that he has an additional hand. Filming this sequence proved to be a problem. There were many retakes because Glenn Strange couldn't stop laughing.

Lou escorts his date Sandra to the masquerade. Sandra, now a full-fledged vampire, is eager to have Costello join the club.

"Look into my eyes," she commands.
Lou looks into her eyes and sees two bats flapping their wings.
Sandra: "Don't you know what's going to happen, now?"
Lou: "I'll bite."
Sandra: "No, I will."

When McDougal is attacked by the Wolfman, Bud is accused of the crime. An angry mob with bloodhounds tracks the boys through the Everglades. Bud and Lou run into Dracula, who hypnotizes them. The Count takes Lou and Joan, also under the vampire's spell, back to the castle by motorboat. Bud and Talbot set out to rescue them. Lou is informed by Sandra that he's about to take part in a brain transplant. Costello is amusing as he pleads to be released. He even tries to reason with the monster. "Don't let 'em do it to you, Frankie," he says. "It's a bad deal. I've had this brain for thirty years and it hasn't worked right yet."

Lou is about to be operated on when Bud and Talbot break into the room. Talbot begins to release Lou when still another full moon appears. Lou, strapped to the operating table, finds himself in the middle of a furious battle between Dracula and the Wolfman. The two creatures push the table back and forth until it begins to spin wildly around the room. The Frankenstein monster also decides to take part in the melee. He gets started by throwing Sandra out the window. Bud and Lou are chased from room to room by the trio of monsters. Lou disguises himself as Dracula to gain control of the monster. Then Lou turns to Bud and proudly says, "He thinks I'm Dracula!" The monster, realizing he's been tricked, is madder than ever. Costello manages to lock the creature in a room but not for long. The creature's fist crashes through the door. (Costello had stepped off his mark during this scene and really got walloped by Glenn Strange's hand.) The Wolfman and Dracula tumble off a balcony and fall into the ocean, curtailing their activities for a while. The boys flee from the castle with the monster in hot pursuit. As Bud and Lou escape in a rowboat, Dr. Stevens finally makes himself useful. He sets fire to the pier, trapping the monster. The flaming pier collapses and the monster falls to its death.

Safely in the rowboat, Bud says, "Now that we've seen the last of Dracula, the Wolfman and the monster, there's nobody to frighten us any more." Suddenly a mysterious voice in the boat ends Bud's false sense of security. The voice (belonging to Vincent Price) says, "Oh, that's too bad. I was hoping to get in on the excitement. Allow me to introduce myself. I'm the Invisible Man!" Bud and Lou jump out of the boat, ending the film.

During the shooting of the climactic chase, Glenn Strange fell and broke his leg. While Strange convalesced, Lon Chaney, Jr., donned the monster's make-up and substituted for him in one brief sequence.

From the animated opening credits to the clever closing gag, ABBOTT AND COSTELLO MEET FRANKENSTEIN is a total delight. All of the gags work and, for a change, they fit into the context of the story. Abbott and Costello showed remarkable restraint, only rarely lapsing into their patter routines. This was easily the best film Bela Lugosi made in years. (At first Universal was reluctant to hire the sixty-six year old actor, afraid that he might be too old for the part. Wisely, they changed their minds.) Glenn Strange proved that he was the best of the post-Karloff Frankenstein monsters and Chaney turned in a competent performance as the troubled Mr. Talbot. When Universal previewed the movie it was an immediate hit. But for some reason Lou still wasn't convinced that it was any good. Lou's mother, sitting next to him at the preview, turned to him and said, "It's the best thing you've ever done." That was enough to convince Lou.

The excitement and hilarity of ABBOTT AND COSTELLO MEET FRANKENSTEIN was never duplicated by the comedians. It enjoyed tremendous success in 1948 and was re-released several times. Abbott and Costello were back on the list of the top ten money-making stars for the first time since 1944. However, the film also initiated their downfall as the screen's leading comedy team. Because, in the Hollywood tradition, the studio began to grind out inferior sequels.

Typical publicity still from ABBOTT AND COSTELLO MEET FRANKENSTEIN. With Glenn Strange, Bela Lugosi, and Lon Chaney, Jr.

Mexican Hayride

MEXICAN HAYRIDE, based on the 1944 Cole Porter musical starring Bobby Clark, has become somewhat of a curiosity over the years. Although the film remained fairly faithful to the book of the Broadway show, it excluded all of the music, even the show's big hit number "I Love You." Universal intended to make it a musical but for some reason the project was never realized. Rather than let the property gather dust on a shelf they decided to make it a vehicle for Abbott and Costello. By this time Abbott and Costello fans were complaining about the preponderance of music in their heroes' movies. So the film was made minus the Cole Porter score. Otherwise it is a refreshing comedy, with moments of inventive foolishness.

Lou is Joe Bascom, alias Humphrey Fish, an American fugitive from justice. He has been accused of putting over a phony stock deal in Iowa but a con artist named Harry Lambert (Abbott) is the guilty one. Lou follows Bud to Mexico to get him to confess. Costello, in turn, is being trailed by two detectives (Tom Powers and Lou's brother Pat Costello). Lou catches up with Bud at a bullfight arena in time to foil another swindle. Lou's girl friend, Mary (Virginia Grey), is now a bullfighter working under the name of Montana. Montana is about to throw her hat to a group of American visitors. Whoever catches that hat will be declared the "Amigo Americana," and will tour Mexico as an honored guest to symbolize Mexican-American good will. When Montana sees Costello in the crowd she becomes so angry that she throws the hat at him. Lou catches it and becomes the "Amigo Americana." Bud and his accomplice, Dagmar (Luba Malina), use Costello's fame to put over another phony stock deal involving a nonexistent silver mine. The police arrest Bud and Lou but they manage to escape. The action culminates in a bullfight with Costello making a very unlikely matador.

The first half of MEXICAN HAYRIDE reaches peaks of hilarity courtesy of four standout sequences. They are:

1. THE REPORTER

Lou is "interviewed" by a newspaper reporter played by Sid Fields. However, the reporter completely dominates the interview, refusing to let Costello answer any questions. "You don't mind if I get a word in here, do you?" asks the talkative reporter.

Abbott and Costello are fugitives in disguise in MEXICAN HAYRIDE, team's twenty-third film.

Lou sarcastically says, "No, you go ahead. I'm getting hoarse." After a lecture on manners, Fields gives Costello a final piece of advice before he leaves: "Remember, in the future, when a reporter comes in and asks you for an interview—don't talk so much!" Many of the gags from the deleted "Language Scene" in IN SOCIETY were included here.

2. IDENTIFICATION

Since Costello is a wanted man, Abbott is worried that he might be recognized in Mexico. So Bud systematically, and hilariously, removes every bit of identification from his helpless partner—until Costello is left standing in his underwear.

Bud, Lou, and Luba Malina in MEXICAN HAYRIDE.

3. SILVER ORE

Bud and Lou have a discussion about silver ore. "Silver or what?" Lou wants to know. Bud tries to explain that silver is made into ornaments by a smith.

Lou: "Couldn't Jones make it?"
Bud: "Oh sure, but he'd still be a smith."
Lou: "How can a Jones be a Smith?"

Bud describes how silver is mined. He tells Lou, "You take a shovel and you go down into the mine. You locate the mother lode. Then you strike the vein." Lou is insulted. "When you say to me that I have to go into a mine with a shovel and hit my mother in the vein while she's carrying a load—that is going too far!"

4. THE ELOCUTION LESSON

In his capacities as the "Amigo Americana," Lou is required to make a series of after-dinner speeches. Bud employs an eccentric elocution teacher, Professor Ganzmeyer (Fritz Feld), to help Lou prepare for speechmaking. The professor tries to show him how to breathe properly. "Hold your breath for five minutes," he instructs his pupil. Lou complies and nearly passes out. "I would like to see you *inhale!*" the professor tells Lou. Comic actor Fritz Feld is delightfully insane in this sketch.

Of course, these four scenes, which supply the film's biggest laughs, are often cut from TV versions of MEXICAN HAYRIDE.

The second half of the film slows up considerably. A lengthy sequence has Dagmar attempting to coax Costello into revealing the whereabouts of some stolen loot. During this she sings a mediocre song, "Is It Yes or Is It No?"

In order to trick the two detectives, Costello assumes a variety of

With Pat Costello, John Hubbard, Virginia Grey and Tom Powers in MEXICAN HAYRIDE.

disguises, including a female tortilla vendor and a mariachi performer.

The shortcomings of the second half of the film are compensated for by the chaotic bullfight sequence. Lou is not only pursued by the bull in and out of the arena, but he rides the animal bareback. Most of the gags employ special effects (Lou dances a samba with the bull via trick photography) but they work quite well.

Virginia Grey as the lady bullfighter, Luba Malina as a Mexican Spitfire type and John Hubbard as a U.S. consul attaché are good in subsidiary roles. It is interesting to see Pat Costello in the film. Pat not only looks like his brother, but he sounds just like him. Lou refers to their similarity in appearance during an early scene.

The New York *Times'* Bosley Crowther, who was one of the team's biggest boosters when they began their film careers, was less enthusiastic about them by the time this film was released in 1948. Crowther wrote, "As surely as corned beef goes with cabbage—or Bud Abbott goes with Lou Costello yet—a good deal of fate bullthrowing goes with any farce set in Mexico. And that's what you get in abundance in the new Abbott-Costello slapstick . . ."

Abbott and Costello Meet The Killer, Boris Karloff

The title of this film is a misnomer. Boris Karloff *isn't* the killer but merely one of the plot's many red herrings. In fact, Karloff barely appears in the film at all. He is relegated to a minor supporting role. The reason for this is that the part of the mysterious swami was not written with Karloff in mind. The film was to be another Abbott and Costello spoof of murder mysteries titled EASY DOES IT. But when ABBOTT AND COSTELLO MEET FRANKENSTEIN became a huge hit, Universal quickly decided to cash in on its success. The studio thought that the best way to do that would be to get the man most identified with the Frankenstein monster. So Boris Karloff was cast in the film and his name was included in the title. THE KILLER is strictly routine, with several ponderous sequences. At times it resembles a black comedy as Bud and Lou tangle with an assortment of dead bodies. But the gags are trite, lacking the spark of the Frankenstein film. Things brighten up, however, in an unusually thrilling finale which takes place in a bottomless cavern.

Costello is Freddie Phillips, an accident-prone bellhop at the Lost Caverns Hotel. Bud is Casey Edwards, the cigar-chomping house detective. A big-shot criminal lawyer, Amos Strickland (Nicholas Joy), arrives at the hotel to spend the weekend. Strickland orders the hotel manager, Mr. Melton (Alan Mowbray), to fire the bumbling Costello. When Strickland is murdered in his room later that night, police inspector Wellman (James Flavin) accuses Costello of the crime. Lou finds a bloodstained handkerchief at the scene of the crime and promptly destroys it. It turns out that Strickland was planning to publish his memoirs and had invited seven of his former clients to meet him at the secluded hotel. All seven were tried on murder charges and they all have a motive if the memoirs are printed. One of the former clients, beautiful Angela Gordon (Lenore Aubert), was defended on a charge of killing her husband with an arsenic cocktail. The seven clients conspire to make Costello the fall guy. Swami Talpur (Karloff) unsuccessfully tries to hypnotize Lou into writing a confession and then committing suicide. In the funniest scene, Angela attempts to serve poison champagne to the innocent bellboy. When another corpse turns up in Costello's room, Bud and Lou can't seem to dispose of it. Lou, disguised as a chambermaid, hides the body in a linen wagon.

The unseen killer, believing Lou has the incriminating handkerchief, lures the little man to the caverns under the hotel. The hooded murderer pursues Costello on the jagged cliffs of the caverns and the results are hair-raising. The production values before this scene are only fair. It seems that producer Robert Arthur was skimping on the budget, saving money for the lavish climax. The eerie cavern sets are beautifully designed and very realistic. The police rescue Lou from falling into the bottomless pit. Back at the hotel, Mr. Melton is revealed as the killer and he is caught by a booby trap devised by Costello.

Besides the suspenseful climax and a good supporting cast of veteran players, THE KILLER has very little going for it and is a decidedly weak entry in the Abbott and Costello "horror" cycle.

Swami Boris Karloff's attempts to hypnotize Costello fail when Costello proves to be too stupid to be hypnotized.

Africa Screams

This film, released by United Artists, is the least known of all the Abbott and Costello comedies. It has been out of circulation on the TV markets for quite a few years. It's a shame because the film is a bright send-up of every Hollywood jungle movie. Abbott and Costello had a grand time filming this one. They were surrounded by good friends, including two future members of their TV stock company, Hillary Brooke and Joe Besser. The team was reunited with Shemp Howard, who is very funny as a nearsighted gunman. Boxing greats Max and Buddy Baer, both friends of Lou Costello's, are also along for the ride, and Frank Buck and Clyde Beatty make brief appearances. Charles Barton directed and kept the nonsensical gags moving at a swift pace.

This was the first time Hillary Brooke worked with Abbott and Costello and she admits that she had some difficulty with them at first. "I never got any cues," says Hillary. Bud and Lou improvised their dialogue and never worried about giving cue lines to their fellow actors. She learned that the key to working with Costello was to wait for a pause in one of his ad-lib routines and then try to get her lines in as best she could.

Bud and Lou play Buzz Johnson and Stanley Livingston, two clerks in the book section of a New York department store. Diana Emerson (Hillary Brooke), a wealthy society woman, is vitally interested in a book titled *Dark Africa,* which has long been out of print. Bud schemes to earn some easy money. He tells Diana that Lou is a big-game hunter and that he accompanied the late author of the book, Cuddleford, on the expedition. She offers to pay Costello twenty-five hundred dollars if he will come to her house and draw a map of the expedition. That night at Diana's mansion the boys meet her henchmen, who are a very odd group indeed. Boots and Grappler (Max and Buddy Baer) are two dim-witted wrestlers, Harry (Joe Besser) is a whining sissy and Gunner (Shemp Howard) is supposedly a sharpshooter but he can't see beyond his nose. When Bud and Lou complete a bogus map, Diana forces them to join her African safari to make certain they're telling the truth. She is secretly looking for a cache of fabulous diamonds in the possession of a Ubangi tribe. In Africa, they join Clyde Beatty, who is stalking a legendary giant ape, Gargantua. After Costello mistakenly rescues a gorilla that has fallen in a trap, the gorilla becomes his friend for life and follows him everywhere. The zany

quest for diamonds results in some narrow escapes from a cannibal tribe, a crocodile and Gargantua the Ape. Bud uncovers the diamonds and greedily hides them in the bushes. Unbeknown to Bud, a chimp removes the gems. Bud returns, can't find the diamonds and becomes hysterical. He departs for America, leaving his partner behind. Lou locates the diamonds and returns to the States a millionaire. He then buys the department store where he was employed and hires Bud as an elevator operator.

The funniest scene in AFRICA SCREAMS, and one of the funniest scenes Lou Costello ever did, has Lou vainly trying to eat his lunch while a gorilla peers out of the jungle at him, observing his every move. Bud and Hillary Brooke are also seated at the dinner table, carrying on an innocuous conversation, unaware of the

A typical slapstick scene from AFRICA SCREAMS.

presence of the ape. Costello wildly gesticulates, trying to warn them of the danger. He is so scared he can't quite seem to get the words out. The best he can muster up is a series of frightened gasps and squeaks.

In another top sequence, Bud puts on a gorilla suit so Lou can prove his courage to the other members of the party. According to the plan, Bud, dressed as the gorilla, will enter the camp and Costello will bravely capture him. As expected, the real ape shows up and Bud passes out. Costello then bullies the ape, thinking it's his partner. Lou is in fine form as he puts on a display of bravado. He is impressed with Bud's realistic performance. Bud not only looks and walks like a gorilla—"You even smell like a gorilla," whispers Lou. Costello locks himself in a cage with the ape and throws

Beautiful Hillary Brooke later became a member of Abbott and Costello's TV stock company. Pictured here with Lou in AFRICA SCREAMS.

away the key. Abbott then appears outside the cage and tries to convince Lou that he's standing next to a real gorilla. The expression on Costello's face when he realizes his predicament is enough to make this film worth seeing.

According to Hillary Brooke and Joe Besser, during production of AFRICA SCREAMS, the off-camera shenanigans were wilder than anything that appeared on film. Bud and Lou were running all over the sound stage with custard pies and seltzer bottles. Jack Dempsey and Gene Tunney dropped by one day to visit the Baer brothers and all four fighters staged bouts to the delight of everyone on the set, especially Lou. One scene required the cast to take a ride on a raft that floated in the studio tank, representing the Congo River. Production was held up for a while because Shemp Howard became seasick.

In his book *Movies Are Better Than Ever,* Andrew Dowdy describes an amusing incident concerning a censorship problem caused by AFRICA SCREAMS. "In a running gag a lady ape periodically chased Lou Costello with evident amorous intentions, but the Breen Office nixed this piece of business, insisting that the gender of the gorilla be changed to male. Presumably the alteration cleaned up the context of the gag, but writers along the Strip were quick to spread the word that this year gay gorillas were in with the censors."

In 1950 AFRICA SCREAMS played theaters on a double bill with a reissue of the Marx Brothers' LOVE HAPPY.

Nearsighted Shemp Howard mistakes a tree for Costello in AFRICA SCREAMS.

Abbott and Costello in the Foreign Legion

ABBOTT AND COSTELLO IN THE FOREIGN LEGION was their only screen offering in 1950. Bud and Lou play two wrestling promoters from Brooklyn. They travel to Algeria to search for one of their wrestlers, Abdullah, who has returned to his homeland. There they become involved with a sultry French spy (Patricia Medina) and the cruel Sergeant Axmann (Walter Slezak), who tricks the boys into joining the Foreign Legion. Axmann has been plotting crimes with the help of an evil sheik (Douglas Dumbrille). For the obligatory chase Lou drives a jeep through the sheik's camp.

This film is just a rehash of the gags from the much funnier LOST IN A HAREM. It moves at a funereal pace, with only a couple of good sequences. In one, the boys spoof a wrestling match. Bud, with script in hand, directs two behemoths in a rehearsal for a bout as if it were a Shakespearean tragedy. Another funny sequence comes much later on. Lou, wandering in the desert, envisions a series of crazy mirages. For instance, he sees a newsboy selling a New York paper in the middle of the desert. "What are you doing way out here?" Lou inquires. The newsboy says, "Can I help it if they gave me a bad corner!"

Abbott and Costello's next endeavor had much happier results.

They're sworn into the Foreign Legion by Walter Slezak.

Abbott and Costello Meet the Invisible Man

Most of these later "horror" spoofs (e.g. THE KILLER, JEKYLL AND HYDE) were weak attempts at duplicating the success of ABBOTT AND COSTELLO MEET FRANKENSTEIN. THE INVISIBLE MAN, however, is a pleasant surprise. Many of the verbal gags misfire but the slapstick is often ingenious. One example is the punching bag sequence early in the film. We see Costello virtually pulverizing a punching bag, although his hands never seem to touch it. He even keeps the bag moving with his head and elbows. Actually the Invisible Man is doing all the work while Lou fakes the action. The climactic boxing match, with the Invisible Man literally carrying a dazed Costello around the ring to avoid his opponent's punches, is masterfully timed and edited. David S. Horsley's photographic tricks manage to surpass those in the 1933 film version of the H. G. Wells story.

Would-be sleuths Abbott and Costello are enrolled in the Dugan Detective Training School, or D.D.T. for short. After graduation (Bud had to slip the instructor twenty dollars to pass Costello) they set up their own detective agency and eagerly await their first client. They don't have to wait long. Tommy Nelson (Arthur Franz), a prizefighter who's been falsely accused of murdering his manager, hires them to prove his innocence. They accompany the fighter to the home of his friend Dr. Philip Gray (Gavin Muir). The doctor has been experimenting with an invisibility formula and Tommy wants to be injected with the serum so he can elude the police. He is warned that the drug might turn him into a raving maniac, as it did to its inventor, John Griffin (a photograph of Claude Rains is hanging on the wall). When the police surround the house, Tommy injects himself with the serum anyway. While this is happening, Bud hears on TV that there is a five-thousand-dollar reward for the capture of Tommy Nelson. Bud locks the fighter in a room with Costello and then alerts Detective Roberts (William Frawley). Lou reaches to shake hands with Tommy and observes that Tommy's hand is missing. Lou watches in astonishment as Tommy gradually disappears. The fighter removes all of his clothing, rendering him invisible. The police break into the room and ask Lou how Nelson got away. "In installments," explains Lou. "He did a Gypsy Rose Lee." When he tries to tell them that Tommy is invisible, the police be-

Full-fledged detectives in ABBOTT AND COSTELLO MEET THE INVISIBLE MAN.

lieve Lou is insane and send him to a psychiatrist. After one session with Costello, the psychiatrist is on the verge of a nervous breakdown.

Back at the detective agency, the boys are visited by Tommy's girl friend, Helen (Nancy Guild). She gives them a five-hundred-dollar retainer and instructions from Nelson to meet him later that evening. They follow orders and rendezvous with the Invisible Man. He confides to the boys that a racketeer named Morgan (Sheldon Leonard) is guilty of killing the fight manager. Morgan wanted Nelson to take a dive in his last bout. When he double-crossed Morgan, the gangster killed Tommy's manager and framed Tommy. The Invisible Man devises a scheme. Lou will pose as a boxer to trap Morgan in another murder attempt.

The following morning the twosome and their transparent friend enter Stillwell's Gym. Lou sees a punch-drunk fighter exercising on a rowing machine. Lou asks him what he's doing. "Rowing," answers the fighter. "I gotta be in Staten Island in twenty minutes." "You'd better hurry," Costello warns him. "The tide's going out." With the aid of the Invisible Man, Lou puts on an incredible exhibition at the punching bag. A crowd of spectators gathers to see this amazing new fighter and a sportswriter dubs him "Louie the Looper." Costello challenges middleweight

A knife wound nearly finishes off the Invisible Man. With Nancy Guild and William Frawley.

Rocky Hanlon to a bout, and Hanlon accepts.

That night the Invisible Man brings the boys to a posh nightclub, hoping to be approached by gangster Morgan. Morgan sends his sexy girl friend, Boots (Adele Jergens), to deliver a message to Costello. Morgan offers to pay him to take a dive in the fifth round. Lou agrees, knowing that he'll win the fight with Tommy's help. Morgan will then try to kill Bud and put the blame on Lou and the police will nab the gangster.

In the nightclub Tommy drinks a couple of bottles of champagne and passes out. Bud and Lou then have the difficult task of carrying the Invisible Man out of the club. They leave him at Dr. Gray's office to recover from his hangover. Because Tommy has been showing signs of madness, the doctor imprisons him in the office until an antidote can be found.

The big fight is approaching and Lou is worried because he hasn't heard from Tommy. Morgan reminds Costello that he'd better take a dive in the fifth round, or else. Lou is forced to enter the ring, without Tommy, and is nearly beaten to a pulp by Rocky Hanlon. Finally the Invisible Man escapes and rushes to the arena just in time to take over the fighting for Costello. "He hits from nowhere," Lou's opponent says at the end of the round. "It's like I'm fighting two guys!" Lou is winning until he accidentally knocks out the Invisible Man. He falls to the floor and Rocky continually trips over his invisible body. Lou manages to revive Tommy, who then wins the fight for Costello.

After the bout, Morgan and one of his henchmen attempt to kill Abbott in the locker room. The Invisible Man scuffles with the two hoods and there is a wild shoot-out as the two gangsters try to hit their unseen attacker. A shot ricochets off a radiator, causing a cloud of steam to fill the room. One of the hoods sees Tommy's silhouette in the steam and throws a knife at him. The police arrest the gangsters and Tommy is rushed to the hospital, where Costello gives him a blood transfusion. Some of Tommy's blood backs up into Lou's system, resulting in Lou's becoming temporarily invisible. When he materializes he finds that his legs are now on backward!

The imaginative sight gags and trick camera work help to make this one of the most entertaining of the team's later efforts. The typecasted Sheldon Leonard is especially enjoyable to watch and Arthur Franz makes an ideal Invisible Man.

Of this film *Variety* wrote, "Abbott and Costello, whose funmaking routines had become decidedly wearing in some of their more recent films, partially redeem themselves in MEET THE INVISIBLE MAN. (The) team's stock double takes and bewhiskered gags are still fulsome, but the hackneyed quips achieve a new gloss in this entry."

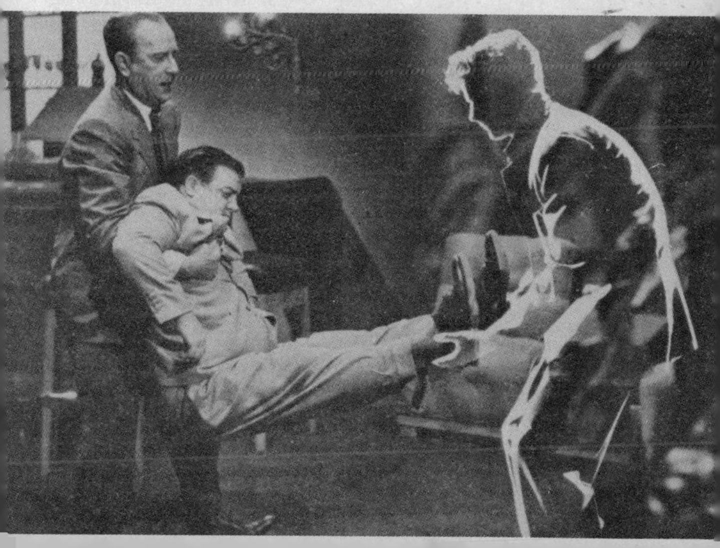

Comin' Round the Mountain

The less said about COMIN' ROUND THE MOUNTAIN the better. The team really hit rock bottom with this hillbilly-feudin'-and-fussin' opus. Charles Lamont's direction is ponderous, although he didn't have much of a script to work with. The film is also hindered by the presence of Dorothy Shay. At one time Miss Shay was an inexplicably popular nightclub singer, billed as "The Park Avenue Hillbilly." She monopolizes the film with four endless songs, including such favorites as "You'll Be Another Notch on Father's Shotgun" and "Sagebrush Sadie." This so-called music is enough to make any Abbott and Costello fan long for the Andrews Sisters and Dick Powell.

Bud is a New York theatrical agent and Lou is one of his acts, a magician. Bud books Lou into a big-time nightclub where Lou performs an escape act, providing the film with its only funny scene. Lou is on the same bill with singer Shay and he learns that he's the long-missing heir to a treasure buried in the Kentucky hills. All three then head for Kentucky, and find themselves in the middle of a feud between the Winfields and the McCoys. Joe Sawyer and Glenn Strange turn up as dumb mountain men, and Margaret Hamilton makes a brief appearance as a witch, naturally. There's the usual assortment of shoot-outs and chases until they find the treasure, which happens to be inside the vaults at Fort Knox.

Ten years after BUCK PRIVATES, COMIN' ROUND THE MOUNTAIN was a sad example of how the quality of the Abbott and Costello comedies had deteriorated. It seemed that John Grant was giving his best gags to Martin and Lewis. Grant wrote their SAILOR BEWARE, released in 1951, which very closely resembles BUCK PRIVATES and IN THE NAVY.

The one and only funny scene in COMIN' ROUND THE MOUNTAIN. Magician Lou attempts a Houdini-like escape.

With ex-Frankenstein monster Glenn Strange and Shaye Cogan.

Jack and the Beanstalk

In 1952 Abbott and Costello signed a deal to make two independent features, to be released by Warner Brothers. According to the deal, Lou owned the first film, JACK AND THE BEANSTALK, and Bud owned the second, ABBOTT AND COSTELLO MEET CAPTAIN KIDD. Bud and Lou profited from both films, which became quite successful.

Lou Costello hired some old friends to work for him on JACK AND THE BEANSTALK. Alex Gottlieb was back as their producer and Jean Yarbrough directed. Although children had always been a large segment of Abbott and Costello's fans, this was the team's first film geared solely to the Saturday afternoon set. In this respect it succeeds very nicely, but it can hardly be termed topnotch Abbott and Costello. For the most part, the film strictly adheres to the original story, affording the boys little opportunity to be funny.

Bud and Lou, as Dink and Jack, visit an employment agency in hopes of landing a job for Costello. Lou is hired to baby-sit with an obnoxious brat who has a penchant for playing practical jokes. Lou attempts to lull the child to sleep by telling him the story of Jack and the Beanstalk. Costello falls asleep instead and dreams that he's the famous giant-killer. (The film has been in black and white until this point but now switches to color.) The remainder of the film recounts the familiar story. Lou is sent by his mother (Barbara Brown) to sell the family cow so they can pay their debts. The local butcher (Abbott) tricks him into selling the cow in exchange for some magic beans. Lou plants the magic beans in his yard and the next morning he is amazed to find a towering beanstalk stretching into the sky. Bud and Lou climb the beanstalk, which leads them to the giant's castle. The giant (Buddy Baer) captures Bud and Lou and forces them to work in the castle. A prince (James Alexander) and a princess (Shaye Cogan) are being held hostage by the cruel giant. Bud and Lou also must contend with a talking harp, a goose that lays golden eggs, and the giant's servant girl (Dorothy Ford). Lou does a comical dance with Dorothy Ford in a scene similar to the dance routine with Joan Davis in HOLD THAT GHOST.

The film is most entertaining during a lengthy chase at the end. Lou, brandishing a huge sword, duels with the giant throughout the castle à la Errol Flynn.

Lou as Jack the Giant Killer.

Abbott and Costello encounter maid Dorothy Ford and a talking harp in JACK AND THE BEANSTALK.

Our heroes help the prince and princess escape from the castle. They fashion catapults by bending back trees and then hurl themselves over the wall. They climb down the beanstalk with the giant following after. Lou chops down the beanstalk, the giant crashes to the ground and Lou happily awakes from his dream.

James Alexander and Shaye Cogan win the title of The Worst of the Romantic Leads in an Abbott and Costello Movie. However Buddy Baer makes a fine giant and Amazonian actress Dorothy Ford works well with Costello. The music isn't as bad as you would expect. Two songs, "He Never Looked Better in His Life" and "I Fear Nothing" (sung by Lou Costello), are nicely done. The film was photographed in something called Super-Cine Color.

JACK AND THE BEANSTALK received some surprisingly good notices. The New York *Herald Tribune* described it as "frequently funny in a highly visual sort of way and there is plenty of action . . . As Jack the Giant-Killer, Costello cuts a very funny figure indeed." Most of the critics gave the film an "A" for effort. They were enthusiastic that Abbott and Costello were at least attempting something new and abandoning their usual formula.

The film earned millions domestically and was Warners' biggest-grossing film in England (where the team has always been very popular) for that year. Bud and Lou stayed on at Warners to complete the second film in their two-picture pact.

Jack (Lou) chops down the beanstalk as Dinklepuss (Bud) and villagers look on.

Abbott and Costello Meet Captain Kidd

ABBOTT AND COSTELLO MEET CAPTAIN KIDD is interesting chiefly because Charles Laughton plays the notorious pirate. Alex Gottlieb remembered how the actor was signed to appear in the film: "I went to see Laughton in Boston, where he was doing a play. I explained to him what the picture was all about and he was fascinated with the idea of doing low comedy. It was a total departure for him. It intrigued him so much that he agreed to do it without reading the script."

Laughton soon discovered that doing "low comedy," particularly with Abbott and Costello, was more than he bargained for. Laughton encountered the same problem that most actors had working with the team for the first time. They never gave him any cues. He was a consummate actor and was naturally used to having his lines down pat. Laughton was not prepared for Abbott and Costello's ad-libbing and he didn't know when to speak his lines. He also learned, to his horror, that rehearsals were a rare occurrence on the set of an Abbott and Costello movie. In all of his years in the theater and films, Charles Laughton had never encountered anything like this. Co-star Hillary Brooke said that he was completely bewildered during the first few days of shooting. Hillary told Laughton not to take it so seriously and just to relax and have a good time. He eventually got used to Bud and Lou's casual work habits and he had the time of his life. In fact, if you see the film, Laughton *does* appear slightly bewildered in the early footage. As the film progresses he gives what is probably the most uninhibited performance of his career. According to Alex Gottlieb, the actor was completely fascinated by Lou Costello. Every day on the set Laughton would sit down with Lou and have the comedian teach him how to do double takes. Imagine Charles Laughton taking lessons from Lou Costello! Laughton proved to be an eager pupil because in CAPTAIN KIDD he does broad takes worthy of a top banana in burlesque.

Bud and Lou, as Rocky and Oliver, are stranded on the pirate island of Tortuga. In order to raise passage to America they work as waiters at an inn which is frequented by Captain Kidd. Captain Kidd and a beautiful female pirate, Captain Bonney (Hillary Brooke), are both vying for a buried treasure. Lady Jane (Fran Warren) has entrusted Bud and Lou with a love letter to be delivered to Bruce Martingale (Bill Shirley). The love letter is acciden-

Posing for the still photographer with Charles Laughton. ABBOTT AND COSTELLO MEET CAPTAIN KIDD (1952).

Joe DiMaggio was a guest of Lou's on the set of CAPTAIN KIDD.

Lou, Charles Laughton and fetching pirate Hillary Brooke.

tally switched with Captain Kidd's treasure map and there's a mad scramble to find the missing map. The pirate then kidnaps Lady Jane and the two waiters and takes them on a voyage to Skull Island, where the treasure is buried. During the voyage Abbott and Costello perform a couple of comedy routines that never really get off the ground. What might have been a great spoof of pirate movies turns out to be another disappointment. Things brighten up with a final chase that evokes some big laughs. The film is handicapped by too much music–six songs altogether, none of which are worth mentioning. Bill Shirley and Fran Warren, furnishing the romantic angle, are typically dull and wooden. It is Laughton's parody of his earlier film role of Captain Kidd that commands the spotlight. *Variety* commented on the actor's performance by saying, "Laughton hams delightfully, thoroughly enjoying himself in abandoning longhair dramatics for low comedy."

ABBOTT AND COSTELLO MEET CAPTAIN KIDD was the comedy team's second and last color film and it is handsomely mounted.

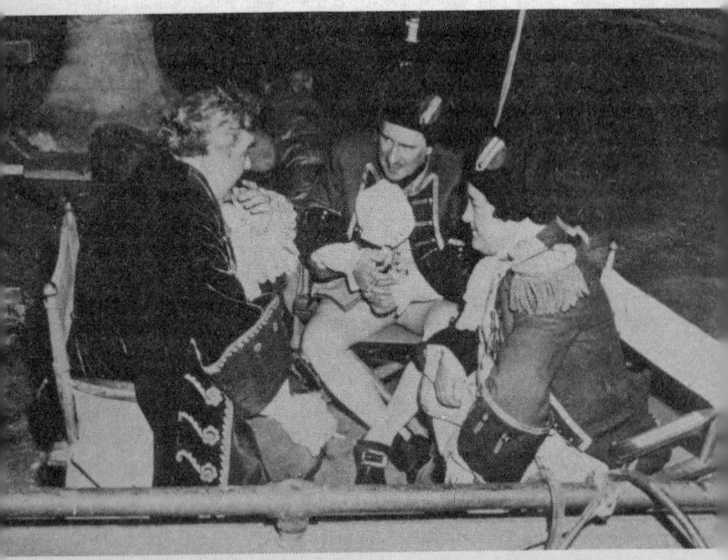

Charles Laughton and Abbott and Costello became good friends while filming CAPTAIN KIDD.

Lost in Alaska

Director Jean Yarbrough hardly has fond memories of LOST IN ALASKA. He read the script and thought it was terrible but agreed to direct the film as a favor to Lou Costello. It's not as bad as COMIN' ROUND THE MOUNTAIN but it's close. By this time Bud and Lou weren't even trying, and it was evident on the screen.

The film opens in San Francisco in the late 1800s. A prospector, Nugget Joe McDermott (Tom Ewell), decides to end it all when his sweetheart Rosette (Mitzi Green) refuses to marry him. He jumps into San Francisco Bay and fireman Lou attempts to rescue him. He manages to save the prospector's life but *Lou* begins to drown in the process. This opening scene is amusing, which is more than can be said for the remainder of the film. Bud, Lou and Nugget Joe head for Alaska, where the latter has stashed two million dollars in gold. They don't exactly receive a warm welcome when they arrive at a rugged Klondike town. It seems that Joe was once a sheriff there and he hanged quite a few relatives of the townspeople so they're all eager to take a shot at him. Everybody is clamoring for the gold, which results in many predictable chases. At the end of the film the gold is lost forever in an ice split, providing a moral lesson, of sorts.

Former child star Mitzi Green came out of a fifteen-year retirement to appear in this. After it was released she promptly went back in. Actually she had an engaging personality but she was forced to sing some awful songs. They must have decided to put music in LOST IN ALASKA since it paid off in the two Warners films. Tom Ewell's talents are wasted and villain Bruce Cabot isn't given much to do either.

Critic Howard Thompson, whose mini film reviews appear on the New York *Times* TV page, rarely has a kind word for Abbott and Costello, but he provided an accurate description of this film: "Lost is right."

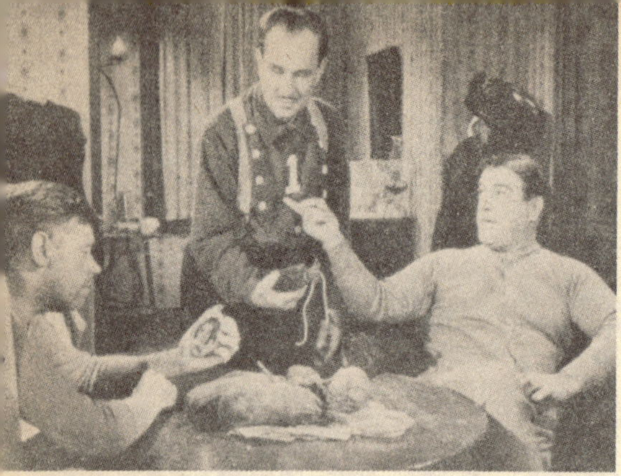

Bud and Lou have just rescued prospector Tom Ewell from a watery grave in LOST IN ALASKA.

Clowning on the set of LOST IN ALASKA. Too bad there wasn't much clowning in the picture.

By 1952 the creative well had run dry: still another variation on the "oyster" routine. This time, Lou attempts to eat a piece of whale meat that continually squirts him in the face.

Abbott and Costello Go to Mars

ABBOTT AND COSTELLO GO TO MARS is their worst film. Even the title is wrong since *Venus* is the planet they visit, not Mars. Bud and Lou appear to be half-asleep during the film. And who can blame them? The story has the pair accidentally launching a rocket ship with themselves on board. The rocket lands in New Orleans during the Mardi Gras. When the boys see everyone dressed in bizarre costumes, they assume they're on Mars. Two escaped convicts (Horace McMahon and Jack Kruschen) rob a bank and force the boys to help them make a getaway. They blast off once again, and this time they land on Venus. As it turns out, Venus is populated entirely by Miss Universe contestants (and Anita Ekberg). The girls must have been sent to Venus as a punishment for their acting.

Some good special effects aren't enough to save the film. An early sequence shows Bud and Lou trapped in the runaway rocket ship as it soars through New York City. (It goes through the Lincoln Tunnel without paying the toll . . . the Statue of Liberty ducks to avoid getting hit by the rocket.) The futuristic sets on Venus look expensive but the film is so silly and so obviously geared to kiddie matinee audiences that it is almost impossible to endure.

Martha Hyer and Robert Paige are on hand briefly for a superfluous romantic interest.

John Grant is credited as one of the writers. This is difficult to believe since nothing of Grant's style of comedy writing is evident in the film.

Lou is a trespasser on a rocket launching pad.

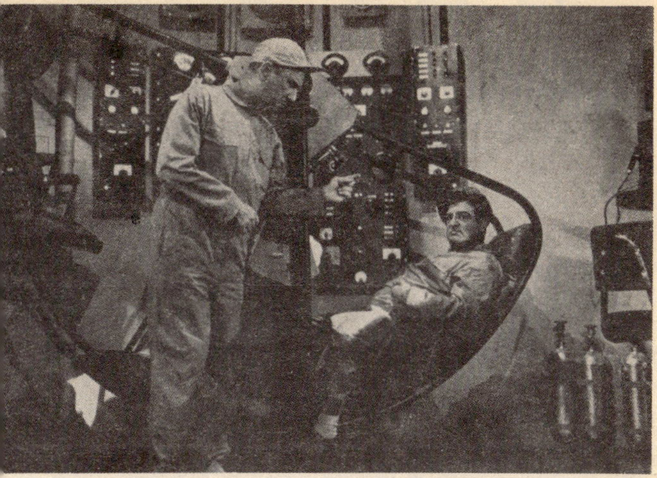

While loading a rocket ship, Abbott and Costello accidentally launch it and themselves. Unfortunately, the film never got off the ground.

Posing with Miss Universe contestants on the set of ABBOTT AND COSTELLO GO TO MARS. Anita Ekberg is fourth from left.

Abbott and Costello Meet Dr. Jekyll and Mr. Hyde

In an interview Sid Fields told me how this film came about. According to Fields, he brought a two-page story treatment to Howard Christie, who produced most of the team's later films. Christie was beginning production on a new Abbott and Costello comedy, FIREMAN SAVE MY CHILD. The sets were built and some chase scenes had been shot with extras doubling for Bud and Lou. But when Christie read Fields' treatment for the JEKYLL AND HYDE film, he liked it so much he decided to make it instead of FIREMAN. Since this film was already into production, two Universal contractees, Hugh O'Brian and Buddy Hackett, were hired to take over Abbott and Costello's roles. O'Brian and Hackett physically resembled the team enough to match the footage already shot. It's just as well that Abbott and Costello didn't appear in FIREMAN SAVE MY CHILD, which turned out to be a bomb. Unfortunately, ABBOTT AND COSTELLO MEET DR. JEKYLL AND MR. HYDE isn't much better. John Grant and Lee Loeb wrote the finished script, which relied solely on Lou Costello's ability to look frightened and take outlandish pratfalls. Boris Karloff, in his only portrayal of the Robert Louis Stevenson characters, conjures up a few chilling moments.

The scene is London, at the turn of the century. Dr. Poole, a noted physician, is brutally murdered by a monster. We soon learn that the monster is the creation of research scientist Dr. Henry Jekyll. He injects a serum into his blood which transforms him into the fiendish Mr. Hyde. As Hyde, he murders his colleagues who have been ridiculing his experiments. These weird experiments include performing brain transplants on animals. He has created a rabbit that barks like a dog and a monkey that moos like a cow.

Jekyll is in love with his young ward, Vicky Edwards (Helen Westcott) who is a champion of equal rights for women. She conducts a rally in Hyde Park, resulting in a brawl. Bud and Lou are Slim and Tubby, two American policemen assigned to study British methods of crime control. They become involved in the riot and are thrown in jail along with Vicky and a handsome newspaper reporter, Bruce Adams (Craig Stevens). The boys are kicked off the police force by the inspector (Reginald Denny). Dr. Jekyll arranges bail money for Vicky and Bruce. Bruce has meanwhile

Bud unmasks Mr. Hyde.

Bud, Lou and Boris Karloff.

fallen in love with Vicky. The doctor, jealous of the reporter, plots to kill him.

That night Bruce visits Vicky, who entertains at a music hall. Bruce doesn't realize he's been followed by Mr. Hyde. Bud and Lou spot Mr. Hyde sneaking into the theater. They figure that if they capture the monster, they will be reinstated on the police force. The boys pursue Hyde backstage at the music hall, and this leads to an exciting rooftop chase as the monster flees from Bud and Lou. In the best scene in the movie, the monster takes refuge in a deserted wax museum, where Costello is also hiding. A broken electrical cable causes the wax figures of Frankenstein and Dracula temporarily to come to life. Lou captures Hyde and locks him in a jail cell and then runs to get the inspector, convinced this will earn him a promotion. When he returns with Abbott and the inspector, they find Dr. Jekyll, who has transformed back from the monster. The inspector scolds Lou for locking up one of London's most distinguished citizens. Jekyll, realizing he must now murder Costello, asks the boys to escort him to his home. When they reach the house he offers to pay them five pounds to stay the night and act as bodyguards. Bud agrees, ignoring Lou's warnings. Unable to sleep, Costello decides to investigate the house and is nearly killed by Jekyll's huge, disfigured servant, Batley (!). Wandering into the laboratory, Lou drinks some of Jekyll's serum by mistake. He runs from the house with Bud following. The serum causes Lou to change into a giant mouse, terrifying Abbott and several customers in a local pub. When the serum wears off, the boys rush to Scotland Yard to warn the inspector about Dr. Jekyll. The inspector doesn't believe them so they return to Jekyll's home to find proof.

Vicky announces to Jekyll that she is going to marry Bruce. The doctor transforms into Hyde once again and tries to kill the young girl. Bruce arrives in time to save Vicky but Hyde escapes. Costello sits on the syringe and he too transforms into a monster.

The remainder of the film is a tedious slapstick chase as the police pursue the two monsters all over Universal's version of London. Hyde returns home and falls out a window to his death. Abbott captures Costello, and with the help of some citizens, brings him to Scotland Yard. For the closing gag, Costello bites the policemen and the inspector and they all turn into monsters. Abbott and Costello crash through a door and escape.

Lou Costello and Boris Karloff don't appear in the chase since it is performed entirely by doubles.

The team's dialogue mainly consists of a series of frightened yelps. The only funny gags are left over from their previous films.

For instance, the boys set out to investigate Jekyll's house. Bud courageously says, "Follow me!" and then pushes Costello in front of him. Lou takes a few dozen pratfalls during the course of the film. He can't seem to take more than three steps without tripping over something.

Karloff's transformations into the monster are accomplished through David S. Horsley's trick photography. Bud Westmore's makeup is all right but can't compare to that in the earlier film versions of DR. JEKYLL AND MR. HYDE.

Surprisingly, this film was a very big hit at the box office. Perhaps this was because it had a large appeal to the Saturday matinee set, and Boris Karloff's name certainly lent marquee value.

Lou is briefly reunited with Frankenstein and Dracula in a wax museum. ABBOTT AND COSTELLO MEET DR. JEKYLL AND MR. HYDE (1954).

Abbott and Costello Meet the Keystone Kops

It was only fitting that the team should "meet" the Keystone Kops since during the forties, Abbott and Costello carried on the brand of slapstick comedy made famous by the Mack Sennett studios. But instead of a satire on the infant movie industry, the film is just a succession of tired sight gags, until the final chase, which is every bit as good as the original Keystone chases.

The film opens in New York, in the year 1912. Bud and Lou, or Harry Pierce and Willie Piper as they're called in this one, are tricked by a con man, Gorman (Fred Clark), into "buying" the Edison Studios in New Jersey. Realizing they've been swindled, they hitch a ride on a freight car heading for Hollywood, where Gorman is masquerading as a Russian film director, Sergei Trumanoff. The boys are given jobs as stunt men at Amalgamated Pictures. They catch Gorman in the act of stealing money from the studio and the bogus director flees to the nearest airport. Abbott and Costello, enlisting the aid of the Keystone Kops, give chase. The villain is apprehended and the boys become silent film comedians.

Mack Sennett himself shows up briefly to throw a custard pie, and three of the original Keystone Kops, Herold Goodwin, Heinie Conklin and Hank Mann, are around to lend authenticity. Lou's pretty daughter Carole appears early in the film as a theater cashier. The real stars of the film, however, are Universal's stunt men, who perform some spectacular feats.

Lou's daughter, Carole, can be seen as a theatre cashier in the opening sequence of KEYSTONE KOPS.

Dressed as hoboes, they steal a ride on a freight car in KEYSTONE KOPS.

Sennett doesn't appear too thrilled to be posing with Bud and Lou and some Universal stunt men impersonating the Keystone Kops.

Abbott and Costello Meet the Mummy

In ABBOTT AND COSTELLO MEET THE MUMMY the team is back in form, aided by some clever dialogue routines by John Grant. It showed they were still capable of making a good comedy. Although it can't compare to their early features, it was certainly a big improvement over some of their more recent efforts. Unfortunately this was their last for Universal. In 1955 Abbott and Costello were fired from the studio that they helped to keep alive for nearly fifteen years.

Due to another bout with rheumatic fever, Lou Costello looks thin and haggard in THE MUMMY and for the first time Abbott appears heavier than Costello. But Lou's performance was not affected and he continued to do much of his own stunt work against doctor's orders.

The story begins with an archaeologist, Dr. Gustav Zoomer, uncovering the mummy of Klaris. He plans to transport the mummy to America. Abbott and Costello, stranded in Egypt, pay a visit to Dr. Zoomer's house, hoping to accompany him on the journey to the States. Shortly before they arrive, two members of a secret society break into the house, kill Zoomer and steal the mummy. In their haste they leave behind a sacred medallion which indicates where a treasure is buried. The leader of the cult, Semu (Richard Deacon), and his followers have been keeping the mummy alive in an underground temple to guard the treasure.

Bud and Lou stumble onto the corpse of the archaeologist and run from the house. The local police suspect Abbott of the murder. Madame Rontru (Marie Windsor) is also interested in Klaris and the treasure. Later that night she and her two henchmen, Charlie (Michael Ansara) and Josef (Dan Seymour), enter Zoomer's house to steal the medallion. They boys have returned to the scene of the crime to find evidence that will clear Bud. Lou comes into possession of the medallion, and a fight ensues, with the boys escaping in the confusion.

When they try to hock the medallion, the pawnbroker warns them that it is cursed. He claims that it brings death to whoever holds it. Lou tries to get rid of the jewel to no avail. At a cafe Bud hides the fatal medallion in Lou's hamburger and Lou swallows it. Madame Rontru lures Costello to her room, where Charley and Josef are hiding in secret panels in the wall. Lou thinks he's imag-

The shock of seeing the Mummy (Eddie Parker) is too much for Costello. With Richard Deacon.

A typical scene from ABBOTT AND COSTELLO MEET THE MUMMY: Mádame Rontru (Marie Windsor) x-rays Costello to read an ancient medallion that he has swallowed!

Bud Abbott in team's last Universal release, ABBOTT AND COSTELLO MEET THE MUMMY.

Abbott and Costello, Michael Ansara, Richard Deacon and Marie Windsor watch as the Mummy is destroyed by explosives in ABBOTT AND COSTELLO MEET THE MUMMY.

ining things when hands continually reach out of the wall and floor, trying to grab him. Lou confesses that he swallowed the jewel and the villains drag him to a doctor's office to X-ray him. The X-ray reveals the location of the temple and the treasure. Semu, posing as an archaeologist, offers to guide Madame Rontru to the treasure. He suggests that they take Bud and Lou along to keep an eye on them. Semu plans to dispose of them all when they reach the temple. At the temple Costello discovers the passageway leading to the tomb of Klaris. In attempting to find his way out, he is frightened by the mummy, a vampire bat, a skeleton and a giant lizard. Madame Rontru and her henchmen tie up Semu and they enter the temple to steal the treasure. Abbott uses bandages to disguise himself as the mummy. To add to the confusion, Charlie is also disguised as the mummy. Madame Rontru can't determine which of the three mummies is Klaris. Lou throws a stick of dynamite at the real Klaris, destroying the mummy and the treasure as well. Bud then decides to turn the temple into a nightclub. The scene disolves to the opening night of Kafe Klaris. Semu is the maître d' and the band is composed entirely of mummies!

This plot is ridiculous even by Abbott and Costello standards. But it's entertaining thanks to a strong supporting cast. Marie Windsor is fine as the sexy villainess, and Richard Deacon, Dan Seymour and Michael Ansara are sufficiently sinister. The mummy is played by Universal's number one stunt man, Eddie Parker, whose makeup is ludicrously bad. For some reason, vocalist Peggy King turns up midway in the movie to sing "You Came a Long Way from St. Louis."

The twosome performs a couple of clever routines along the way. In one, Abbott has a conversation with a beautiful girl who speaks only French. Bud apparently understands the language and repeatedly tells her, "No, I can't–No, I can't!" Finally Lou interrupts: "Hey, Abbott, what's she saying? Maybe *I* can!"

When Madame Rontru orders them to dig a hole, Lou offers several implements to Bud and tells him to take his choice. Bud chooses a shovel, explaining that "the shovel is my pick." "How can a shovel be a pick!" yells Lou and they launch into a routine in the best tradition of Abbott and Costello.

THE MUMMY did only passable business despite some decent reviews. *Variety* called it "one of their best comedies in some time." The team then left their home studio with little or no prospects of continuing their film careers. Almost a year passed before they were approached by producer Bob Goldstein to make another film, which would be their last together.

Dance With Me, Henry

This United Artists release is a dreary swan song for Abbott and Costello. It is so cloyingly sentimental that it is often embarrassing to watch. The team's lack of enthusiasm for their material has never been more evident. Lou looks better than he did in THE MUMMY, but he gives a curious, low-keyed performance. And for some reason he remained remarkably faithful to the script, rarely ad-libbing. The title has nothing to do with the story. "Dance with Me, Henry" was the name of an early rock 'n' roll tune that was passé long before the film was released in December 1956.

Lou plays the owner of a small-town amusement park, Kiddyland. He is a kindhearted soul who has the habit of collecting strays–including two orphans (Rusty Hamer, Gigi Perreau), a dog, a canary and a chronic gambler (Abbott). A welfare worker (Mary Wickes) threatens to take the children away from Costello, claiming he's a bad influence on them. Costello should be glad to get rid of these two kids since they're constantly delivering nauseating dialogue like, "Gee, Popsy, I don't want to leave you!"

Abbott further complicates matters. He owes a gangster, Big Frank (Ted de Corsia), twenty thousand dollars. To pay off the debt, Bud agrees to deliver some stolen bank money to a hood in Chicago. The district attorney (Robert Shayne) is tipped off to the scheme and one of Big Frank's henchmen murders him at the amusement park. Lou is accused of the killing and is arrested. When the police release Costello, he's kidnapped by the mob. The stolen money has been stashed somewhere in Kiddyland, and Big Frank believes that Lou knows where it is. The gangster interrogates Costello in the best scene in the movie, and the only scene in which Costello really comes alive.

The amusement park is the setting for the final chase, with the neighborhood kids joining in to help Lou rout the gangsters. The loot is recovered and Big Frank is tricked into making a full confession. Lou becomes a hero and the welfare board allows him to take custody of the children.

It is to Abbott and Costello's credit that they were able to breathe some life into a script that was almost totally devoid of humor. The film did, however, get its share of favorable reviews. The critic for the New York *Herald Tribune* wrote, "This time the team is more sedate. Mr. Costello doesn't take a pushing around

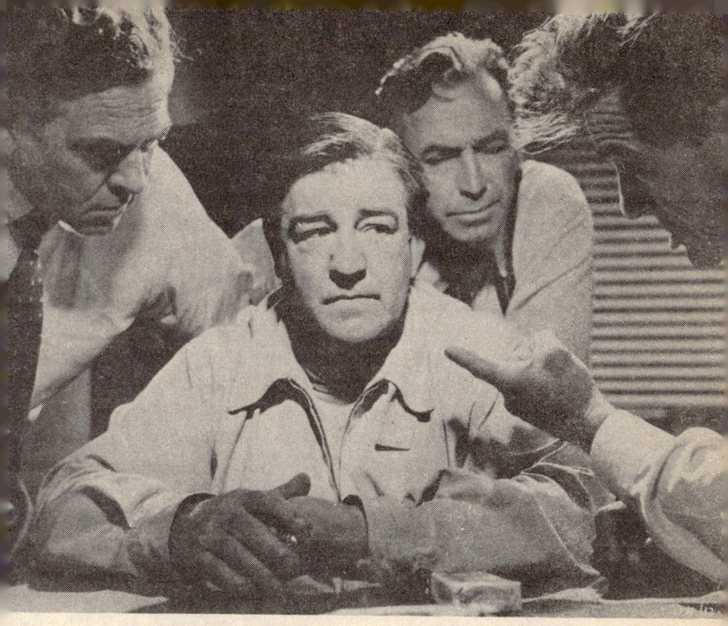

Lou is grilled by police.

In a deleted sequence from DANCE WITH ME, HENRY, Lou dreams that he's an orchestra conductor. Several other sequences should have been deleted from this film, one of the team's worst.

Costello runs a carnival in DANCE WITH ME, HENRY, team's final film.

Gangster Ted de Corsia kidnaps Bud and Lou.

Lou tries to impress welfare worker Mary Wickes, with the usual results.

from Mr. Abbott, who has mellowed to the extent of feeling sorry for the rotund comedian. In fact, Mr. Costello is developing along the lines of a Chaplinesque character, pathetic and the victim of a conniving world."

DANCE WITH ME, HENRY, meant to be their comeback film after a year-and-a-half absence from the screen, performed poorly at the box office and was a prime reason for the team's splitting up six months later.

At least the film reunited Abbott and Costello with one of their favorite directors, Charles Barton. Barton went on to direct several of the most successful of the Disney comedies.

ABBOTT AND COSTELLO ON TELEVISION

"The Colgate Comedy Hour" was one of the most popular variety shows in the early days of television. Eddie Cantor devised the format of alternating guest hosts. It was his contention that one comedian couldn't sustain a TV show on a weekly basis. Abbott and Costello were the last to join the roster of guest hosts, which included Cantor, Bob Hope, Jimmy Durante, Donald O'Connor and Martin and Lewis. (Fred Allen was one of the first hosts of the show but he didn't care for the format and departed in 1950.) Abbott and Costello made a much-publicized TV debut on "Colgate," January 7, 1951. They insured their first venture into the new medium with tried-and-true material. In the course of the one-hour show they did virtually all of their best routines—"Who's on First," "Mustard," the "Lemon Bit," "Crazy House" and the "moving candle" gag from HOLD THAT GHOST. Sharing the bill with the team were Sid Fields, Joe Besser and singer Evelyn Knight. Reviewing the team's debut, New York *Times* critic Jack Gould said that "their medium was much newer than their material." Summing up his review, Gould stated, "All in all, the first Abbott and Costello show was sort of like putting on Loew's State from coast to coast." *Variety* said, "The boys were in there pitching Sunday—and practically threw the timeworn book at the viewers." This critic doubted if the team would have sufficient material left to sustain a second Colgate appearance. Bud and Lou continued to host the "Comedy Hour" for the next three years and all of their appearances were highly rated.

The critics continually panned the team for doing their old burlesque routines on television, but Abbott and Costello did a great deal of new material written especially for the "Colgate" shows. One of the best sketches they ever did on the show was written by Sid Fields. The sketch has Lou attempting to give Bud a rubdown in their garage. Lou follows the instructions of a radio announcer, "Fatless Frankie," who explains how to give a massage properly. The announcer (Fields) starts off by saying, "Remember—do *everything* I say!" His first instruction is to get a bottle of rubbing alcohol or witch hazel. Lou asks Bud which one he wants and Bud replies, "Use either." Lou thinks Bud said, "Use *ether.*" He gets a bottle of the anesthetic and begins pouring it on Bud, rendering him unconscious. Lou momentarily steps out of the garage and a commercial for a body and fender shop interrupts Fatless

Frankie. The announcer then proceeds to give instructions on how to paint your car at home. Lou returns in time to hear the announcer say, "Put everything else aside and get some sandpaper." The remainder of the sketch is hilarious as the baffled Costello follows the strange instructions. "Look the body over for dents or bulges. Have you found any bulges?" the radio voice asks. Lou looks at Abbott's body and nods. "Get a hammer and hammer them out," instructs Fields. "Does the body have a spare tire?" "Yeah, a beaut," Lou answers. "Then remove it," orders Fields. Lou then applies a coat of paint to his sleeping partner.

In October 1953, "the Colgate Comedy Hour" celebrated its one hundredth show. This anniversary special starred all of the hosts on one show–Abbott and Costello, Hope, Martin and Lewis, Durante, Cantor and O'Connor. Since two acts couldn't be in the same sketch, they were each given eight-minute segments. In the article "Those Feudin' Comics," October 16, 1953, *TV Guide* claimed that a feud existed between Abbott and Costello and Martin and Lewis. Although there was never any love lost between the two teams, they certainly didn't carry on a feud.

In 1954, Abbott and Costello had to cancel their regular "Colgate" chores due to Lou's illness.

In 1951, the team began production on their own weekly TV series. Sid Fields recalled that when he was working on "The Jackie Gleason Show" in the sixties, every day at five o'clock sharp Gleason could not be reached for production meetings or rehearsals. He was in his office with a magnum of champagne, watching reruns of the Abbott and Costello series on TV. Jackie Gleason was a big fan of the team and was influenced by Lou Costello.

"The Abbott and Costello Show," which was syndicated by Revue and sponsored by Chevrolet, made its debut December 5, 1952. Fifty-two episodes were filmed, airing Friday night at ten-thirty on CBS. This was an odd time slot for the comedians since a large part of their audience was comprised of children. Simultaneously, they were continuing to host many of the "Colgate Comedy Hours," which appeared on a rival network, NBC, Sunday nights. The series was a pastiche of all their old routines. Lou Costello owned the show outright. He insisted on repeating these classic routines so he'd own them on film. The first show that aired, "The Wrestling Match," featured a variation of the great wrestling scene from HERE COME THE CO-EDS. In fact, the series was crammed with material "borrowed" from all the Abbott and Costello movies. Entire scenes from the films were lifted, word for word. John Grant didn't supervise the writing and his talent for integrating routines into some kind of a story was sorely missing. Al-

though the jokes and routines were usually out of context, the program could be screamingly funny. As usual, the critics were not enthusiastic. They repeated their complaint that the boys were doing old material. *Variety* said the show resembled the weakest of the two-reeler comedies of the thirties.

Alex Gottlieb produced the first six shows. When the format was established, Lou's brother, Pat, took over as executive producer. Lou hired another good friend, Jean Yarbrough, to direct. At this time Yarbrough also received an offer to direct "I Love Lucy," but he decided to work for Bud and Lou, who were still the

Lou strikes a familiar pose.

Lou's brother-in-law, Joe Kirk, played MT. Bacciagalupe.

highest-paid performers in show business. The shows were filmed like movies. They often filmed segments from three different shows in one day, making it very confusing for the actors. Yarbrough shot all the scenes in the boardinghouse for several different episodes. Then he shot all the scenes out on the mock street at Universal, and so forth. The filming was done very quickly and the entire season was completed in just a few months. The budget was about fifteen thousand dollars per show. Two cameras were used. Yarbrough always kept one camera on Costello so as not to miss any of his bits of business.

The team played two unemployed actors, who happened to be named Abbott and Costello. Lou wore a modified version of the costume he wore in burlesque—a checkered coat, a necktie that hung down to his knees and a derby that was one size too small. He said he liked to wear the derby because it put him "in the mood." The necktie was his favorite prop. He was constantly fidgeting with it, stuffing it in his mouth or waving goodbye with it.

The comedians were aided by an impeccable stock company of second bananas, all of whom had worked with Bud and Lou in the past. Sid Fields appeared as the landlord who was forever hounding the boys for rent. The boys were generally six months behind in their payments.

In "The Birthday Party" Fields did a routine that he created in burlesque. In the routine, Fields takes umbrage at whatever Costello says to him. For example, Lou invites him to a birthday party.

Fields: "I suppose you want me to bring a present?"

Lou: "Look, Mr. Fields, a lot of people are going to bring me presents. You don't have to bring me one."

Fields: "I see. Everybody brings a present but you want me to come empty-handed. People should look at me and say, 'Sidney Fields is a cheapskate!' "

The team's TV debut on "The Colgate Comedy Hour."

Lou tells the landlord that he can bring his children to the party and they can eat anything they want.

Fields: "Sure, you'll have my kids eat first—then if that bad food you have doesn't give *my* kids ptomaine, then the other people will eat!"

Besides the landlord, Fields played a variety of other characters—doctors, druggists, dentists, psychiatrists, used-car salesmen, singing instructors and lawyers. These characters' resemblance to the landlord was explained by simply saying they were relatives of Mr. Fields! In addition to this, Sid Fields wrote many of the best shows. Sadly, Sid Fields died in October, 1975. He had spent the last years of his life in Las Vegas where he wrote a weekly humor column for a local newspaper.

Hillary Brooke was featured in the first twenty-six episodes. A statuesque blonde, Hillary played Bud and Lou's neighbor across the hall. It was never explained exactly who she was supposed to be or what she did for a living, but Hillary's cultured demeanor made her an excellent foil for the comedians. Hillary has said that she loved working with Lou Costello. She told me that they often went over budget because everyone kept breaking up at Lou's ad libs and they had to do many retakes. Some of Hillary's memorable film credits include THE ADVENTURES OF SHERLOCK HOLMES, MINISTRY OF FEAR, THE ENCHANTED COTTAGE and THE MAN WHO KNEW TOO MUCH. She was also featured as "Roberta" on the popular television series, "My Little Margie."

Gordon Jones was Mike the cop, Bud and Lou's perennial nemesis. Jones was a fine comic actor and he certainly made the most of his part. Jones appeared with the team in THE WISTFUL WIDOW OF WAGON GAP, in which he was the villain. His other film credits include MY SISTER EILEEN (1942), THE ABSENT-MINDED PROFESSOR, SON OF FLUBBER and McCLINTOCK. He also co-starred in the TV series "Meet Mr. McNulty."

Joe Besser was an old friend of Costello's. He first met Costello in the 1920s when Besser did a show in Paterson, New Jersey. Besser was Stinky, a malevolent brat who lived in the boardinghouse. Besser's choleric performance was often hilarious. He would pinch Lou's arm and threaten, "I'll harm you!" The sight of a forty-year-old-man running around in a Little Lord Fauntleroy suit was very bizarre. In fact, almost everything about this series was bizarre. Besser had performed the character, Stinky, three

Bud and Lou on the first episode of their TV series.

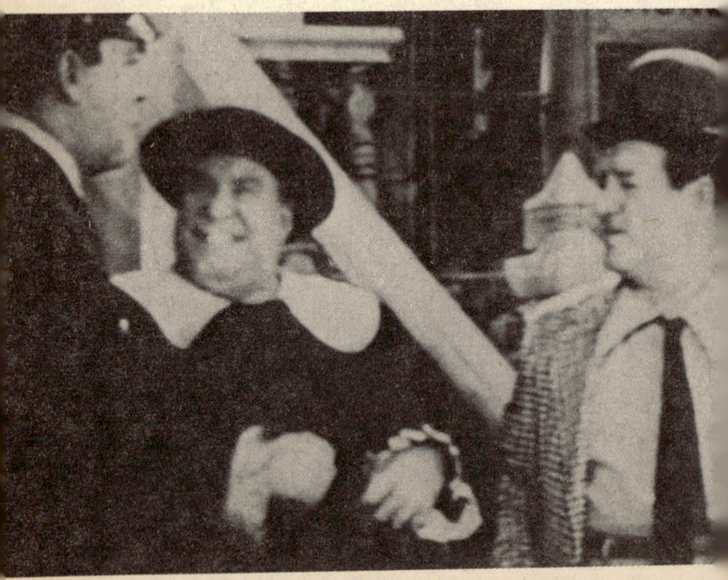

With regulars Gordon Jones and Joe Besser in "The Wrestling Match" episode.

times on the Alan Young TV show. Lou saw these shows and asked him to be a regular on the series. Joe Besser later replaced Shemp Howard as one of the Three Stooges and was a regular on Joey Bishop's situation comedy series in the early sixties.

Joe Kirk played Mr. Bacciagalupe. Kirk was Lou's brother-in-law and Lou found bit parts for him in many of the films. Kirk was also a writer on the radio show. In various episodes Mr. Bacciagalupe worked as a barber, a grocer, an ice cream man, a peanut vendor, a baker and a salesman in a music store. Apparently, Bacciagalupe had difficulty holding a job.

Joan Shawlee can be seen in quite a few episodes. She was often cast as a gum-popping hussy who would ogle the innocent Costello and exclaim, "Say, he's cute!" Joan was under contract to Lou Costello in the forties. With Lou's help she was signed by Universal and acted in a number of films, using her maiden name, Joan Fulton. She also co-starred with the team in BUCK PRIVATES COME HOME. When Bud and Lou were putting together the TV series they naturally called Joan to help out. Besides being an excellent dramatic actress, Joan Shawlee is an equally talented comedienne. In one episode she played twin waitresses, re-creating the sketch the boys did with Martha Raye in KEEP 'EM FLYING. Joan recalled that working on that particular show was the most fun she ever had. "Lou was so good at improvisation," recalls Joan. "Lou took what I considered a rank script and he played with it and he was able to make absolutely nothing into something. He was terribly conscientious, more so than Bud." Joan Shawlee was also a frequent guest on "The Colgate Comedy Hour," acting as a foil for Abbott and Costello, Bob Hope and Martin and Lewis. More recently, she has become one of Hollywood's top character actresses. She's had some choice supporting roles in three Billy Wilder comedies, SOME LIKE IT HOT (as Sweet Sue), THE APARTMENT and IRMA LA DOUCE. She is also fondly remembered as Morey Amsterdam's scatterbrained wife, Pickles, on the original "Dick Van Dyke Show." Joan feels that she owes a great deal of her success to Bud and Lou.

Another regular was a man named Bobby Barber. He was short, bald, and usually played shifty-looking con men. In a racetrack scene, he sold Costello a dopesheet for a day-old race. Bobby Barber's full-time job was being Lou Costello's "legman," running errands for the comedian. Barber can also be seen in many films of the thirties and forties, including The Marx Brothers' MONKEY BUSINESS, DODSWORTH, THE ROAD TO SINGAPORE and THE LADY EVE. During production of the TV series, Bud and Lou were constantly playing practical jokes on the little man.

Joe Besser as Stinky.

One day the whole cast was assembled at the Universal commissary. Bobby Barber was having a bowl of soup and when he wasn't looking, Lou emptied an entire saltshaker into the soup. When Barber tasted the soup, he gasped. Then Bud handed him a glass of water, shouting, "Quick! Drink this!" Barber downed the water, which, of course, Bud had also spiked with salt. Barber was the "court jester" around the set. He was often the recipient of custard pies and seltzer water in the face. Bud and Lou didn't limit their practical jokes to little Bobby Barber. Joe Besser remembered a scene in which Lou was a soda jerk in a drugstore. Besser, as Stinky, was supposed to ask Costello for a soda with castor oil in it. During one of the takes, Besser drank down the soda and turned a light shade of green. Lou had put real castor oil in it. "You had to be ready for anything on that set," said Joan Shawlee.

The oddest member of the stock company was a chimpanzee named Bingo. He wore a derby and checkered coat, matching Lou's outfit. Lou was deathly afraid of the chimp and the chimp sensed it. One day on the set, the chimp bit Lou and that was the end of Bingo's acting career.

The show opened with its theme song, "Jazz Babies' Ball," which was played over a montage of clips from the Abbott and Costello movies. After the credits, Bud and Lou emerged from behind a curtain and set up the premise for the episode. Some of the premises were funnier than the shows themselves. For instance, in "Safari," the boys decide, on the spur of the moment, to go to Africa to locate Bingo's father. In less than a minute, Bud and Lou and the entire cast are standing in the middle of the African jungle! It is fascinating to watch some of these earlier episodes. They rarely made sense and had absolutely no continuity. At times, they were almost surrealist.

If Lou strayed from the script in the movies, he ran amok on TV. He even carried a little cap pistol which he would start shooting off whenever he felt like it. Bud would just warn him to "put that thing away." Jean Yarbrough said he could never get Lou to rehearse. "We had one scene with Lou on the telephone. It was a fairly straight scene and I insisted that he rehearse it a few times. He did and when he performed it in front of the cameras, he was lousy. So there was very little rehearsal on the set after that." Lou was in rare form during the first twenty-six shows. It seemed that his enthusiasm was back in his work. He was having a lot of fun with old friends and this spirit of camaraderie came across on the TV screen. Many of the team's burlesque cronies frequently turned up, such as Murray Leonard and Milt Bronson, who was also the dialogue director.

The earlier shows didn't bother with plots. If there was a plot, it was usually abandoned in midstream. The boys would simply walk down the street and things would begin to happen. For example, an angry man grabs Lou in front of the boardinghouse and presents him with some compromising photographs. The photos show Lou on a park bench, kissing a girl. The man announces that he's the girl's boy friend and wants to know what Lou is going to do about it. Lou points to the photos and says, "I'll take two of these, one of these, you can have this one enlarged . . ."

Or a panhandler stops Lou and begs him for a dime. Lou, the Good Samaritan, gives him his last dime. Then the panhandler puts the dime in a parking meter, next to which is parked his big, expensive car.

Lou helps an elderly woman cross a busy street, in the best tradition of the Boy Scouts. When he gets her on the other side, she informs him that she didn't want to cross and hits Costello with her cane.

In "The Politician," Lou, who's running for public office, campaigns for votes in the park. His campaign manager, Bud, tells the audience, "Is he a Republican? No! Is he a Democrat? No! He is a combination of a Republican and a Democrat!" A heckler in the audience (Milt Bronson) shouts, "He sure is! He eats like an elephant and thinks like a jackass!" This scene provides a good spoof of political campaigns. Bud brings out Lou's saintly fourth-grade teacher to elicit voter sympathy. Unfortunately, the old woman doesn't remember Costello. "You remember me, don't you?" coaxes Lou. "I was the little boy who always had his hand up." (He demonstrates.) "Oh yes," she says mechanically. "You may go now."

One of the best episodes, "Television," lampoons TV quiz shows. The boys are contestants on "Hold That Cuckoo," with a typically obnoxious MC putting them through a series of embarrassing stunts. The second half of this show is a hilarious travesty of just about every movie courtroom scene.

In "The Haunted House," Hillary Brooke will inherit an old mansion if she spends one night in it. Bud and Lou offer to keep her company. They took this as another opportunity to reprise the "moving candle" gag.

"The Western Story" has Hillary inviting them to her uncle's dude ranch. In a saloon, Costello spots a mean hombre "with a price on his head." Sure enough, it's Bobby Barber and printed on his bald pate is "$7.49."

My favorite is "Getting a Job," which I think captures burlesque comedy better than anything ever done on television. It in-

Mr. Fields tries to talk Bud and Lou into taking jobs selling "No Peddlers Allowed" signs.

Bud, Lou and Bobby Barber.

Lou and Bingo on the set of the TV series, circa 1951.

cludes three classic burlesque scenes, "The Baker Scene," "Floogle Street," and "Get Out of the Office."

Another show, titled "The Birthday Party," also ranks as one of the best. Bud ejects Lou from his own birthday party and there are some unusually poignant moments as Costello tries to celebrate by himself.

In "Bingo" Lou is informed that he must get a license for his pet chimp. So Lou goes to City Hall to get the license, but accidentally walks into the marriage bureau. This leads to an amusing segment with a very confused clerk (Joan Shawlee).

"Little Old Lady" deals with the boys' efforts to raise cash to prevent an old woman in the neighborhood from being evicted. Upon presentation of the hard-earned money to the little old lady, she calls her bookie and makes a wager on a horse race. In this one, Lou tells Mike the cop that when he was a little kid in Paterson, New Jersey, he was unjustly accused of stealing thirty-eight cents and had to run away from home. Mike, feeling sorry for Costello, asks, "Where did you go?" "Where was I gonna go on thirty-eight cents?" shouts Costello.

The team revived "Crazy House" in a show titled "Peace and Quiet." Murray Leonard, Sid Fields, Hillary Brooke, Milt Bronson and Bobby Barber joined in the lunacy.

Lou dances with Lon Chaney, Jr., as Bud and Jarmila Novotna look on; from the "Colgate Comedy Hour."

In a similar episode, "The Actors' Home," Lou goes to visit his partner, who is a patient there. Lou encounters some of the strange inhabitants of the home, two of whom are having a baseball game with an imaginary ball. This episode also contains "Who's on First."

Sid Fields and Lou Costello do the "Slowly I Turned" routine in "Jail," and no one ever did it better.

Preparing for a vacation in Phoenix, Bud decides to rent a U-Drive. "Why do I have to drive?" Lou wants to know. "Why can't you drive?" Bud says, "You don't understand, it's a Hertz U-Drive." Lou complains, "Well, if it hurts, I'm not gonna drive." Bud, exasperated, explains that "every company has to have a head and this company's head's Hertz!" Costello shouts, "Why don't the guy take an aspirin!"

During the filming of the program, the sound stage resembled a circus. One can just picture the chaos on the set, involving chimps, old burlesque comics, gamblers, Bobby Barber and Abbott and Costello themselves. As usual there was a high-stakes card game going on between shots. Occasionally Lou would become so involved in the game, the assistant director couldn't get him to resume work. Whenever this happened, Hillary Brooke was dispatched to talk to Lou. She was the only one on the set who could

One of the funnier episodes, "Safari," with Bobby Barber, Hillary Brooke and Joe Kirk.

talk him into leaving the game. "Bud and Lou bet on anything," Joan Shawlee told me. "They'd bet a hundred and fifty dollars that you wouldn't make it on the first take or five hundred dollars that a light bulb would blow out."

If the stagehands got a tip on a racehorse they were careful not to tell Lou. Otherwise he'd bet four thousand dollars on it and the odds would go down.

Jean Yarbrough decided that the show needed a change in format for its second season. He wanted to get away from unrelated burlesque skits and do stories instead. He cut the opening and closing segments with the team performing routines on stage. *TV Guide* reported that the comedians knew that audiences wanted "sight stuff" and they were concentrating on immediate and total action. Yarbrough hired Clyde Bruckman, a vastly experienced gagman, to write the scripts. The show became a more restrained half hour. Joe Besser, Hillary Brooke and Joe Kirk were missing from the cast, with only Sid Fields and Gordon Jones remaining. These episodes lacked the genial lunacy of the early ones. Obviously, they needed to try something new since the comedians had nearly exhausted their old routines. The idea of doing stories was certainly a welcomed one. But the plots were trite and hampered Bud and Lou, who were better off left to their own devices. The first twenty-six shows didn't make sense, but at least they moved at a good clip and contained many laughs. The last twenty-six are lethargic and some are, quite frankly, unfunny. The energy that Lou Costello displayed during the earlier episodes was gone. Because of poor health he was no longer up to the physical demands of his kind of comedy. Abbott, ten years older than his partner, and by now sporting a pencil-thin moustache, was also slowing up. The show was also marred by a shrieking laugh track that sounded as if it was recorded in the audience at the Roller Derby.

Clyde Bruckman, who wrote and directed many memorable comedies in the twenties and thirties, had the habit of lifting gags from these films and reworking them into the Abbott and Costello scripts. One show was a virtual re-enactment of Buster Keaton's ONE WEEK. In this classic short, Keaton builds a "do it yourself" house for his bride, only to have it sabotaged by a jealous suitor. In the Abbott and Costello episode, "Honeymoon House," Lou is the builder, repeating several gags from ONE WEEK.

Another show featured a scene from an early Keaton short, THE BALLOONATIC. We see Costello and his new girlfriend on a boat, happily entering the tunnel of love in an amusement park. A few seconds later we see the two coming out of the other end of

Ruth Lee, Maureen Nash, Walter Catlett, Lou, Bud, and Gloria Saunders. A scene from the "Fall Guy" episode.

One of the later episodes. With Sid Fields.

the tunnel, but now Lou has a big black eye.

The boys participate in a Civil War melodrama in the "South of Dixie" episode, which was just an excuse to use gags from Keaton's famous silent comedy THE GENERAL.

Although most of these shows were disappointing, there were some bright moments. One of the better episodes found the duo working as pest exterminators. While on a job fumigating a psychiatrist's office, the telephone rings. The woman calling assumes that Costello is a psychiatrist and asks him to help her with her "aunts." The aunts are two elderly eccentrics who behave like children. Costello thinks she means "ants" and volunteers his services.

Bud and Lou are hired to pose as British noblemen at a reception in "In Society." Lou regales the other guests with a lengthy shaggy-dog story (unfortunately he doesn't know how the story ends). The party turns into a pie-throwing melee thanks to Costello.

In "Public Enemies" the pair becomes involved with a gang of crooks who are planning a warehouse robbery. There's a chase in a warehouse, utilizing gags from several different silent comedies.

Typical is an episode in which Lou falls for a blonde who's engaged to a wrestler, Bone-Bender Brodsky. The usual slapstick ensues, which was, by now, dull and repetitive.

"The Abbott and Costello Show" featured an impressive guest list of veteran character actors. Among them: Walter Catlett, Joe Sawyer, Charlie Hall, Allen Jenkins, Dorothy Granger, Percy Helton, Byron Foulger, Paul Fix, George Chandler, Benny Rubin, Virginia Christine, Glenn Strange, Veda Ann Borg, Thurston Hall, James Flavin, Joyce Jameson, Marjorie Reynolds, Jane Frazee, Lucien Littlefield and Burt Mustin.

The show ended its course on CBS (it was replaced by Edward R. Murrow's "Person to Person") and the profits from the reruns helped to solve Lou Costello's tax problems. Costello also owned another series at the time, the popular crime drama "I'm the Law," which starred George Raft.

After twenty years, "The Abbott and Costello Show" is still one of the most widely syndicated series in the country. (It was recently estimated that WPIX-TV in New York reran each episode over two hundred times!) Viewing the shows today, many of them hold up remarkably well. They haven't dated at all. Fortunately, they never used any topical references. As Sid Fields said, "It was just pure, hokum comedy."

THE FINAL CHAPTER

Following the release of DANCE WITH ME, HENRY, Lou made a series of memorable solo appearances on "The Steve Allen Show." In 1957 and 1958 he was a frequent guest on this classic variety hour. "Lou was very effective on the show," recalls Steve Allen, "and he made our jobs easy because he always brought his own material." That he did. Lou re-created all of his favorites—the drill routine, the "Lemon Bit," "Crazy House" and others. Two of the show's regulars, Louis Nye and Tom Poston, played Abbott's part in these sketches. Lou also appeared in the fondly remembered "Man on the Street" segments. I think these shows amounted to Lou Costello's finest work in his later years. He participated in the sketches with renewed energy and enthusiasm, perhaps because he was embarking on a second career. In 1958, while the United States was still on friendly terms with Cuba, Steve Allen took the whole cast to Havana for a special show. Lou was one of the guest stars on that show and he performed the dice game scene from BUCK PRIVATES, with Tom Poston as his straight man. Lou's daughter, Carole, who pursued a singing career in the fifties, was featured several times on "The Steve Allen Show."

In July of 1957 it became official. Bud Abbott and Lou Costello had split up. An Associated Press reporter asked Lou why he broke up with his longtime partner. "It's funny," Lou replied, "but I was seen as a single by millions of people on 'The Steve Allen Show' . . . and you're the first one who's asked me why. I guess after twenty years, no one would believe that Abbott and Costello split up." The reason he gave was that Bud was tired of working and wanted to take it easy for a while.

When asked what his future plans were, Lou joked, "Oh, I might try and work with Dean Martin." Martin and Lewis had dissolved their partnership months before. Ironically, Martin and Lewis, who eclipsed Abbott and Costello at the movie box office in the fifties, might never have teamed if it wasn't for Lou. Lou discovered Dean Martin in a small nightclub in New York where the singer was earning about fifty dollars a week. Lou signed him to a personal contract and gave him five hundred dollars to have his nose fixed. He then arranged important nightclub bookings for Dean in Philadelphia and New York. Lou felt that Dean was ungrateful and he eventually tore up the contract.

Lou performing the "Lemon Bit" with Tom Poston and Louis Nye on "The Steve Allen Show."

The Havana trip, with Steve Allen, Louis Nye and Tom Poston.

Lou performing "Crazy House" on the Steve Allen TV show in 1957. Louis Nye substituted for Abbott.

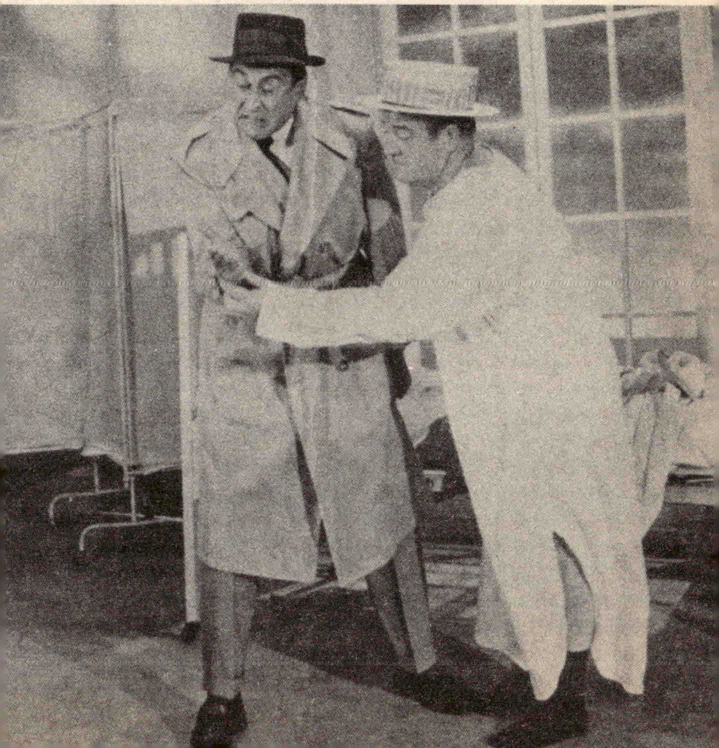

Unlike Martin and Lewis', Abbott and Costello's separation was an amicable one. Regardless of varying accounts of feuds between Bud and Lou, they always managed to get along quite well together. Of course, they did have their differences. One of the things that bothered Lou more and more over the years was his billing. He resented Bud's name coming first. Children often ran up to Lou and asked, "Can I have your autograph, Mr. Abbott?"—which never failed to annoy him. The children assumed that his name came first since he was the funny one. Even *Variety,* the show business bible, had difficulty getting their names straight. A review of the act in *Variety,* October 19, 1938, describes *Bud* as the bombastic comic and *Lou* as the straight man. Lou felt that he was losing his identity and by the 1950s he was anxious to work as a single.

Lou also resented the fact that in the early days of their partnership, Bud commanded sixty percent of the salary. Even while they were working at Universal Bud was getting the larger share. During their tour for the Lou Costello Jr. Youth Foundation, Lou finally demanded a fifty-fifty split. Bud was more than happy to oblige. The press distorted this incident, claiming Bud and Lou were threatening to break up the act.

Wherever they went, Bud and Lou were invariably followed by a large entourage of friends and relatives. Some of their so-called friends were jealous of the team's success and tried to instigate arguments between the two. All of these problems—plus the fact that their film careers were waning—contributed to the split in 1957. Bud and Lou still remained friends afterward and saw each other frequently. Lou commented on their relationship in a *TV Guide* interview: "Bud was a dandy, a real sharp dresser. Easygoing kind of a guy. Me, I'm a worrier. I worried about Bud for twenty years. Would he be there for rehearsal? Would he make the airport on time? Did he know the new material?"

After the breakup, Lou busied himself with a great number of projects. At one point he said he was planning to emcee a comedy-quiz program but nothing came of it. More than anything else, Lou wanted to star in a film based on the life of Fiorello La Guardia. This pet project was never realized and it is indeed a great shame. He would have been the perfect choice to play New York's colorful mayor since he closely resembled La Guardia. This might very well have been the crowning achievement of Lou's career. To give you an idea just how bright Lou was, another one of his dreams was to portray Sancho Panza in a movie version of *Don Quixote.* This too would have been the ideal role for Lou, combining humor and pathos. Unfortunately this never came to fruition either and he landed up making his "dramatic" debut on TV's "General Electric Theatre" in 1958. In a story titled "Blaze of Glory," Costello played a bumbling plumber held prisoner by a gang of crooks. This show failed to be either funny or dramatic. Lou's co-star Joyce Jameson contributed a few laughs as a gangster's moll.

His second straight acting role came later that year in a "Wagon Train" episode, "The Tobias Jones Story." It was considerably better than the "GE Theatre" show but it was still disappointing. Lou played Tobias Jones, a pathetic drunk falsely accused of murder. His performance was convincing but the script was clichéd and at times maudlin. However, Lou received a good set of reviews from TV critics for a change, which pleased him. In the *TV Guide* interview he spoke of his fling at dramatic acting: "It's easy to me. No falls, no pushing around, no seltzer in the face. But I had a real tough time with this guy inside me at first. This guy inside, he kept saying, 'What a perfect spot for a tumble, kiddo! Go ahead.' And then, eight to one you forget the next line."

After this Lou returned to the kind of performing he did best—burlesque comedy. He starred in a burlesque revue at the Dunes Hotel in Las Vegas, "Minsky's Follies of 1958." Sid Fields played straight man for Lou in familiar scenes like "Crazy House" and the "Lemon Bit." The show, scheduled to run six weeks, broke all house records at the Dunes. The owners of the Dunes hoped to extend the show another six weeks and they offered to give Costello a brand-new white Thunderbird if he would stay on. Lou wanted to continue the show but he had been feeling ill and knew he wasn't up to it. His last bout with rheumatic fever had left him very weak. Doctors repeatedly warned him not to put a strain on his heart but Lou insisted on doing scenes like "Crazy House" which required him to take many pratfalls. The hotel owners found it such a pleasure to work with Lou that they gave him the Thunderbird anyway and he departed for Hollywood. This would be his last stage appearance, and his last success. Ironically it was in a burlesque show bearing the name "Minsky," a name which helped to launch his fabulous career.

Back in Hollywood, Lou began production on his first and only film without Bud Abbott, titled LOU COSTELLO AND HIS THIRTY FOOT BRIDE. It was an innocuous little film similar to the Disney comedies. It is startling to see Lou in the film. He was only fifty-two but due to illness he looked years older, and he had lost a lot of weight. This Columbia release is the story of Artie Pinsetter (Lou), a junk collector in the desert town of Candy Rock. He is also an amateur inventor and has created a time machine. Lou is

At Havana hotel. With Nye and Poston.

in love with Emmy Lou (Dorothy Provine), a niece of the town's corrupt mayor, Raven Rossiter (Gale Gordon). When Emmy Lou runs into the magical "dinosaur springs," she emerges a thirty-foot giantess. The rest of the film recounts Lou's efforts to restore his girl friend back to normal size. Costello is aided by a good supporting cast including Charles Lane, Jimmy Conlin, Peter Leeds and Bobby Barber. Columbia didn't release the film until two years after it was completed and by then the title had been changed to THE THIRTY FOOT BRIDE OF CANDY ROCK. The New York *Daily News* commented, "Lou Costello's last legacy to his fans is something to leave them laughing . . . In THE THIRTY FOOT BRIDE OF CANDY ROCK he signs off in high spirits as a man on the threshold of a blissful everafter."

On February 26, 1959, soon after finishing the film, Lou suffered a heart attack in his home. He was rushed to Doctor's Hospital in Beverly Hills, where his condition was declared to be "satisfactory." Bud visited Lou several times at the hospital and his partner's health seemed to be improving. Then on March 3, Lou died of a second heart attack. Earlier that day he had been laughing and joking with his manager, Eddie Sherman. Lou's wife Anne had left his hospital room just minutes before the final attack. Three days later would have been Lou's fifty-third birthday.

Photograph taken for Lou's final stage appearance at the Dunes Hotel in Las Vegas, 1958.

Bud sobbed when he heard the news. "My God, what can I say? My heart is broken. I've lost the best pal anyone ever had." Lou was buried March 7, after a requiem mass in North Hollywood.

Lou left behind his widow Anne, three daughters, three grandchildren, a mother, a brother and sister, and millions of fans who were stunned at the untimely death of this great comedian. Local TV stations all around the country had well-intentioned tributes to Lou, showing clips from Abbott and Costello movies and TV episodes. Anne Costello, who also suffered heart ailments, died the following December 5.

Shortly before his death, Lou talked about his stage and screen personality in *TV Guide:* "I'm a wistful little guy . . . I'm the underdog, the guy nobody pays much attention to until something happens to him. I'd be way out of place trying to play some guy like a big hero . . . I've been doing comedy for maybe thirty years now. People know what I look like and what kind of a little guy I am. They wouldn't accept too much different from that, would they?"

Throughout the 1950s, Abbott and Costello had a running battle with the Internal Revenue Service, stemming from deductions they made for the Lou Costello Jr. Youth Foundation, and from other deductions. Lou managed to settle up with the IRS, which

Lou and Beverly Washburn in the "Wagon Train" episode "The Tobias Jones Story."

claimed a good share of his personal wealth. In 1959 Bud was hit with a bill for seven years of back taxes, with penalties and interest. To meet the payments Bud was forced to sell his $125,000 home in Encino at a loss and he and his wife Betty moved into a small house in Woodland Hills.

Bud remained pretty much in retirement until early in 1961 when he teamed with a comic named Candy Candido, who closely resembled Lou Costello. They put together a forty-minute act consisting of many of the old Abbott and Costello routines, and played a few nightclubs around the country. *Variety,* reviewing Abbott and Candido, said, "Bud Abbott is back with a new partner, Candy Candido, and it's as close as it could possibly be without the late Lou Costello. The same routines that made the team famous are used, Candido doing a letter-perfect impression of Costello and retaining his own identity by doing a spot before the classic 'Who's on First.' " Despite good reviews, the act failed to work out. Bud later remarked that nobody could ever live up to Lou.

April 16, 1961, Bud made a dramatic appearance on "General Electric Theatre," as his partner had done three years earlier. The show, titled "The Joke's on Me," was the story of an obnoxious insult comic, played by Lee Marvin, whose on-stage personality began running into his personal life. Bud played Marvin's long-suffering manager, Sid Benton. Bud's return to TV might have sparked a new career for him as a character actor. He showed how good he could be in LITTLE GIANT and THE TIME OF THEIR LIVES. But he looked nervous and ill at ease on the show, which was understandable since it was the first TV show he had done without Lou Costello.

Bud then stayed retired until Hanna-Barbera produced the Abbott and Costello cartoon series in 1967. The only interesting feature of these hundred and fifty-six color cartoons was that Bud provided the voice of his own animated character. The cartoons themselves were mediocre but it was a treat for Abbott and Costello fans to hear Bud's familiar, gravelly voice shouting, "Talk sense, Costello!" (The voice of Costello was supplied by Stan Irwin.) Bud profited from these cartoons, which are often replayed on local stations all over the country.

Abbott and Costello had turned up once before in animated form via a number of clever Warner Brothers cartoons in the forties. In these cartoons they were portrayed as a couple of conniving alley cats. The first of these, A TALE OF TWO KITTIES, introduced another popular Warner Brothers character named Tweetie Pie.

Kathleen Hughes, Lee Marvin and Bud in the "General Electric Theatre" show "The Joke's On Me."

Lou and cast (Jonathan Harris on top) from the "General Electric Theatre" show "Blaze of Glory."

Lou's only film without Bud Abbott—THE THIRTY FOOT BRIDE OF CANDY ROCK. With (left to right) Joey Faye, Bobby Barber, Doodles Weaver and Charles Lane.

Costello as Napoleon in THE THIRTY FOOT BRIDE OF CANDY ROCK.

Hanna-Barbera produced a series of Abbott and Costello cartoons in 1967.

Bud Abbott, age sixty-three, attends his partner's funeral in 1959. UPI photo.

In 1965, Universal turned out a "tribute" to the team, THE WORLD OF ABBOTT AND COSTELLO. This hastily produced film, narrated by Jack E. Leonard, was a compilation of scenes from eighteen of their Universal comedies. It briefly played neighborhood theaters on the bottom half of a double bill top-lining something called MCHALE'S NAVY JOINS THE AIR FORCE. The film did contain some of their best scenes—the boxing match from BUCK PRIVATES. "Who's on First" from THE NAUGHTY NINETIES and "Floogle Street" from IN SOCIETY. But, strangely, it also featured a great deal of footage from their *worst* films like ABBOTT AND COSTELLO GO TO MARS, THE KEYSTONE KOPS, LOST IN ALASKA and COMIN' ROUND THE MOUNTAIN. It was further hindered by a narration that attempted to be funny, but wasn't. The film was frustrating for Abbott and Costello fans. If someone who was familiar with the team had produced the film, it could have been excellent.

All through his life Bud had suffered a long series of ailments. He was an epileptic and he found alcohol to be an escape from this illness. Doctors warned him to stop drinking or he'd die. He kept drinking and he outlived the doctors. In 1967, he had the first of several strokes and in 1972, he fell and broke his hip and was confined to a wheelchair thereafter.

Bud Abbott died of cancer in his home in Woodland Hills, April 24, 1974. He was seventy-eight. A few months before, Bud and Betty Abbott had celebrated their fifty-fifth wedding anniversary with family and friends. Besides his widow he was survived by two adopted children, Rae Victoria Wheeler and Bud Abbott, Jr., and four grandchildren.

Abbott and Costello were the last of the great movie comedy teams. Dean Martin and Jerry Lewis were very successful in the fifties but it's hard to consider them a "team" on film since Jerry was the whole show. Most of the time, Dean was just around to supply the love interest and sing a couple of tunes. Martin and Lewis failed to establish the kind of rapport in the movies that made Abbott and Costello so great. Since then, other comedy teams, such as Rowan and Martin and even Allen and Rossi(!), have attempted to fill the void left by Abbott and Costello, with dismal results.

Bud and Lou are both gone now but they'll always be with us through their films and television shows. They enjoyed their greatest popularity in the early 1940s when the world desperately needed laughter. Considering the current state of the world and the current state of comedy, I'd say that we need them more today than we ever did before.

AN INDEX
TO THE FILMS OF
ABBOTT AND COSTELLO

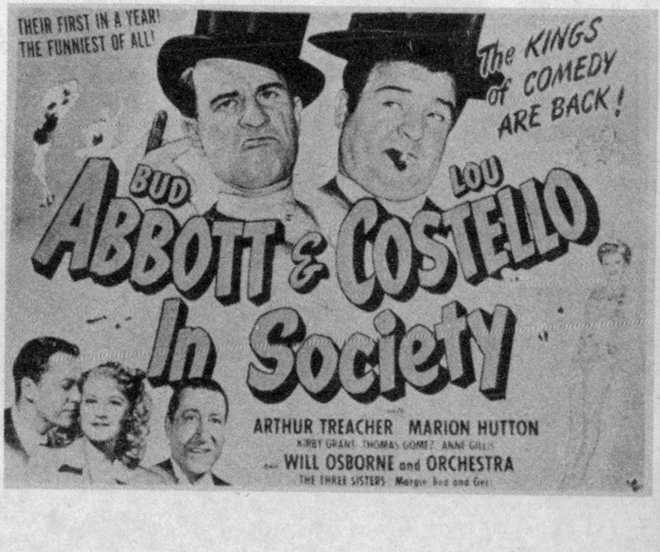

ONE NIGHT IN THE TROPICS

(UNIVERSAL–1940)
Directed by A. Edward Sutherland
Produced by Leonard Spigelgass
Screenplay by Gertrude Purcell and Charles Grayson
Adapted by Kathryn Scola and Francis Martin
From the novel *Love Insurance,* by Earl Derr Biggers
Director of Photography: Joseph Valentine, ASC
Musical Direction by Charles Previn
Orchestrations by Frank Skinner
Dances by Larry Ceballos
Film Editor: Milton Carruth
Song by Jerome Kern, Dorothy Fields, Oscar Hammerstein
Running Time: 82 minutes

CAST

JIM MOORE .... Allan Jones
STEVE HARPER .... Robert Cummings
CYNTHIA.................. Nancy Kelly
AUNT KITTY .... Mary Boland
ABBOTT .... Bud Abbott
COSTELLO .... Lou Costello
MICKEY FITZGERALD .... Peggy Moran
ROSCOE.................. William Frawley
SENOR ESCOBAR......... Leo Carrillo
RUDOLFO .... Don Alvarado
THE THEODORES .... Theodore Rand
Mina Farragut
MR. MOORE.............. Richard Carle
MAN .... Edgar Dearing
THOMPSON .... Barnett Parker
ESCOBAR'S AIDE .... Francis McDonald
VENDOR .... Jerry Mandy
EDWARDS................ Eddie Dunn
DANCER .... Vivian Fay
STEWARD................ Eddie Acuff
WAITER.................. Frank Penny
ORCHESTRA LEADER ..... William Alston
DRUNK .... Charles B. Murphy
STEWARD................ Charlie Hall

BUCK PRIVATES

(UNIVERSAL–1941)
Directed by Arthur Lubin
Produced by Alex Gottlieb
Original Screenplay by Arthur T. Horman
Special Material for Abbott and Costello by John Grant
Director of Photography: Milton Krasner, ASC
Songs by Hughie Prince and Don Raye
Dance Director: Nick Castle
Film Editor: Philip Cahn
Running Time: 82 minutes

CAST

SLICKER SMITH .... Bud Abbott
HERBIE BROWN .... Lou Costello
ANDREWS SISTERS........ Themselves
RANDOLPH PARKER III ... Lee Bowman
BOB MARTIN.............. Alan Curtis
JUDY GRAY .... Jane Frazee
MICHAEL COLLINS........ Nat Pendleton
DICK BURNETTE.......... Don Raye
MISS DURLING............ Dora Clemant
CAPTAIN WILLIAMS....... J. Anthony Hughes
HENRY .... Hughie Prince
BRIGGS .... Leonard Elliott
HOSTESSES................ Jeanne Kelly
Elaine Morey
Kay Leslie
SERGEANT CALLAHAN ... Harry Strang
HARMONICA PLAYER..... Frank Cook
MAJOR EMERSON......... Samuel S. Hinds
COOK .... Shemp Howard
SERGEANT .... James Flavin
ANNOUNCER.............. Mike Frankovich
MEDICAL EXAMINER ..... Jack Mulhall
MRS. PARKER .... Nella Walker
MR. PARKER .... Douglas Wood
EDMUNDS.................. Charles Coleman
CAPTAIN .... Selmer Jackson
INSTRUCTOR.............. Tom Tyler
SERGEANT .... Herold Goodwin
PORTER .... Bud Harris
TOUGH FIGHTER .... Al Billings

SERGEANT MARKS........Frank Penny
SMALL BOXER.............Frank Grandetta
LIEUTENANT..............Bob Wayne

IN THE NAVY

(UNIVERSAL–1941)
Directed by Arthur Lubin
Produced by Alex Gottlieb
Screenplay by Arthur T. Horman and John Grant
Original Story by Arthur T. Horman
Director of Photography: Joseph Valentine, ASC
Songs: Gene de Paul and Don Raye
Technical Advisor: H. E. Harris, U.S.N.
Film Editor: Philip Cahn
Running Time: 85 minutes

CAST

SMOKEY ADAMS..........Bud Abbott
POMEROY WATSON.......Lou Costello
TOMMY HALSTEAD.......Dick Powell
DOROTHY.................Claire Dodd
ANDREWS SISTERS........Themselves
DYNAMITE DUGAN.......Dick Foran
DIZZY.....................Shemp Howard
BUTCH...................Billy Lenhart
BUDDY...................Kenneth Brown
CONDOS BROTHERS......Themselves
CAPTAIN RICHARDS......William Davidson
HEAD OF COMMITTEE....Thurston Hall
TRAVERS..................Robert Emmet Keane
COMMANDER.............Edward Fielding
FLOOR MANAGER........Don Terry
LANCER..................Sunnie O'Dea
TICKET TAKER............Eddie Dunn
TRAFFIC COP............Ralph Dunn
BIG BRUISER.............Dick Alexander
SMALL MEEK HUSBAND..Lorin Raker
BOS'N.....................Frank Penny
SENTRY..................Pat Gleason
LIEUTENANT SCOTT......Jack Mulhall
TOUGH CIVILIAN.........Mickey Simpson

MARINE	Lyle Latell
TRUCK DRIVER	Chuck Morrison
BANDLEADER	Lee Kass
POLICEMAN	James Sullivan
FAT WOMAN	Edna Hall
GUSHING MOTHER	Claire Whitney
MESS BOY	Joe Bautista
MOTHER	Doris Herbert
SAILOR	Charles Sullivan

HOLD THAT GHOST

(UNIVERSAL–1941)
Directed by Arthur Lubin
Produced by Alex Gottlieb
Screenplay by Robert Lees, Frederic I. Rinaldo and John Grant
Original Story by Robert Lees and Frederic I. Rinaldo
Director of Photography: Elwood Bredell, ASC
Film Editor: Philip Cahn
Running Time: 86 minutes

CAST

CHUCK MURRAY	Bud Abbott
FERDINAND JONES	Lou Costello
DOCTOR JACKSON	Richard Carlson
NORMA LIND	Evelyn Ankers
CAMILLE BREWSTER	Joan Davis
ANDREWS SISTERS	Themselves
TED LEWIS	Himself
MAITRE D'	Mischa Auer
CHARLIE SMITH	Marc Lawrence
HARRY HOSKINS	Milton Parsons
SNAKE-EYES	Frank Penny
IRONDOME	Edgar Dearing
STRANGLER	Don Terry
HIGH COLLAR	Edward Pawley
GLUM	Nestor Paiva
LAWYER	Russell Hicks
MOOSE MATSON	William Davidson
LEFTY	Paul Fix
JUDGE	Howard Hickman
JENKINS	Harry Hayden

STATE TROOPER .... William Forrest
BIG FINK.................. Paul Newlan
LITTLE FINK .... Joe LaCava
BIT WAITER .... Bobby Barber

KEEP 'EM FLYING

(UNIVERSAL–1941)
Directed by Arthur Lubin
Produced by Glenn Tryon
Screenplay by True Boardman, Nat Perrin and John Grant
Original Story by Edmund L. Hartmann
Director of Photography: Joseph Valentine, ASC
Special Effects by John Fulton
Aerial Photography by Elmer Dyer
Songs by Don Raye, Gene de Paul, Ned Washington and George Bassman
Chase and Flying Sequences Directed by Ralph Ceder
Film Editors: Philip Cahn and Arthur Hilton
Running Time: 86 minutes

CAST

BLACKIE .... Bud Abbott
HEATHCLIFFE............. Lou Costello
BARBARA/GLORIA .... Martha Raye
LINDA..................... Carol Bruce
CRAIG MORRISON .... William Gargan
JINX...................... Dick Foran
BUTCH .... Truman Bradley
JIM .... Charles Lang
GONIGAL .... William Davidson
SPEALER .... Frank Penny
MAJOR BARSTOW .... Loring Smith
CADETS .... Stanley Smith
James Horne, Jr.
Charlie King, Jr.
Regis Parton
USO GIRLS .... Dorothy Darrell
Marcia Ralston
LADY WITH LIPSTICK..... Doris Lloyd
MAN IN GORILLA SUIT ... Emil Van Horn
LIEUTENANT.............. James Seay

CAPTAIN .... William Forrest
ATTENDANT .... Earle Hodgins
TRUCK DRIVER .... Harry Strang
ORCHESTRA LEADER ..... Carleton Young
ANNOUNCER.............. Harold Daniels
CADET STEVENS .... Dick Crane
DOCTOR .... Paul Scott
HATCHECK GIRL .... Virginia Engels
BRUNETTE .... Dorothy L. Jones

RIDE 'EM COWBOY

(UNIVERSAL–1942)
Directed by Arthur Lubin
Produced by Alex Gottlieb
Screenplay by True Boardman, John Grant
Adaptation by Harold Shumate
Original Story by Edmund L. Hartmann
Director of Photography: John W. Boyle, ASC
Songs by Don Raye and Gene de Paul
Musical Numbers Staged by Nick Castle
Running Time: 82 minutes

CAST

DUKE .... Bud Abbott
WILLOUGHBY.............. Lou Costello
ANNE SHAW .... Anne Gwynne
SAM SHAW .... Samuel S. Hinds
BRONCO BOB .... Dick Foran
PETER CONWAY .... Richard Lane
TOM......................... Judd McMichael
DICK .... Ted McMichael
HARRY...................... Joe McMichael
DOTTY DAVIS............. Mary Lou Cook
ALABAM .... Johnny Mack Brown
RUBY........................ Ella Fitzgerald
JAKE RAINWATER .... Douglas Dumbrille
MOONBEAM................ Jody Gilbert
ACE ANDERSON........... Morris Ankrum
MARTIN MANNING ...... Charles Lane
ANNOUNCER............... Russell Hicks
RODEO MANAGER .... Wade Boteler

RAILROAD DETECTIVE ... James Flavin
DOCTOR .... Boyd Davis
DETECTIVE #2........... Eddie Dunn
LADY...................... Isabel Randolph
ANNOUNCER.............. Tom Hanlon
RANGER CAPTAIN .... James Seay
REPORTER .... Harold Daniels
FIRST HENCHMAN .... Ralph Peters
SUNBEAM .... Linda Brent
SECOND INDIAN GIRL .... Lee Sunrise
CHIEF TOMAHAWK .... Chief Yowlachie
MIDGET.................. Harry Monty
SQUARE DANCE CALLER . Sherman E. Sanders
FIRST INDIAN GIRL....... Carmela Cansino

RIO RITA

(METRO-GOLDWYN-MAYER–1942)
Directed by S. Sylvan Simon
Produced by Pandro S. Berman
Screenplay by Richard Connell and Gladys Lehman
Special Material for Abbott and Costello by John Grant
Director of Photography: George Folsey, ASC
Songs by Harold Arlen, E. Y. Harburg, Harry Tierney and Joseph McCarthy
Music Directed by Herbert Stothart
Special Effects by Warren Newcombe
Editor: Ben Lewis
Running Time: 91 minutes

CAST

DOC...................... Bud Abbott
WISHY .... Lou Costello
RITA WINSLOW .... Kathryn Grayson
RICARDO MONTERA...... John Carroll
LUCILLE BRUNSWICK..... Patricia Dane
MAURICE CRAINDALL .... Tom Conway
JAKE .... Peter Whitney
TRASK .... Arthur Space
DOTTY .... Joan Valerie
GUS .... Dick Rich
HARRY GANTLEY......... Barry Nelson

MARIANNA.................Eva Puig
JULIO......................Mitchell Lewis
DANCER...................Eros Volusia
MEXICAN GENT...........Julian Rivero
CONTROL MAN............Douglass Newland
LITTLE MEXICAN.........Lee Murray
PULQUE....................Inez Cooper
CHEF.......................Frank Penny

PARDON MY SARONG

(UNIVERSAL–1942)
Directed by Erle C. Kenton
Produced by Alex Gottlieb
Screenplay by True Boardman, Nat Perrin and John Grant
Director of Photography: Milton Krasner, ASC
Songs by Don Raye, Gene de Paul, Milton Drake, Ben Oakland, Stanley Cowan and Bobby North
Musical Direction by Charles Previn
Editor: Arthur Hilton
Assistant Director: Howard Christie
Running Time: 83 minutes

CAST

ALGERNON SHAW........Bud Abbott
WELLINGTON PHLUG.....Lou Costello
JOAN MARSHALL.........Virginia Bruce
TOMMY LAYTON..........Robert Paige
DOCTOR VARNOFF.......Lionel Atwill
WHABA....................Leif Erickson
DETECTIVE KENDALL....William Demarest
CHIEF KOLUA.............Samuel S. Hinds
INK SPOTS................Orville Jones
Charles Fuqua
Bill Kenney
Deek Watson
TIP, TAP, TOE.............Raymond Winfield
Sammy Green
Teddie Fraser
PROPRIETOR..............Irving Bacon
LUANA....................Nan Wynn
FERNA....................Marie McDonald

AMO .... Elaine Morey
TAGALONG .... Susan Levine
TABOR .... Jack La Rue
MOSS......................... Hans Schumm
HENCHMAN................. Joe Kirk
HENCHMAN................. Frank Penny
SUPERINTENDENT .... Charles Lane
CHECKER .... Chester Clute
SVEN .... Tom Fadden
NEWSMAN .... George Chandler
MAN .... Eddie Acuff
MARCO .... Sig Arno
GIRL .... Jane Patten
GIRL .... Florine McKinney
GIRL .... Marjorie Reardon
GIRL .... Audrey Long
NEMO .... Teddy Infuhr
SHARKEY THE SEAL ...... Himself

WHO DONE IT?

(UNIVERSAL–1942)
Directed by Erle C. Kenton
Produced by Alex Gottlieb
Screenplay by Stanley Roberts, Edmund Joseph and John Grant
Original Story by Stanley Roberts
Director of Photography: Charles Van Enger, ASC
Music by Frank Skinner
Running Time: 77 minutes

CAST

CHICK LARKIN .... Bud Abbott
MERVYN MILGRIM .... Lou Costello
LIEUTENANT MORAN..... William Gargan
JANE LITTLE .... Louise Allbritton
JIM TURNER .... Patric Knowles
ART FRASER .... Don Porter
MARCO HOLLER .... Jerome Cowan
BRANNIGAN .... William Bendix
JULIET COLLINS .... Mary Wickes
COLONEL J. R. ANDREWS . Thomas Gomez

DOCTOR ANTON MAREK .	Ludwig Stossel
JENKINS....................	Edmund MacDonald
THOMPSON	Joe Kirk
ELEVATOR BOY	Walter Tetley
RADIO ACTOR	Crane Whitley
RADIO ACTRESS	Margaret Brayton
ACROBATS	The Pinas
CORONER..................	Milton Parsons
CARTER....................	Edward Keane
ANNOUNCER..............	Ed Emerson
SECOND ANNOUNCER	Buddy Twiss
TELEPHONE OPERATOR ..	Gladys Blake
BIT MAN	Eddie Bruce
TRUCK DRIVER	Harry Strang
SPINELLI..................	Frank Penny
CUSTOMER #2............	Jerry Frank
TECHNICIAN IN BOOTH...	Bobby Barber

IT AIN'T HAY

(UNIVERSAL–1943)
Directed by Erle C. Kenton
Produced by Alex Gottlieb
Screenplay by Allen Boretz and John Grant
Based on a Story by Damon Runyon
Director of Photography: Charles Van Enger, ASC
Songs by Harry Revel and Paul Francis Webster
Editor: Frank Gross
Running Time: 79 minutes

CAST

GROVER MOCKRIDGE .... Bud Abbott
WILBUR HOOLIHAN....... Lou Costello
KITTY MCGLOIN.......... Grace McDonald
GREGORY WARNER ...... Eugene Pallette
PRIVATE JOE COLLINS.... Leighton Noble
KING O'HARA............. Cecil Kellaway
PRINCESS O'HARA .... Patsy O'Connor
UMBRELLA SAM .... Shemp Howard
HARRY THE HORSE....... Eddie Quillan
CHAUNCEY THE EYE ..... Dave Hacker
SLICKER .... Richard Lane
COLONEL BRAINARD ..... Samuel S. Hinds
STILT-WALKER........... Harold De Garro
MUSICAL SPECIALTY ..... The Vagabonds
BIGHEARTED CHARLIE ... Andrew Tombes
MAJOR HARPER .... Pierre Watkin
BANKER.................. William Forrest
MAN AT MIKE .... Ralph Peters
REILLY.................... Wade Boteler
CLERK .... Bobby Watson
COP .... James Flavin
DRUNK .... Jack Norton
RADIO ANNOUNCER...... Tom Hanlon
SHORTY................... Harry Harvey
MAN IN MIKE ROOM ..... Herbert Vigran
GRAFTER .... Ed Foster
POLICEMAN............... Harry Strang
BOUNCERS................ Mike Mazurki
Sammy Stein
MANAGER .... Herbert Heyes
HACK DRIVER .... Barry Macollum

GOOD HUMOR MAN ...... Eddie Bruce
TOUT...................... Paul Dubov
S.P.C.A. DRIVER .... Charles Bennett
JOCKEY .... Rod Rogers
LITTLE GIRL .... Janet Ann Gallow
MATRON .... Kate Lawson
TICKET SELLER........... Frank Penny
ATTENDANT .... Fred Cordova
NEWSBOY .... Spec O'Donnell
CHILD...................... Stephen Gottlieb
THE STEP BROTHERS ..... Themselves

HIT THE ICE

(UNIVERSAL–1943)
Directed by Charles Lamont
Produced by Alex Gottlieb
Screenplay by Robert Lees, Frederic I. Rinaldo and John Grant
Original Story by True Boardman
Director of Photography: Charles Van Enger, ASC
Songs by Harry Revel and Paul Francis Webster
Musical Numbers Staged by Sammy Lee
Musical Director: Charles Previn
Skating Number Staged by Harry Losee
Editor: Frank Gross
Assistant Director: Howard Christie
Running Time: 81 minutes

CAST

FLASH FULTON .... Bud Abbott
TUBBY MCCOY........... Lou Costello
MARCIA MANNING ...... Ginny Simms
DR. BILL BURNS .... Patric Knowles
PEGGY OSBORNE .... Elyse Knox
BUSTER .... Joseph Sawyer
PHIL....................... Marc Lawrence
SILKY FELLOWSBY....... Sheldon Leonard
JOHNNY LONG........... Himself
SECOND CONDUCTOR .... Joseph Crehan
COP .... Edward Gargan
POLICE LIEUTENANT ..... Pat Flaherty
BIT COP .... Eddie Dunn

NURSE	Dorothy Vaughn
WIFE	Minerva Urecal
REDCAP	Mantan Moreland
PORTER ON TRAIN	Bobby Barber
FIRST CONDUCTOR	Wade Boteler
FIRE CHIEF	Ken Christy
MAN IN BED	Billy Wayne
WOMAN IN BED	Rebel Randall
SKATER	Cordelia Campbell
AMBULANCE DRIVER	Eddie Parker

IN SOCIETY

(UNIVERSAL–1944)
Directed by Jean Yarbrough
Produced by Edmund L. Hartmann
Screenplay by John Grant, Edmund L. Hartmann and Hal Fimberg
Additional Comedy Material for Abbott and Costello by Sid Fields
Original Story by Hugh Wedlock, Jr., and Howard Snyder
Director of Photography: Jerome Ash, ASC
Songs: Mann Curtis and Vic Mizzy
Musical Director: Edgar Fairchild
Musical Numbers Devised and Staged by George Dobbs
Film Editor: Philip Cahn
Assistant Director: Howard Christie
Dialogue Director: Carter DeHaven
Special Photography: John P. Fulton, ASC
Running Time: 75 minutes

CAST

EDDIE HARRINGTON ..... Bud Abbott
ALBERT MANSFIELD...... Lou Costello
ELSIE HAMMERDINGLE. . . Marion Hutton
PETER EVANS .... Kirby Grant
GLORIA WINTHROP....... Ann Gillis
PIPPS THE BUTLER........ Arthur Treacher
DREXEL................... Thomas Gomez
BARON SERGEI .... George Dolenz
COUNT ALEXIS............ Steven Geray
MRS. WINTHROP .... Margaret Irving
MARLOW................... Murray Leonard
MR. VAN CLEVE........... Thurston Hall
MRS. VAN CLEVE .... Nella Walker
PARKER................... William B. Davidson
BIT WOMAN............... Elvia Allman
BIT MAN .... Milt Bronson
DRUNK IN POOL .... Don Barclay
COP .... Edgar Dearing
WOMAN................... Ann Roberts
SECOND BUTLER.......... Ian Wolfe
POLICEMAN............... Charles Sherlock
SECOND BIT MAN......... Al Thompson

LUIGI .... Luis Alberni
FIRE CHIEF .... Tom Fadden

LOST IN A HAREM

(METRO-GOLDWYN-MAYER–1944)
Directed by Charles Riesner
Produced by George Haight
Screenplay by John Grant, Harry Crane and Harry Ruskin
Director of Photography: Lester White, ASC
Music Supervised by Johnny Green
Songs by Don Raye, Gene de Paul, Sammy Fain, Ralph Freed and Toots Camarata
Film Editor: George Hively
Running Time: 89 minutes

CAST

PETER JOHNSON .... Bud Abbott
HARVEY GARVEY .... Lou Costello
HAZEL MOON .... Marilyn Maxwell
PRINCE RAMO .... John Conte
NIMATIV .... Douglas Dumbrille
JIMMY DORSEY .... Himself
TEEMA .... Lottie Harrison
BOBO .... J. Lockard Martin
THE DERELICT .... Murray Leonard
CHIEF GHAMU .... Adia Kuznetzoff
CRYSTAL GAZER .... Milton Parsons
MR. ORMULU .... Ralph Sanford
CHASE GUARDS .... Bud Wolfe
Carey Loftin
POLICE CHIEF .... Harry Cording
NATIVE .... Eddie Abdo
NATIVE JAILOR .... Sammy Stein
JAILOR .... Duke York
BEAUTIFUL GIRL .... Katharine Booth
BEARDED VENDOR .... Frank Penny
FRUIT VENDOR .... Frank Scannell
NATIVE .... Nick Thompson
MAJORDOMO .... Tor Johnson
NATIVE LAUNDRY
WOMAN .... Jody Gilbert

GUARD.................... Tiny Newland
SENTRY .... Eddie Dunn
ZAIDA, MAID.............. Sondra Rogers
EXECUTIONER .... Dick Alexander
DRUNK .... Tom Herbert
NATIVES IN CAFE......... Heinie Conklin
Ernest Brenck
SLAVE GIRLS............. Toni LaRue
Frances Ramsden
Margaret Savage
Jan Bryant
Margaret Kelly
Elinor Troy
Symona Boniface
ACROBATIC ACT .... The Pinas

HERE COME THE CO-EDS

(UNIVERSAL–1945)
Directed by Jean Yarbrough
Produced by John Grant
Screenplay by Arthur T. Horman and John Grant
Based on a Story by Edmund L. Hartmann
Director of Photography: George Robinson, ASC
Songs by Jack Brooks and Edgar Fairchild
Special Camera Work by John P. Fulton
Film Editor: Arthur Hilton
Running Time: 88 minutes

CAST

SLATS .... Bud Abbott
OLIVER QUACKENBUSH .. Lou Costello
PATTY.................... Peggy Ryan
MOLLY .... Martha O'Driscoll
DIANE.................... June Vincent
JOHNSON .... Lon Chaney, Jr.
BENSON.................. Donald Cook
JONATHAN KIRKLAND ... Charles Dingle
NEARSIGHTED MAN ...... Richard Lane
HONEST DAN .... Joe Kirk
PHIL SPITALNY AND
HIS BAND .... Themselves

ANNOUNCER.............. Bill Stern
TIMEKEEPER.............. Anthony Warde
BERTHA.................... Dorothy Ford
TIGER MCGURK .... Sammy Stein
BASKETBALL COACH ..... Carl Knowles
AMAZON BASKETBALL
PLAYERS................ Martha Garotto
Naomi Stout
June Cuendet
Muriel Stetson
Marilyn Hoeck
Margaret Eversole
Lorna Peterson
MISS HOLFORD .... Ruth Lee
DIAMOND.................. Don Costello
WOMAN.................... Rebel Randall
WOMAN.................... Maxine Gates
WOMAN.................... Dorothy Granger
WOMAN IN TRAILER...... Marie Osborn
RING ANNOUNCER .... Milt Bronson

THE NAUGHTY NINETIES

(UNIVERSAL–1945)
Directed by Jean Yarbrough
Produced by Edmund L. Hartmann and John Grant
Screenplay by Edmund L. Hartmann, John Grant, Edmund Joseph and Hal Fimberg
Additional Comedy Sequences by Felix Adler

Director of Photography: George Robinson, ASC
Musical Director: Edgar Fairchild
Songs by Edgar Fairchild and Jack Brooks
Assistant Director: Howard Christie
Film Editor: Arthur Hilton
Running Time: 76 minutes

CAST

DEXTER BROADHURST ... Bud Abbott
SEBASTIAN DINWIDDIE ... Lou Costello
CRAWFORD .... Alan Curtis

BONITA	Rita Johnson
CAPTAIN SAM	Henry Travers
CAROLINE	Lois Collier
BAILEY	Joe Sawyer
CROUPIER	Joe Kirk
DRUNK	Jack Norton
MATT	Sam McDaniel
MINSTREL	Billy Green
CROUPIERS	Bud Wolfe
	Henry Russell
	Bud O'Connor
	Jack Worth
EFFIE	Lillian Yarbo
CITIZEN	Emmet Vogan
GAMBLER	Milt Bronson
SHERIFF	John Hamilton
BAXTER	Ed Gargan
WAITER	Jack Chefe

ABBOTT AND COSTELLO IN HOLLYWOOD

(METRO-GOLDWYN-MAYER–1945)
Directed by S. Sylvan Simon
Produced by Martin A. Gosch
Screenplay by Nat Perrin and Lou Breslow
Original Story by Nat Perrin and Martin A. Gosch
Director of Photography: Charles Schoenbaum, ASC
Songs by Ralph Blane and Hugh Martin
Dances Directed by Charles Walters
Film Editor: Ben Lewis
Running Time: 84 minutes

CAST

BUZZ KURTIS .... Bud Abbott
ABERCROMBIE............ Lou Costello
CLAIRE WARREN .... Frances Rafferty
JEFF PARKER .... Robert Stanton
RUTHIE .... Jean Porter
NORMAN ROYCE.......... Warner Anderson
RAGS RAGLAND .... Himself
LUCILLE BALL .... Herself
PRESTON FOSTER......... Himself
ROBERT Z. LEONARD ..... Himself
BUTCH JENKINS .... Himself
KLONDIKE PETE .... Mike Mazurki
GREGORY LEMAISE....... Carleton G. Young
DENNIS KAVANAUGH .... Donald MacBride
2ND STUDIO COP .... Robert Emmet O'Connor
DIRECTOR .... Arthur Space
LOUISE..................... Katharine Booth
1ST STUDIO COP .... Edgar Dearing
QUARTETTE................ The Lyttle Sisters
MISS MILBANE............ Marion Martin
CHILD STAR .... Dean Stockwell
KAVANAUGH'S
ASSISTANT .... Bill Phillips
MR. BURVIS .... Chester Clute
SECRETARY .... Marie Blake
TAXI DRIVER .... Harry Tyler
ASSISTANT DIRECTOR .... Skeets Noyes
PROP MAN .... Dick Alexander
ORCHESTRA LEADER .... Dick Winslow
CIGARETTE GIRL .... Jane Hale
WAITER .... Frank Scannell

LITTLE GIANT

(UNIVERSAL–1946)
Directed by William A. Seiter
Produced by Joe Gershenson
Screenplay by Walter DeLeon
Original Story by Paul Jarrico and Richard Collins
Music Score and Direction by Edgar Fairchild
Director of Photography: Charles Van Enger, ASC
Film Editor: Fred R. Feitshans
Running Time: 91 minutes

CAST

JOHN MORRISON &
TOM CHANDLER........ Bud Abbott
BENNY MILLER .... Lou Costello
RUBY.................... Brenda Joyce
HAZEL .... Jacqueline De Wit
UNCLE CLARENCE........ George Cleveland
MARTHA HILL .... Elena Verdugo
MOM MILLER............ Mary Gordon
PRESIDENT VAN LOON ... Pierre Watkins
PULLMAN CONDUCTOR .. Donald MacBride
GUS .... Victor Kilian
MRS. HENDERSON .... Margaret Dumont
O'BRIEN................. George Chandler
SECRETARY .... Beatrice Gray
POLICEMAN.............. Ed Gargan
JIM...................... Ralph Peters
BARTENDER .... Bert Roach
HERCULES .... George Holmes
DRIVER .... Eddie Waller
MAN IN LOWER BERTH... Ralph Dunn
WIFE.................... Dorothy Christy
TAILOR .... Chester Conklin
FARMER PERKINS .... William "Red" Donahue

THE TIME OF THEIR LIVES

(UNIVERSAL–1946)
Directed by Charles Barton
Produced by Val Burton
Original Screenplay by Val Burton, Walter DeLeon and Bradford Ropes
Additional Dialogue for Abbott and Costello by John Grant
Director of Photography: Charles Van Enger, ASC
Running Time: 82 minutes

CAST

CUTHBERT AND DOCTOR GREENWAY	Bud Abbott
HORATIO PRIM	Lou Costello
MELODY ALLEN	Marjorie Reynolds
MILDRED	Binnie Barnes
SHELDON GAGE	John Shelton
TOM DANBURY	Jess Barker
EMILY	Gale Sondergaard
MAJOR PUTNAM	Robert Barrat
LIEUTENANT MASON	Donald MacBride
NORA	Anne Gillis
JUNE PRESCOTT	Lynne Baggett
CONNERS	William Hall
SERGEANT MAKEPEACE	Rex Lease
CURATOR	Selmer Jackson
LEIGH	Vernon Downing
BESSIE	Marjorie Eaton
GUARD	Wheaton Chambers
DANDIES	Myron Healy John Crawford

BUCK PRIVATES COME HOME

(UNIVERSAL–1947)
Directed by Charles Barton
Produced by Robert Arthur
Screenplay by John Grant, Frederic I. Rinaldo and Robert Lees
Based on a Story by Richard MacCauley and Bradford Ropes
Director of Photography: Charles Van Enger, ASC
Music by Walter Schumann

Art Direction by Bernard Herzbrun and Frank A. Richards
Special Photography by David S. Horsley, ASC
Film Editor: Edward Curtiss
Running Time: 77 minutes

CAST

CORPORAL SLICKER SMITH . . . . Bud Abbott
HERBIE BROWN . . . . Lou Costello
BILL GREGORY . . . . Tom Brown
SYLVIA HUNTER . . . . Joan Fulton (Joan Shawlee)
SERGEANT COLLINS . . . . . . Nat Pendleton
YVONNE LEBRU (EVEY) . . . Beverly Simmons
MR. ROBERTS . . . . Don Beddoe
CAPTAIN . . . . Don Porter
POLICE CAPTAIN . . . . Donald MacBride
FIRST LIEUTENANT . . . . Lane Watson
SECOND LIEUTENANT . . . . William Ching
STEVE . . . . Peter Thompson
CAL . . . . George Beban, Jr.
WHITEY . . . . Jimmie Dodd
HANK . . . . Lennie Bremen
MURPHY . . . . Al Murphy
STAN . . . . Bob Wilke
HUSBAND . . . . William Haade
WIFE . . . . Janna deLoos
NEW YORK COP . . . . Buddy Roosevelt
SECOND NEW YORK COP . Chuck Hamilton
YOUNG GIRL . . . . Patricia Alphin
REAL ESTATE MAN . . . . Joe Kirk
MR. QUINCE . . . . Charles Trowbridge
APPLEBY . . . . Russell Hicks
ED . . . . Ralph Dunn
DREW . . . . John Sheenan
QUENTIN . . . . Cliff Clark
DUPREZ . . . . Jean Del Val
TIE BUYER . . . . Frank Marlowe
FRENCH MATRON . . . . Ottola Nesmith
MULRONEY . . . . Eddie Dunn
MEDICS . . . . Harlan Warde
Lyle Lattel
Myron Healy
BANK GUARD . . . . James Farley
CHAUFFEUR . . . . Rex Lease

TIE BUYER .... Ernie Adams
ANNOUNCER.............. Milburn Stone
COMMENTATOR .... Knox Manning

THE WISTFUL WIDOW OF WAGON GAP

(UNIVERSAL–1947)
Directed by Charles Barton
Produced by Robert Arthur
Screenplay by Robert Lees, Frederic I. Rinaldo and John Grant
Based on a Story by D. D. Beauchamp and William Bowers
Director of Photography: Charles Van Enger, ASC
Associate Producer: Sebastian Cristillo
Dialogue Director: Norman Abbott
Running Time: 78 minutes

CAST

DUKE EGAN .... Bud Abbott
CHESTER WOOLEY........ Lou Costello
WIDOW HAWKINS......... Marjorie Main
JUANITA HAWKINS .... Audrey Young
JUDGE BENBOW .... George Cleveland
JAKE FRAME.............. Gordon Jones
JIM SIMPSON.............. William Ching
PHIL...................... Peter Thompson
UNDERTAKER .... Olin Howlin
MATT HAWKINS .... Bill Clauson
BILLY HAWKINS .... Billy O'Leary
SARAH HAWKINS .... Pamela Wells
JEFFERSON HAWKINS .... Jimmie Bates
LINCOLN HAWKINS....... Paul Dunn
SALLY HAWKINS.......... Diane Florentine
HANK .... Rex Lease
LEFTY.................... Glenn Strange
DRUNK .... Dewey Robinson
LEM...................... Edmund Cobb
SQUINT .... Wade Crosby
BARTENDER .... Murray Leonard
OLD CODGER .... Emmett Lynn
HOSTESS .... Iris Adrian
SHOTGUN RIDER .... Lee Lasses White
COWPUNCHER........... George Lewis

COWBOY .... Charles King
TOUGH MINER............ Jack Shutta
CARD DEALER .... Harry Evans
BIG MINER................ Mickey Simpson
COWBOYS .... Frank Marlo
Ethan Laidlaw

THE NOOSE HANGS HIGH

(EAGLE-LION–1948)
Produced and Directed by Charles Barton
Screenplay by John Grant and Howard Harris
Adapted from a Screenplay by Charles Grayson and Arthur T. Horman
Based on a Story by Daniel Taradash, Julian Blaustein and Bernard Fins
Director of Photography: Charles Van Enger, ASC
Running Time: 77 minutes

CAST

TED HIGGINS .... Bud Abbott
TOMMY HINCHCLIFFE.... Lou Costello
CAROL SCOTT............. Cathy Downs
MIKE CRAIG .... Joseph Calleia
JULIUS CAESAR MCBRIDE. Leon Errol
CHUCK.................... Mike Mazurki
JOE....................... Jack Overman
PSYCHIATRIST .... Fritz Feld
ELEVATOR GIRL .... Vera Martin
GANGSTERS............... Joe Kirk
Matt Willis
STEWART .... Ben Weldon
MESSENGERS .... Jimmy Dodd
Ben Hall
MAID...................... Ellen Corby
MISS VAN BUREN .... Isabel Randolph
POSTMAN .... Frank O'Connor
PATIENT .... Bess Flowers
CRAZY DENTIST .... Murray Leonard
TOUGH DRIVER........... Pat Flaherty
BIT WOMAN............... Elvia Allman
WOMAN ON STREET ...... Lois Austin

MAN WITH COAT .... Herb Vigran
TRAFFIC COP .... James Flavin
HUSKY WOMAN........... Minerva Urecal
MANAGER .... Russell Hicks
HEADWAITER............. Arno Frey
JEWELRY PROP .... Paul Maxey
WORKMAN................ Lyle Latell

ABBOTT AND COSTELLO MEET FRANKENSTEIN

(UNIVERSAL–1948)
Directed by Charles Barton
Produced by Robert Arthur
Original Screenplay by Frederic I. Rinaldo, Robert Lees and John Grant
Director of Photography: Charles Van Enger, ASC
Music by Frank Skinner
Special Photography by David S. Horsley, ASC
Film Editor: Frank Gross
Make-up: Bud Westmore
Running Time: 83 minutes

CAST

CHICK YOUNG............ Bud Abbott
WILBUR GREY .... Lou Costello
LAWRENCE TALBOT ...... Lon Chaney, Jr.
DRACULA.................. Bela Lugosi
THE MONSTER............ Glenn Strange
SANDRA MORNAY .... Lenore Aubert
JOAN RAYMOND.......... Jane Randolph
MR. MCDOUGAL.......... Frank Ferguson
DOCTOR STEVENS .... Charles Bradstreet
MR. HARRIS............... Howard Negley
MAN .... Joe Kirk
MAN IN ARMOR .... Clarence Straight
PHOTOGRAPHER.......... Harry Brown
WOMAN AT BAGGAGE
COUNTER .... Helen Spring
MAN .... George Barton
MAN .... Carl Sklover
SERGEANT .... Paul Stader
MAN .... Joe Walls

JEEPERS!
The CREEPERS are after BUD & LOU!!
BUD ABBOTT & LOU COSTELLO meet FRANKENSTEIN
The Wolfman PLAYED BY LON CHANEY
Dracula PLAYED BY BELA LUGOSI
The Monster PLAYED BY GLENN STRANGE
LENORE AUBERT · JANE RANDOLPH

WAITER .... Bobby Barber
VOICE OF INVISIBLE MAN . Vincent Price

MEXICAN HAYRIDE

(UNIVERSAL–1948)
Directed by Charles Barton
Produced by Robert Arthur
Screenplay by Oscar Brodney and John Grant
Based on the Musical Play by Herbert and Dorothy Fields and Cole Porter
Director of Photography: Charles Van Enger, ASC
Running Time: 77 minutes

CAST

HARRY LAMBERT .... Bud Abbott
JOE BASCOM/HUMPHREY FISH..................... Lou Costello
MONTANA .... Virginia Grey
DAGMAR.................. Luba Malina
DAVID WINTHROP .... John Hubbard
SENOR MARTINEZ .... Pedro de Cordoba
PROFESSOR GANZMEYER. Fritz Feld
ED MASON .... Tom Powers
TIM WILLIAMS .... Pat Costello
GUS ADAMSON .... Frank Fenton
REPORTER .... Sid Fields
MARIACHI LEADER .... Chris Pin Martin
TRIO .... Flores Brothers Trio
INDIAN WOMAN .... Argentina Brunetti
GIRLS .... Mary Brewer
Marjorie L. Carver
Lucille Casey
Toni Castle
Lorraine Crawford
MR. CLARKE .... Eddie Kane
MAGICIAN .... Ben Chavez
PROPRIETOR .... Pedro Regas
MR. LEWIS .... Charles Miller
BUSINESSMAN .... Harry Brown
SECOND BUSINESSMAN ... Joe Kirk
TICKET SELLER .... Julian Rivero

BLANKET WEAVER........ Tony Roux
BASKET WEAVER .... Roque Ybarra
ARTIST.................... Joe Dominguez
SIVERSMITH DEALER ..... Felipe Turich
MAN .... Alex Montoya
WOMAN.................... Julia Montoya
PHOTOGRAPHER.......... George Mendoza
MEXICAN BOY .... Robert Elias
MEXICAN CHILD.......... Rose Marie Lopez
BELLBOY.................. Earl Spainard
ARTIST'S MODEL.......... Suzanne Ridgway
HEADWAITER .... Cosmo Sardo

ABBOTT AND COSTELLO MEET THE KILLER, BORIS KARLOFF

(UNIVERSAL–1949)
Directed by Charles Barton
Produced by Robert Arthur
Screenplay by Hugh Wedlock, Jr., Howard Snyder and John Grant
Original Story by Hugh Wedlock, Jr., and Howard Snyder
Director of Photography: Charles Van Enger, ASC
Music by Milton Schwarzwald
Special Effects by David S. Horsley
Make-up by Bud Westmore
Film Editor: Edward Curtiss
Running Time: 94 minutes

CAST

CASEY EDWARDS .... Bud Abbott
FREDDIE PHILLIPS........ Lou Costello
SWAMI TALPUR........... Boris Karloff
ANGELA GORDON .... Lenore Aubert
JEFF WILSON .... Gar Moore
BETTY CRANDALL .... Donna Martell
MELTON .... Alan Mowbray
INSPECTOR WELLMAN.... James Flavin
T. HANLEY BROOKS ...... Roland Winters
AMOS STRICKLAND....... Nicholas Joy
SERGEANT STONE .... Mikel Conrad
GREGORY MILFORD...... Morgan Farley

MRS. HARGREAVE .... Victoria Horne
ABERNATHY .... Percy Helton
MRS. GRIMSBY............ Claire Du Brey
LAWRENCE CRANDALL... Harry Hayden
MIKE RELIA............... Vincent Renno
MANICURIST.............. Patricia Hall
JOE.......................... Murray Alper
MAID........................ Marjorie Bennett
MEDICAL EXAMINER ..... Harry Brown
WOMAN.................... Beatrice Gray
1ST REPORTER............ Billy Snyder
2ND REPORTER .... Eddie Coke
BOZZO .... Frankie Van
BARBER..................... Jack Chefe
PHOTOGRAPHER.......... Arthur Hecht
BOOTBLACK .... Ed Randolph
BELLBOY.................. Phil Shepard

AFRICA SCREAMS

(UNITED ARTISTS–1949)
A Huntington Hartford Production
Directed by Charles Barton
Produced by Edward Nassour
Written by Earl Baldwin
Director of Photography: Charles Van Enger, ASC
Special Effects by Carl Lee
Film Editor: Frank Gross
Assistant Director: Joe Kenny
Dialogue Director: Norman Abbott
Running Time: 79 minutes

CAST

BUZZ JOHNSON .... Bud Abbott
STANLEY LIVINGSTON.... Lou Costello
DIANA EMERSON .... Hillary Brooke
BOOTS....................... Max Baer
GRAPPLER .... Buddy Baer
GUNNER .... Shemp Howard
HARRY...................... Joe Besser
CLYDE BEATTY .... Himself
FRANK BUCK .... Himself

BIT MAN .... Bobby Barber

ABBOTT AND COSTELLO IN THE FOREIGN LEGION

(UNIVERSAL–1950)
Directed by Charles Lamont
Produced by Robert Arthur
Screenplay by John Grant, Martin Ragaway and Leonard Stern
From a Story by D. D. Beauchamp
Director of Photography: George Robinson, ASC
Film Editor: Edward Curtiss
Running Time: 79 minutes

CAST

JONESY .... Bud Abbott
LOU HOTCHKISS .... Lou Costello
NICOLE .... Patricia Medina
AXMANN .... Walter Slezak
HAMUD EL KHALID ...... Douglas Dumbrille
HASSAM .... Leon Belasco
FRANKIE .... Marc Lawrence
ABOU BEN .... Tor Johnson
ABDULLAH .... Wee Willie Davis
BERTRAM .... Sam Menacker
COMMANDANT .... Fred Nurney
IBN .... Paul Fierro
IBRIM .... Henry Corden
ALI AMI .... Jack Raymond
THUGS .... Jack Shutta
Ernesto Morelli
Chuck Hamilton
JOSEF .... Dan Seymour
LIEUTENANT .... Alberto Morin
SALEEM .... Guy Beach
PROPRIETOR .... Ted Hecht
REFEREE .... Mahmud Shaikhaly
ORDERLY .... Buddy Roosevelt
ARAB GIRL .... Charmienne Harker
NEWSBOY .... David Gorcey
BIT MAN .... Bobby Barber

ABBOTT AND COSTELLO MEET THE INVISIBLE MAN

(UNIVERSAL–1951)
Directed by Charles Lamont
Produced by Howard Christie
Screenplay by Robert Lees, Frederic I. Rinaldo and John Grant
From a Story by Hugh Wedlock, Jr., and Howard Snyder
Suggested by H. G. Wells' *The Invisible Man*
Director of Photography: George Robinson, ASC
Music by Joseph Gershenson
Film Editor: Virgil Vogel
Running Time: 82 minutes

CAST

BUD ALEXANDER . . . . Bud Abbott
LOU FRANCIS . . . . Lou Costello
HELEN GRAY . . . . Nancy Guild
BOOTS MARSDEN . . . . Adele Jergens
MORGAN . . . . Sheldon Leonard
DETECTIVE ROBERTS . . . . . William Frawley
DOCTOR PHILIP GRAY . . . . Gavin Muir
TOMMY NELSON . . . . Arthur Franz
RADIO ANNOUNCER . . . . . . Sam Balter
WAITER . . . . Sid Saylor
SNEAKY . . . . Bobby Barber
ROONEY . . . . Billy Wayne
ROCKY HANLON . . . . John Day
TORPEDO . . . . George J. Lewis
REFEREE . . . . Frankie Van
LOU'S HANDLER . . . . Carl Sklover
ROCKY'S HANDLER . . . . Charles Perry
DOCTOR TURNER . . . . Paul Maxey
MILT . . . . Ed Gargan
STILLWELL . . . . Herbert Vigran
MOTORCYCLE COP . . . . Ralph Dunn
BARTENDER . . . . Herold Goodwin
BALD-HEADED MAN . . . . . . Richard Bartell
COP . . . . Perc Launders
NURSE . . . . Edith Sheets
RING ANNOUNCER . . . . Milt Bronson

COMIN' ROUND THE MOUNTAIN

(UNIVERSAL–1951)
Directed by Charles Lamont
Produced by Howard Christie
Screenplay by Robert Lees and Frederic I. Rinaldo
Additional Dialogue by John Grant
Director of Photography: George Robinson, ASC
Film Editor: Edward Curtiss
Running Time: 77 minutes

CAST

AL	Bud Abbott
WILBERT	Lou Costello
DOROTHY MCCOY	Dorothy Shay
CLARK WINFIELD	Kirby Grant
KALEM	Joe Sawyer
AUNT HUDDY	Margaret Hamilton
GRANNY	Ida Moore
DEVIL DAN WINFIELD	Glenn Strange
JUDGE	Russell Simpson
MATT	Shaye Cogan
LUKE	Robert Easton
UNCLE CLEM	Guy Wilkerson
JASPER WINFIELD	Virgil "Slats" Taylor
ZEKE	O. Z. Whitehead
ZEB	Norman Leavitt
GANGSTERS IN NIGHTCLUB	Jack Kruschen
	Peter Mamakos
	Barry Brooks
MAN	Joe Kirk
OLD MOUNTAIN MAN	William Fawcett
SECOND MOUNTAIN MAN	Herold Goodwin

JACK AND THE BEANSTALK

(Warner Brothers–1952)
Directed by Jean Yarbrough
Produced by Alex Gottlieb
Screenplay by Nat Curtis
From a Story by Pat Costello
Music Composed and Conducted by Heinz Roemheld
Film Editor: Otto Lovering
Running Time: 78 minutes; color

CAST

DINKLEPUSS .... Bud Abbott
JACK .... Lou Costello
SERGEANT RILEY/GIANT . Buddy Baer
POLLY..................... Dorothy Ford
MOTHER .... Barbara Brown
DONALD .... David Stollery
THE KING................. William Farnum
ELOISE LARKIN/
PRINCESS .... Shaye Cogan
ARTHUR ROYAL/PRINCE . James Alexander
VILLAGER.................. Joe Kirk
–and–
Johnny Conrad and Dancers

ABBOTT AND COSTELLO MEET CAPTAIN KIDD

(WARNER BROTHERS–1952)
Directed by Charles Lamont
Produced by Alex Gottlieb
Screenplay by Howard Dimsdale and John Grant
Director of Photography: Stanley Cortez, ASC
Songs by Bob Russell and Lester Lee
Musical Score by Raoul Kraushaar
Film Editor: Edward Mann
Running Time: 70 minutes; color

CAST

ROCKY STONEBRIDGE.... Bud Abbott
OLIVER "PUDDIN' HEAD"
JOHNSON .... Lou Costello

CAPTAIN KIDD	Charles Laughton
CAPTAIN BONNEY	Hillary Brooke
LADY JANE	Fran Warren
BRUCE MARTINGALE	Bill Shirley
MORGAN	Leif Erickson
PIRATES	Sid Saylor
	Frank Yaconelli
	Rex Lease
BIT MAN	Bobby Barber

LOST IN ALASKA

(UNIVERSAL–1952)
Directed by Jean Yarbrough
Produced by Howard Christie
Screenplay by Martin Ragaway and Leonard Stern.
From a Story by Elwood Ullman
Director of Photography: George Robinson, ASC
Music by Joseph Gershenson
Film Editor: Leonard Weiner
Running Time: 76 minutes

CAST

TOM WATSON	Bud Abbott
GEORGE BELL	Lou Costello
ROSETTE	Mitzi Green
NUGGET JOE MCDERMOTT	Tom Ewell
JAKE STILLMAN	Bruce Cabot
SHERMAN	Emory Parnell
HENCHMAN	Jack Ingram
OLD-TIMER	Rex Lease
HENCHMAN	Joe Kirk
MRS. MCGILLICUDDY	Minerva Urecal
HIGGINS	Howard Negley
WOMAN IN WINDOW	Maudie Pricket
CROUPIER	Billy Wayne
CAPTAIN CHISHOLM	Paul Newlan
WILLIE	Michael Ross
ESKIMO WOMAN	Julia Montoya
NANOOK	Iron Eyes Cody
BEARDED PROSPECTOR	Fred Aldrich

MULTOLAH .... Donald Kerr
BIT .... George Barton
BIT CHEF.................. Bobby Barber

ABBOTT AND COSTELLO GO TO MARS

(UNIVERSAL–1953)
Directed by Charles Lamont
Produced by Howard Christie
Screenplay by D. D. Beauchamp and John Grant
Original Story by Howard Christie and D. D. Beauchamp
Director of Photography: Clifford Stine, ASC
Special Photography by David S. Horsley
Music Directed by Joseph Gershenson
Film Editor: Russell Schoengarth
Running Time: 77 minutes

CAST

LESTER.................... Bud Abbott
ORVILLE .... Lou Costello
DOCTOR WILSON .... Robert Paige
ALLURA.................... Mari Blanchard
JANIE .... Martha Hyer
MUGSY..................... Horace McMahon
HARRY .... Jack Kruschen
GUARD..................... Anita Ekberg
GUARD..................... Jackie Loughery (Miss USA)
CAPTAIN .... Jean Willes
DOCTOR ORVILLA .... Joe Kirk
DOCTOR COLEMAN .... Herold Goodwin
DOCTOR NEDRING .... Hal Forrest
DOCTOR HOLTZ .... Jack Tesler
FIRST POLICEMAN
IN BANK .... James Flavin
MAN AT FOUNTAIN....... Sid Saylor
2ND POLICEMAN
IN BANK .... Russ Conway
TRAFFIC COP .... Paul Newlan
CASHIER .... Tim Graham
POLICE OFFICER.......... Ken Christy
FRENCH GIRL............. Grace Lenard
DRUNK .... Billy Newell

FRENCH WAITER .... Harry Lang
ANNOUNCER.............. Milt Bronson
OBSERVER .... Robert Forrest
PORTER .... Dudley Dickerson
POLICE SERGEANT........ Rex Lease
BARTENDER .... Frank Marlowe
BIT MAN .... Bobby Barber
VENUSIAN
HANDMAIDENS .... Miss Universe Contestants

ABBOTT AND COSTELLO MEET DR. JEKYLL AND MR. HYDE

(UNIVERSAL–1954)
Directed by Charles Lamont
Produced by Howard Christie
Screenplay by Lee Loeb and John Grant
Original Story by Sid Fields and Grant Garrett
From the novel *Dr. Jekyll and Mr. Hyde,* by Robert Louis Stevenson
Director of Photography: George Robinson, ASC
Musical Director: Joseph Gershenson
Special Effects: David S. Horsley
Make-up by Bud Westmore
Dialogue Director: Milt Bronson
Film Editor: Russell Schoengarth
Running Time: 76 minutes

CAST

SLIM .... Bud Abbott
TUBBY .... Lou Costello
JEKYLL AND HYDE .... Boris Karloff
BRUCE ADAMS............. Craig Stevens
VICKY EDWARDS .... Helen Westcott
INSPECTOR................ Reginald Denny
BATLEY .... John Dierkes
CANCAN DANCER......... Patti McKaye
CANCAN DANCER......... Lucille Lamarr
JAVANESE.................. Carmen de Lavallade
JAVANESE ACTOR......... Henry Corden
MILITANT WOMAN .... Marjorie Bennett
ROUGH CHARACTER ..... Harry Cording

BARTENDER .... Arthur Gould-Porter
DRUNKS IN PUB .... Clyde Cook
John Rogers
VICTIM...................... Herbert Deans
WOMAN ON BIKE .... Judith Brian
MAN ON BIKE............. Gil Perkins
NURSEMAID .... Hilda Plowright
JAILER .... Keith Hitchcock
CHIMNEY SWEEP .... Donald Kerr
BOBBIES.................... Clive Morgan
Tony Marshe
Michael Hadlow

ABBOTT AND COSTELLO MEET THE KEYSTONE COPS

(UNIVERSAL–1955)
Directed by Charles Lamont
Produced by Howard Christie
Screenplay by John Grant
From a Story by Lee Loeb
Music by Joseph Gershenson
Director of Photography: Reggie Lanning, ASC
Film Editor: Edward Curtiss
Running Time: 79 minutes

CAST

HARRY PIERCE............ Bud Abbott
WILLIE PIPER .... Lou Costello
JOSEPH GORMAN .... Fred Clark
LEOTA VAN CLEEF........ Lynn Bari
HINDS...................... Maxie Rosenbloom
MR. SNAVELY .... Frank Wilcox
CAMERAMAN .... Herold Goodwin
MACK SENNETT .... Himself
OLD WAGON DRIVER..... Roscoe Ates
JASON...................... Paul Dubov
THE HUNTER .... Joe Besser
PIANO PLAYER............ Harry Tyler
SECOND BRAKEMAN...... Henry Kulky
POLICEMAN................ Joe Devlin
TRAMP .... William Haade
BURGLAR .... Jack Daly

OFFICER .... Byron Keith
PILOT .... Houseley Stevens
STUDIO COP .... Murray Leonard
STOUT WOMAN .... Marjorie Bennett
WATERMELON PEDDLER . Charles Dorety
PROJECTIONIST .... Donald Kerr
COPS .... Heinie Conklin
Forrest Burns
Don House
1ST BRAKEMAN .... Jack Stoney
CASHIER IN THEATER .... Carole Costello
AD LIB .... Hank Mann

ABBOTT AND COSTELLO MEET THE MUMMY

(UNIVERSAL—1955)
Directed by Charles Lamont
Produced by Howard Christie
Screenplay by John Grant
Story by Lee Loeb
Director of Photography: George Robinson, ASC
Music by Joseph Gershenson
Film Editor: Russell Schoengarth
Running Time: 79 minutes

CAST

BUD .... Bud Abbott
LOU .... Lou Costello
MADAME RONTRU .... Marie Windsor
CHARLIE .... Michael Ansara
JOSEF .... Dan Seymour
DOCTOR GUSTAV
ZOOMER .... Kurt Katch
HETSUT .... Richard Karlan
SEMU .... Richard Deacon
IBEN .... Mel Welles
VOCALIST .... Peggy King
DANCE TROUPE........... Mazzone-Abbott Dancers
DANCE TROUPE........... The Chandra-Kaly and
Hi Dancers
HABID....................... George Khoury
KLARIS (THE MUMMY) ... Eddie Parker

WAITER .... Jan Arvan
ANZI .... Ted Hecht
DOCTOR AZZUI .... Michael Vallon
POLICEMEN .... Kem Dibbs
Mitchell Kowal
Ken Alton
BLOND GIRL .... Lee Sharon
NATIVE .... Hank Mann
NEWSPAPERMAN.......... Donald Kerr

DANCE WITH ME, HENRY

(UNITED ARTISTS–1956)
Directed by Charles Barton
Produced by Bob Goldstein
Screenplay by Devery Freeman
Original Story by William Kozlenko and Leslie Kardos
Music by Paul Dunlap
Film Editor: Robert Golden
Script Supervisor: Eleanor Donahue
Running Time: 79 minutes

CAST

BUD FLICK................ Bud Abbott
LOU HENRY.............. Lou Costello
SHELLEY .... Gigi Perreau
DUFFER.................... Rusty Hamer
MISS MAYBERRY......... Mary Wickes
BIG FRANK .... Ted de Corsia
ERNIE...................... Ron Hargrave
BOOTSIE .... Sherry Alberoni
FATHER MULLAHY ...... Frank Wilcox
MUSHIE .... Richard Reeves
DUTCH..................... Paul Sorenson
PROCTOR .... Robert Shayne
KNUCKS .... John Cliff
MICKEY.................... Phil Garris
DRAKE..................... Walter Reed
GARVEY .... Eddie Marr
SAVOLDI .... David McMahon
MCKAY .... Gil Rankin
PORTER.................... Rod Williams

Lou Costello made the following film without Bud Abbott:

THE THIRTY FOOT BRIDE OF CANDY ROCK

(COLUMBIA–1961)
Directed by Sidney Miller
Executive Producer: Edward Sherman
Produced by Lewis J. Rachmil
Screenplay by Rowland Barber and Arthur Ross
Story by Lawrence L. Goldman
Director of Photography: Frank G. Carson
Running Time: 75 minutes

CAST

ARTIE PINSETTER......... Lou Costello
EMMY LOU RAVEN .... Dorothy Provine
RAVEN .... Gale Gordon
MAGRUDER............... Jimmy Conlin
STANDARD BATES .... Charles Lane
FIRST GENERAL .... Robert Burton
PENTAGON GENERAL .... Will Wright
SERGEANT .... Lenny Kent
AUNT MAY................ Ruth Perrott
BILL BURTON .... Peter Leeds
BOOSTERS................. Bobby Barber
Joey Faye
Doodles Weaver
Jack Rice
Russell Trent
Joe Greene
BANK MANAGER.......... Robert Nichols
JACKIE DELANEY .... Veola Vonn

THE WORLD OF ABBOTT AND COSTELLO

(UNIVERSAL–1965)
Produced by Max J. Rosenberg and Milton Subotsky
Narration Written by Gene Wood
Narrated by Jack E. Leonard
Editorial Direction by Sidney Meyer
Music Supervision by Joseph Gershenson
Running Time: 75 minutes

This compilation film contained footage from the following Abbott and Costello movies: BUCK PRIVATES, IN THE NAVY, RIDE 'EM COWBOY, WHO DONE IT?, HIT THE ICE, IN SOCIETY, THE NAUGHTY NINETIES, LITTLE GIANT, BUCK PRIVATES COME HOME, THE WISTFUL WIDOW OF WAGON GAP, ABBOTT AND COSTELLO MEET FRANKENSTEIN, MEXICAN HAYRIDE, ABBOTT AND COSTELLO IN THE FOREIGN LEGION, COMIN' ROUND THE MOUNTAIN, LOST IN ALASKA, ABBOTT AND COSTELLO GO TO MARS, ABBOTT AND COSTELLO MEET THE KEYSTONE KOPS, ABBOTT AND COSTELLO MEET THE MUMMY.

Abbott and Costello appeared in the following short subjects:

PICTURE PEOPLE

(RKO–1941)

An eight-minute short featuring several Hollywood celebrities, including Ray Bolger, Abbott and Costello and Rita Hayworth.

SCREEN SNAPSHOTS

(COLUMBIA–1941)

Abbott and Costello appeared in this one-reeler with other Hollywood stars shown entertaining at army bases in the United States. Burns and Allen, Rita Hayworth were among the other stars.

MEET THE PEOPLE

(REPUBLIC–1941)

Judy Garland, Mickey Rooney, Abbott and Costello, Milton Berle and others are shown at a Los Angeles newspaper benefit in this one-reeler.

NEWS OF THE DAY

(METRO-GOLDWYN-MAYER–1952)

The team appeared with Charles Laughton in this newsreel to promote the sale of U.S. bonds.

"THE ABBOTT AND COSTELLO SHOW" SERIES SYNOPSES AND CASTS

First Season

(All of the following episodes were directed by Jean Yarbrough. Scripts for the first season were written by Eddie Forman and Sid Fields. Clyde Bruckman, Felix Adler, and Sid Fields contributed the scripts for the second season.)

1. THE DRUGSTORE–*Hillary Brooke, Gordon Jones, Sid Fields, Joe Kirk, Joe Besser, Iris Adrian, Elvia Allman*

Bud and Lou get jobs in Fields' drugstore and with typical Abbott and Costello brand of service, they all but destroy the store.

2. THE DENTIST OFFICE–*Hillary Brooke, Gordon Jones, Sid Fields, Joe Kirk, Virginia Christine, Ray Walker, Vera Marsh, Bobby Barber*

Lou has a giant-size toothache and Bud takes him to a nearsighted dentist. However, the operation is unsuccessful and Lou tries to get arrested so he can get free treatment. Instead he lands up preventing a bank robbery.

3. JAIL–*Hillary Brooke, Gordon Jones, Sid Fields, Joe Kirk, Elvia Allman, Stanley Andrews*

Lou is arrested for shooting a hole into a pail belonging to his next-door neighbor, Mrs. Crumbcake. The case goes to court and Lou discovers that Mrs. Crumbcake is the judge. Lou is thrown into jail and his cellmate shows homicidal tendencies at the mere mention of the words "Niagara Falls."

4. THE VACATION–*Hillary Brooke, Gordon Jones, Sid Fields, Joe Kirk, Bobby Barber*

The boys decide to spend their vacation at the Biltmore Hotel near Phoenix. Bud becomes worried that Mr. Fields will rent their apartment while they're gone. Lou continually packs and unpacks each time Bud changes his mind. They finally set out for the trip and Lou drives the distance of one half a block down the street to the Biltmore Hotel next door to the Phoenix Cafe.

5. THE BIRTHDAY PARTY–*Hillary Brooke, Gordon Jones, Sid Fields, Joe Kirk, Joe Besser, Elvia Allman, Milt Bronson, Glenn Strange, Joyce Jameson*

It's Lou's birthday and he invites the whole gang to his apartment for a party. Lou mistakes ant paste for antipasto, causing everyone to become ill. Bud throws Lou out of his own birthday party and he visits Mr. Bacciagalupe's bakery and orders a tremendous cake in which Lou becomes the principal ingredient.

6. ALASKA–*Hillary Brooke, Gordon Jones, Sid Fields, Joe Kirk, Joe Besser*

Costello's uncle strikes gold in Alaska and the boys decide to visit him and share in the wealth but before they get started they become involved in a holdup.

7. THE VACUUM CLEANER SALESMAN–*Hillary Brooke, Gordon Jones, Sid Fields, Joe Kirk, Joe Besser, Robin Raymond, Vera Marsh, Dorothy Ford, Bobby Barber*

Lou tries his hand at selling vacuums door-to-door. This leads to a disastrous encounter at a farmhouse.

8. THE ARMY STORY–*Hillary Brooke, Gordon Jones, Sid Fields, Joe Kirk, James Alexander, Joe Besser, Robert Cherry*

Bud and Lou join the reserves. At army camp they recreate the dice game routine and the drill routine.

9. POTS AND PANS–*Hillary Brooke, Gordon Jones, Sid Fields, Joe Kirk, Anthony Caruso*

This time Costello attempts to sell pots and pans door-to-door. Later that day Lou uses the utensils to prepare dinner for the neighbors. Needless to say the evening is a disaster.

10. THE CHARITY BAZAAR–*Hillary Brooke, Gordon Jones, Sid Fields, Joe Kirk, Joe Besser, Nicla Di Bruno*

The boys participate in the annual charity bazaar. Costello spends most of his money at the kissing booth. The boys then do the "Lemon Bit."

11. THE WESTERN STORY–*Hillary Brooke, Gordon Jones, Sid Fields, Joe Kirk, James Alexander, Anthony Caruso, Minerva Urecal, Anthony Hughes, Bobby Barber*

Hillary invites Abbott and Costello to visit her at her uncle's dude ranch. After several attempts at milking a cow the boys are forced to join the posse tracking down cattle rustlers. Costello tangles with the leader of the outlaw gang in a Western saloon, resulting in a shoot-out.

12. THE HAUNTED HOUSE–*Hillary Brooke, Gordon Jones, Sid Fields, Joe Kirk, Joan Shawlee, Joe Besser, Bobby Barber*

Hillary will inherit a mansion if she agrees to spend one night in the house. Lou and Bud tag along to keep her company and encounter a ghost, a mysteriously moving candle and a gorilla. Bud uncovers a cache of money and they flee from the house.

13. PEACE AND QUIET–*Hillary Brooke, Gordon Jones, Sid Fields, Joe Kirk, Marjorie Reynolds, Joe Besser, Murray Leonard, Veda Ann Borg, Eddie Parker, Lillian Bronson, Milt Bronson, Bobby Barber*

Lou is suffering from a terrible case of insomnia so Bud takes him to a psychiatrist. The doctor gives Lou a sleep-inducing record but this fails to work. Finally Bud takes his partner to a sanitarium for a night's rest.

14. HUNGRY–*Hillary Brooke, Gordon Jones, Sid Fields, Joe Kirk, Joan Shawlee*

Bud and Lou visit two restaurants. In one, they become involved with twin waitresses, and in the other, Lou battles with a pugilistic oyster.

15. THE MUSIC LOVERS–*Hillary Brooke, Gordon Jones, Sid Fields, Joe Kirk, Joe Besser, Raymond Hatton, Minerva Urecal, Rennie Riano, Frank Yaconelli*

Hillary's father will only allow her to marry a man with musical talent so Costello goes to a singing instructor, who resembles Mr. Fields. Later Bud arranges to play a recording of piano music while Lou mimics the action. Lou impresses Hillary's father until the father discover the scheme.

16. THE POLITICIAN–*Hillary Brooke, Gordon Jones, Sid Fields, Joe Kirk, Joan Shawlee, Selena Walters, Charles Cane, John Shoemaker*

Lou runs for public office and gives a speech in the park which causes a brawl.

17. THE WRESTLING MATCH–*Hillary Brooke, Gordon Jones, Sid Fields, Joe Kirk, Joe Besser, Dorothy Granger, Emory Parnell, Ben Weldon, Milt Bronson, William Newell, Bobby Barber, Bingo the Chimp*

Stinky and Lou agree to a wrestling match for the policemen's benefit. Stinky becomes ill from drinking too many sodas so his "kid brother" (Ivan the Terrible) substitutes for him. Lou is nearly killed in the ring but somehow manages to win the bout.

(This was the first episode to be aired.)

18. GETTING A JOB–*Hillary Brooke, Gordon Jones, Sid Fields, Joe Kirk, Joe Besser, Veda Ann Borg, Vera Marsh, Milt Bronson, Lucien Littlefield, Anthony Hughes, Sid Saylor*

Bud explains to his partner that he has a job as a loafer in a bakery, which confuses Costello. The boys are then hired to deliver a box of straw hats to the Susquehanna Hat Company. On the street they encounter several lunatics who become violent whenever Lou mentions the Susquehanna Hat Company. In a last desperate attempt to find work they visit Fields' employment agency.

19. BINGO–*Hillary Brooke, Gordon Jones, Sid Fields, Joe Kirk,*

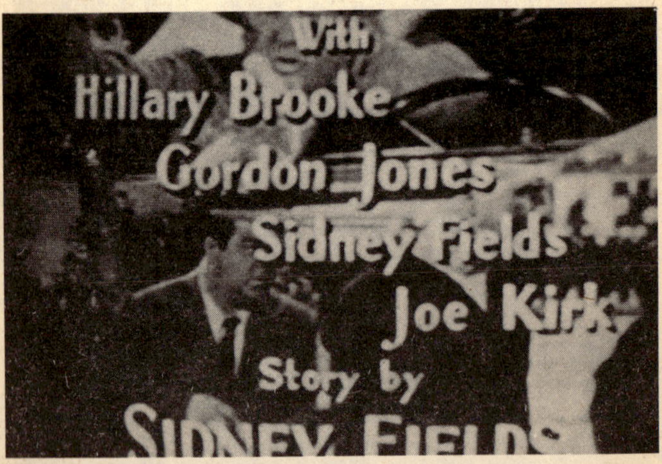
With
Hillary Brooke
Gordon Jones
Sidney Fields
Joe Kirk
Story by

Produced and Directed
by
JEAN YARBROUGH

Executive Producer
PAT COSTELLO

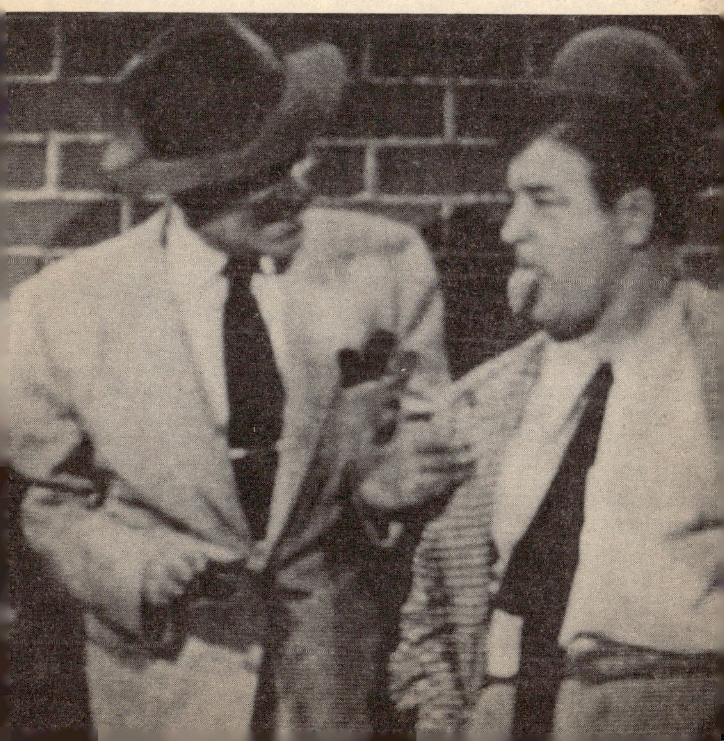

Joan Shawlee, Joe Besser, Isabel Randolph, Bingo the Chimp

Lou learns that he must get a license for his pet chimp, Bingo. So Bud and Lou go to the license bureau, where they cause a great deal of confusion.

20. HILLARY'S BIRTHDAY–*Hillary Brooke, Gordon Jones, Sid Fields, Joe Kirk, Joan Shawlee, Chick Chandler, Lee Patrick, Anthony Hughes, Bingo the Chimp*

Abbott and Costello, planning a surprise birthday party for Hillary Brooke, head for the supermarket, and as usual, Costello causes chaos. That night at the party Lou plays the radio so the others can dance. The music bothers the landlord and he begins to beat up Lou. The team then revives "Go Ahead and Sing."

21. TELEVISION–*Hillary Brooke, Gordon Jones, Sid Fields, Joe Kirk, Joan Shawlee, Bob Hopkins, Bobby Barber, Veda Ann Borg, James Alexander, Ben Weldon, Milt Bronson, Bingo the Chimp*

Lou is chosen as a contestant on his favorite TV quiz show. He must perform a series of embarrassing stunts, only to discover he has won a package of bubble gum for his trouble. The next day Bud and Lou find themselves in court over the small matter of a lawsuit involving their neighbor, John Rednose.

22. LAS VEGAS–*Hillary Brooke, Gordon Jones, Sid Fields, Joe Kirk, Lucien Littlefield, Renie Riano, Joyce Compton, Virginia Christine, Joe Devlin, Bobby Barber*

Our heroes rent a car from Friendly Fields and drive to Las Vegas where Lou engages in a violent game of billiards with a gambler.

23. LITTLE OLD LADY–*Hillary Brooke, Gordon Jones, Sid Fields, Joe Kirk, George Chandler, Dorothy Granger, Burt Mustin, Benny Rubin, Murray Leonard, Judy Clark, Helene Halston*

The boys want to help an old woman who has just been dispossessed. Lou tries panhandling with a tin cup to raise money for the woman. When this doesn't work, Bud and Lou win the needed cash at a charity bazaar. They hand over the money to the old woman and she calls her bookie and bets the money on a racehorse, which comes in first.

24. THE ACTORS' HOME—*Hillary Brooke, Gordon Jones, Sid Fields, Joe Kirk, Joe Besser, Thurston Hall, Allen Jenkins, Joan Shawlee, Lucien Littlefield, Ray Walker, Jarma Lewis, Jo Carol Dennison, Milt Bronson, Bingo the Chimp*

Costello tries hawking newspapers to raise rent money. A millionaire approaches him and presents him with a five-hundred-dollar bill. The same man also gives Bud five hundred dollars. Then two men come along and tell the boys that the man had escaped from a sanitarium and the money is counterfeit. Bud, in a rage, tears up the money. The men return saying that they were mistaken and the gentleman was really a wealthy philanthropist. When Bud can't piece together the money he gets hysterical and is carted away to the old actors' home. Lou visits Bud and they perform "Who's on First" for the other residents of the home.

25. POLICE ROOKIES—*Hillary Brooke, Gordon Jones, Sid Fields, Joe Kirk, Emory Parnell, Robert Cherry, Bingo the Chimp*

With the help of Mike the cop the boys enroll in the police academy. Lou manages to blow up the school with a hand grenade!

26. SAFARI—*Hillary Brooke, Gordon Jones, Sid Fields, Joe Kirk, Bobby Barber, Bingo the Chimp*

Bingo has been ill and running a very high temperature. Costello figures that Bingo misses his father so the whole gang goes to Africa to locate the chimp's parents.

Second Season

27. THE PAPERHANGERS—*Sid Fields, Gordon Jones, Bill Varga, Bob Wilke, Henry Kulky, Jane Frazee, Sarah Haden, Rex Lease*

Mr. Fields forces the boys to do the wallpapering in one of his apartments to pay off some of their back rent. After making a shambles of the apartment, the boys get jobs as waiters in a seafood restaurant. In the restaurant they become involved in a brawl with some hoodlums.

28. UNCLE BOZZO'S VISIT–*Sid Fields, Gordon Jones, Fortunio Bonanova, G. Pat Collins, Milt Bronson, Pat Flaherty, Max Wagner, Anthony Hughes*

Lou's Uncle Bozzo visits him from Italy. Uncle Bozzo is an unemployed opera singer with a loud, booming voice. Every day for hours he practices singing, which annoys Mr. Fields. Fields threatens to throw Lou and his uncle out of the apartment. After a run-in with Mike the cop, Bud, Lou and Uncle Bozzo are arrested. In jail they become involved in a jailbreak engineered by one of the prisoners. The escape is frustrated when Lou's uncle breaks into song, alerting the guards.

29. IN SOCIETY–*Sid Fields, Gordon Jones, Isabel Randolph, Sheila Bromley, Alix Talton, Jack Rice, Tristram Coffin*

A wealthy society lady recruits Bud and Lou to act as British noblemen at a banquet.

30. LIFE INSURANCE–*Sid Fields, Gordon Jones, Murray Leonard, Dorothy Granger, Minerva Urecal, Milt Bronson, Anthony Hughes, Joe La Cava, Bobby Barber*

Mr. Fields demands some security for all the back rent that Bud and Lou owe him. He suggests that the boys take out life insurance, making it payable to the landlord. Because of high blood pressure Bud cannot get insured, so he decides to insure Costello. Bud takes his partner to an unusual doctor for an insurance examination, which Lou fails to pass. The doctor informs Abbott that if Lou spends a few weeks in the country he'll be able to pass. Bud takes Lou on a hunting trip, with rifles. Lou believes that Bud is trying to kill him for the insurance money and he runs away, only to tangle with a bear.

31. PEST EXTERMINATORS–*Sid Fields, Creighton Hale, Dorothy Vaughn, Florence Auer, Helen Millard, Bobby Barber*

Abbott and Costello, as pest exterminators, are mistaken for psychiatrists when they call at the home of Mrs. Featherton to "take care of her ants." The exterminating job finished, they announce to their employer that they have killed her ants, and Mrs. Featherton thinks they have murdered her two maiden aunts. The mix-up is straightened out and the boys take the two aunts out for a night on the town.

32. KILLER'S WIFE–*Sid Fields, Gordon Jones, Max Baer, Mary Beth Hughes, Lou Nova*

A heavyweight prizefighter and his beautiful blond wife rent the apartment across the hall from our heroes. The fighter, "Killer," is a very jealous man and suspects that Lou is carrying on with his wife.

33. CHEAPSKATES–*Sid Fields, Gordon Jones, Paul Fix, Phyllis Coates, Tony Ward, Ralph Gamble, Bobby Barber, Milt Bronson, Teddy Infuhr, Bingo the Chimp*

At an auction Bud and Lou accidentally buy a crate and its contents, sight unseen. Back at the boardinghouse they discover that the crate contains hundreds of roller skates. Gangsters are after the skates because they have hidden stolen diamonds inside them. The leader's girl friend works on Lou in an effort to learn of the skates' whereabouts, and Costello incurs the gangster's jealousy and is nearly murdered.

34. SOUTH OF DIXIE–*Sid Fields, Gordon Jones, Gene Baird, Bob Hopkins, Jean Porter, Glenn Langan, Dick Gordon, Bobby Barber, Milt Bronson*

Lou overhears a man and a young girl rehearsing a Civil War melodrama. Outside their apartment Lou listens to the man threaten the girl's life as they rehearse the play. He breaks into her room to save her and he's so magnificent in his rescue role that he is given a part in the play.

35. FROM BED TO WORSE–*Sid Fields, Gordon Jones, Dan Weiss, Lucien Littlefield*

The boys are currently working in a garden supplies store. They learn that a civic group is offering a cash prize to the citizen who raises the finest backyard home garden. They try planting a garden in order to win the money and provoke a feud with their next-door neighbor.

36. $1000 TV PRIZE–*Sid Fields, Gordon Jones, Bob Hopkins, Ralph Sanford, Milt Bronson*

Bud and Lou attempt to repair the landlord's television and wind up destroying the set. Fields' phone rings and the caller is the host of a TV game show. Lou answers the thousand-dollar question quite accidentally. The prize money will be delivered that evening. The boys manage to get the landlord out of his apartment but he returns unexpectedly and a fight ensues.

37. AMNESIA–*Sid Fields, Gordon Jones, Joel Mulhall, Katharine Sheldon, Charles Cane*

Lou is about to marry a girl with whom he has corresponded through a lonely-hearts magazine, although he has never even seen her. Abbott in an attempt to break up the romance, makes Costello believe he has amnesia. He convinces Lou that he has actually married the girl of his dreams. Bud has hired an actress to pose as the wife. She henpecks and browbeats Lou until he runs away.

38. EFFICIENCY EXPERTS–*Sid Fields, Jean Willis, Lucille Barkley, Theodore Von Eltz, Herbert Hayes, Lillian Bronson, Frank Scanell, Joe Ray, Bobby Barber*

Somehow the duo has landed jobs as efficiency experts. Their first client has two daughters who are spending money faster than he can make it. The boys are hired to keep a financial rein on his spendthrift daughters. However, the girls trick Bud and Lou into taking them to a gambling casino, where they lose all their money and start a fire.

39. CAR TROUBLE–*Sid Fields, Gordon Jones, Emory Parnell, Percy Helton, Horace Murphy, Milt Bronson, Ted Stanhope, Bobby Barber, Sid Saylor*

Lou wins an automobile in a box-top contest. The car turns out to be a lemon and the boys drive to Flint, Michigan, to buy a new car. In Flint they nearly run over Mike the cop's twin brother. On the trip back to L.A. the boys encounter some hoboes and an angry sheriff.

40. WIFE WANTED–*Sid Fields, June Vincent, Frank Jarra, Tracy Roberts, Claudia Barrett*

Lou will inherit ten thousand dollars from his grandfather if he gets married. Costello attempts to marry his old girl friend, Agnes, but she is now dating a wrestler, Bone-Bender Brodsky. The jealous wrestler beats up Costello and deposits him in a trash can.

41. UNCLE FROM NEW JERSEY–*Sid Fields, Gordon Jones, Tim Ryan, Ralph Gamble*

Abbott and Costello, about to be evicted for nonpayment of their rent, convince Mr. Fields that Lou has a millionaire uncle and Lou is sole heir. Costello disguises himself as his own uncle and everything goes well until the landlord believes that the mythical character has been murdered by the boys for his money.

42. PRIVATE EYE–*Sid Fields, Gordon Jones, Lynn Thomas, Milt Bronson, Bill Varga, Frank Richards, Bobby Barber*

Lou takes a correspondence course to become a detective. His first job is to help a young girl find some bonds that are hidden in a mysterious house belonging to an eccentric relative.

43. THE TAX RETURN–*Sid Fields, Gordon Jones, Thurston Hall, Bennie Bert, Al Hill, Bobby Barber*

The income tax office, through an error, sends Lou a tax refund check for one million dollars. After Lou cashes the check at the bank, he is followed home by gangsters, who try to steal the money.

44. PUBLIC ENEMIES–*Sid Fields, Gordon Jones, Joe Sawyer, Clair Carleton, Mike Ross*

A group of safecrackers and their molls have moved into the apartment house where Bud and Lou live. They mistake Costello for a fellow crook and he is forced to join in the robbery of a warehouse.

45. BANK HOLDUP–*Sid Fields, Gordon Jones, Douglas Fowley, Milt Bronson, Bobby Barber*

The boys are hired to act as guards by two men who explain that their business is transporting money to and from banks. Actually they are stickup men and Bud and Lou have unwittingly assisted in a robbery.

46. WELL OILED–*Sid Fields, Gordon Jones, Connie Cezon, William Fawcett*

Mr. Fields is threatened with a breach of promise suit and the boys try to help him out. Lou poses as a Texas millionaire and courts the woman who is suing Mr. Fields.

47. THE PIGEON–*Sid Fields, Gordon Jones, Gloria Henry, Ted Hecht, Ray Montgomery, Harry Clexx, Hank Patterson, Bobby Barber*

Lou's next-door neighbor, the beautiful Ruby Norton, has long been the sweetheart of a mobster. Ruby has fallen in love with another man and wants to break off with the gang leader. She decides to lure Costello into a romance with her, figuring the mobster will kill him and then the police will arrest her former boy friend. Lou manages to live through the ordeal by sheer luck.

48. HONEYMOON HOUSE–*Sid Fields, Karen Sharpe, George Chandler, Renie Riano, Danny Morton, Tommy Farrell*

Lou, with the help of Fields and Abbott, constructs a prefabricated house for his fiancée, Sally. A former boy friend of Sally's sabotages the house. Sally's parents arrive to inspect the house and are nearly killed. The father refuses to allow Costello to marry his daughter.

49. FENCING MASTER–*Sid Fields, Gordon Jones, Fortunio Bonanova, Byron Foulger*

Abbott volunteers Costello to aid in a bizarre experiment by a scientist. The scientist believes that he can make Lou immune to physical injury. Sure enough, the experiment works until Lou becomes involved in a duel.

50. BEAUTY CONTEST STORY–*Sid Fields, James Flavin, Sandra Spence, Claudia Barrett, Dick Wessel, Jane Cane, Ralph Gamble, Charles Hatton*

The boys are judges for the "Miss Mud Turtle" beauty pageant, in which Mr. Fields' niece is a contestant.

51. FALL GUY–*Sid Fields, Walter Catlett, Charlie Hall, Maureen Nash, Gloria Saunders, Frank Marlowe, Joe Haworth, Ruth Lee, John Bernadino, Bobby Barber, Milt Bronson*

After a trying day selling "No Peddlers Allowed" signs, the boys are approached by two men. The men are in love with two sisters, but the father of the girls dislikes the men. They offer Bud and Lou two hundred dollars if they will take the sisters out on a date; then the two men will take the girls off their hands. Bud and Lou take the job and when they arrive at the house the father talks them into putting up a new TV antenna on the roof.

52. BARBER LOU–*Renie Riano, Sid Fields, Bobby Barber*

After helping out in an amateur theatrical directed by their neighbor, Mrs. Bronson, Bud decides that he needs a relaxing rubdown. He makes the mistake of enlisting Costello to give him the massage. (This episode was written by Sid Fields and Lou Costello.)

With Martha Raye in the fun house scene.

During the filming of RIDE 'EM COWBOY, Bud and Lou paid a visit to comic Hugh Herbert, who was playing a bartender in a Universal western.

Lou is a study in loneliness in HIT THE ICE.

Mack Sennett made a brief appearance in a disappointing comedy, ABBOTT AND COSTELLO MEET THE KEYSTONE KOPS.

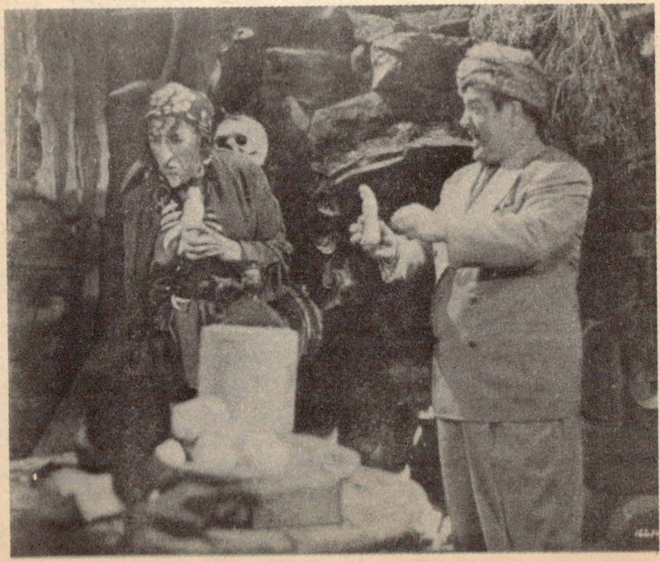

Margaret Hamilton and Lou have a "duel" with voodoo dolls resembling each other in COMIN' ROUND THE MOUNTAIN.

Lou and his "thirty foot bride" (Dorothy Provine).